THE DEAT

THE DEATH OF UNCLE JOE

Alison Macleod

MERLIN PRESS

The Merlin Press
2 Rendlesham Mews Rendlesham Woodbridge
Suffolk IP12 2SZ

©1997 The Merlin Press

ISBN 085036 467 1

Printed in Finland by WSOY

Acknowledgements

In 1989, when I dug out the notes I had made in 1956 and 1957, I set out to trace my fellow-witnesses of these events. Almost all of those then alive were willing to answer my letters and talk to me, if only on the phone. One of these phone conversations led me to the story of Rosa Rust, another to the story of Otto Sling. Many of those who helped me have since died: Mick Bennett, James Friell (better known as the cartoonist Gabriel), Llew Gardner, Leon Griffiths, Frank Lesser, Malcom MacEwen, Phil Piratin and Louis Simmonds.

Still alive to receive my thanks are: Chimen Abramsky, Phil Bolsover, Paddy Goldring, Stanley Harrison, Christopher Hill, Derek Kartun, Florence Keyworth, Bob Leeson, George MacDougall, George Matthews, Dennis Ogden, Betty Reid, Sam Russell, Rosa Rust, Eric Scott, Jane and Dennis Swinnerton and Ray Waterman.

Francis Beckett, author of *The Enemy Within* (John Murray, 1995) was kind enough to share with me some fascinating documents he had discovered. Monty Johnstone has done a service to every researcher by bringing back to England microfiches of the documents he found in the Comintern archives.

Peter Fryer has been an unfailing help. He has given me permission to quote his own writings. Dora Scarlett has given me permission to quote hers. Brian Pearce has contributed his historian's expertise, as well as his memories. No detail has been too small or too tiresome for him to check.

To Alexander Baron, who tried to shake my illusions before I was willing to give them up, I express my gratitude.

Above all I thank my husband, Jack Selford, to whom this book is dedicated.

Preface

Who can ever say what the Soviet Union had been for me? Far more than the country of my choice, an example and an inspiration – it represented what I had always dreamed of but no longer dared hope; it was something towards which all my longing was directed; it was a land where I imagined Utopia was in process of becoming reality.

André Gide, in *The God that Failed* (Hamish Hamilton, 1950)

Stalin's eminence rests on his solution of two big problems. Confronted with the orthodox theory that Socialism is impossible in a single State surrounded by capitalist States, and that 'the revolution' must be international, he decided to try, and established the Single Socialist State in the teeth of the Trotsky opposition.

The second was the agricultural problem, which our chosen fainéant Prime Ministers failed so dangerously to solve. Stalin solved it by collective farming...

What Stalin has not feared to face is a general election in each of his four new Baltic republics, with adult suffrage and secret ballot...

George Bernard Shaw, in a letter to the *New Statesman*, 31 May 1941.

1

At the end of the 19th Congress of the Communist Party of the Soviet Union, Comrade Stalin came up to me and said: 'There is a light in your eyes, Harry. Are you happy?' Of course, I was happy.

Harry Pollitt, in the *Daily Worker*, 7 March 1953.

The fashion in anti-Soviet books is changing.

Insurrection in Poshansk, by Robert Neumann (Hutchinson, 12s. 6d.) is a crude imitation of Koestler.

Russians have slave camps in Siberia, their beds are full of bugs, their hospitals have no doctors, and any foreigner who still likes the Soviet Union after seeing it must be a half-wit.

But that sort of thing is on the way out...

Alison Macleod, in the *Daily Worker*, 14 June 1952.

So the boys without an overcoat
Have got an Uncle Jo.

Paul Potts, *We Lepers*, A Poet's Testament, 1940.

What on earth was the matter with us all? Others have tried to diagnose the illness. All I can do is describe events which were, for some of us, the cure.

I

From the index of Foreign Office papers for 1944:

> Rust, Rosa, Miss.
>
> (Daughter of Editor of *Daily Worker):* return to U.K. from Soviet Union: holder of Soviet document for persons without nationality.
>
> K603/K2832/4584/603/238.

The numbers refer to documents which ought to be at the Public Record Office. They are not. The staff said they had never arrived from the Foreign Office.

I turned to the next item on the index, which looked as if it might refer to the same case. (Though, as I learned later, the initials were wrong.)

> Rust, R.J. (Mrs. and daughter).
>
> British passport. T14944/81/378.

Here the staff could help me. They produced a file containing the papers of people who, in 1944, claimed to be British. The Rust papers were missing. Stolen? Or lost?

This was 1991, and the papers should have been available for inspection by the public since 1974, thirty years after the event. Documents are sorted out by 'reviewers' in each department, three years before they are due to become public.

I wrote to the Foreign Office librarian, Ian Davenport. He made a search for the papers and assured me that they were not in the Foreign Office. Only papers of historical value, he wrote, were sent to the Public Record Office. 'We can only assume that in 1971, i.e. 27 years after the papers were originated, the reviewer would have had no knowledge of Rust and his daughter and thought the papers were of no value.'

It took me a year to find Rosa Rust. She was not hiding, but living in contented obscurity. It had not occurred to her that anyone would want to hear her story.

Rosa (called after Rosa Luxemburg) was born on 26 April 1925. When she was seven months old her father, Bill Rust, was one of 12 British Communist leaders sent to prison for a year, under the Incitement to Mutiny Act of 1797. Her mother took her to see her father in prison. The couple had to talk under the eye of a warder, across a table. On this table Rosa got up and walked for the first time.

In 1928 Bill Rust took his family to Moscow, where he worked for the youth section of the Communist International. Rosa grew up speaking Russian, and shared the normal experiences of a Soviet child, such as having her tonsils out without an anaesthetic.

When her parents' marriage broke up, Rosa lived in one room with her mother. At the age of eight she was sent to a very splendid boarding school for the children of foreign Communists, at Ivanovo-Vosnesensk. The son of the Hungarian Communist Rakosi was there; so was the son of the man who was then known as Josip Broz, but later as Marshal Tito. After Hitler came to power in 1933 the pupils included numerous German children. The main foreign language taught was German. Rosa was quick to learn that, though her outstanding talents were for music and dancing.

Bill Rust returned to England with a Georgian lady, Tamara, who became his second wife. Rosa's mother stayed in

Moscow until 1937, when she too returned to England, telling Rosa that she would be back to fetch her.That became impossible once Britain was at war.

The school's pupils, on reaching the age of 15, continued their education in Moscow. So Rosa was there on 22 June 1941, when Hitler attacked the Soviet Union. With some of her German fellow-pupils, she was sent down the Volga to safety. By this chance, they came to share the fate of the Volga German Autonomous Soviet Socialist Republic.

About 330,000 people, descendants of the settlers brought by Catherine the Great from Darmstadt and the nearby villages, lived in this republic with their own schools and newspapers. They still spoke German, or rather an eighteenth-century dialect, which Rosa found unintelligible. As farmers, the Volga Germans had suffered terribly in Stalin's forced collectivisation and the consequent famine. But there was no evidence (the Soviet Government admitted later) that they were preparing to welcome the German Army.

Nevertheless, on 28 August 1941, Stalin accused them of harbouring 'thousands and tens of thousands of diversionists and spies'. He decreed that the whole population should be sent to 'other areas'.

A second, secret decree spelt out the methods:

> The entire family will be transported to the entrainment station in one vehicle, but at the depot the family heads will be loaded into special, preselected railway cars... their families will be deported to special settlement locales in remote areas... They must not be told of their impending separation from the family head.

The deportation began on 10 September 1941. It applied not only to the Volga Germans, but to any other Germans who happened to be about – including Rosa's fellow-pupils. Rosa protested to the local police. These were not Volga Germans.

How could the decree apply to them? She soon found that it applied to her too. Though not a German, she was rounded up with the rest.

They were taken down the Volga to Astrakhan, and then by ship, on the Caspian Sea, to Guryev. 'It doesn't look very far on the map,' Rosa said to me in 1992. 'But it took five days. And we were lucky; we were on a proper boat. There was a sort of barge being towed behind us; the people on that were out in the open, day and night. Two women gave birth to babies on that barge.'

At Guryev the people were loaded on to cattle trucks. They began to move east, but very slowly, because they were shunted out of the way whenever the line was needed for a troop train. These halts, however tedious, were welcome. The people would pour out, the men on one side and the women on the other, because there were no lavatories on the train.

Sometimes they would stop at a station. All Russian stations have hot water on tap, and there was generally some food to buy, for those with money and ration cards. A woman with a baby, in the same cattle truck as Rosa, had a supply of condensed milk. At one of the halts the mother was left behind, and Rosa found herself looking after the baby, who was only three months old. Rosa did her best with the condensed milk. When the train stopped near a stream she tried to wash the baby's nappies. The frantic mother caught up with the train five days later. The baby, unlike many other people, survived the journey.

After six weeks, the train came to its final halt, at a place which hardly seemed to be a place, Ust-Kaminogorsk, in Kazakhstan. Local officials billeted the new arrivals, very simply. An official would bang on a door, yell the name of the person inside, and give the order: 'Receive two people!' Nobody argued, but nobody was very welcoming. All the people from the cattle trucks were covered with lice. Rosa, and a German woman who had become her friend, slept on the floor of an old woman's one-room dwelling. They had carefully guarded their clean clothes, and they were able to burn the verminous ones, visit the village bath-house and get paraffin to help them delouse each other's hair.

They had reached their destination, such as it was, before the winter set in. Later trainloads were not so lucky. Rosa later met people who admitted throwing Granny off the train, once she had died of cold. 'Well! She was dead, wasn't she?' If they did not report the matter, they could go on using Granny's ration card.

Even in this remote place, Rosa had no language difficulty. Russian was the language of the official class. Russians treated the local people with a contempt which disgusted Rosa. At school she had been taught the internationalism which was supposed to be the creed of Soviet man.

For a time she worked on a collective farm. Then she did a six-month course in metallurgy. The men who worked in the copper mine at Belousovka, a village near the Chinese border, were called up for the army. The students of metallurgy were told it was their patriotic duty to take the men's place in the copper mine. So Rosa went down the mine too.

All this time the sufferings of many people round her had been more terrible than her own. So it had not occurred to Rosa to feel sorry for herself. But now she was becoming ill from malnutrition. She began to wonder what on earth she was doing in Belousovka. She wrote to a girl she had known at the boarding school, whom she believed to be still in Moscow.

Because of this letter, things began to happen. Money arrived. Travel papers arrived. One of them was signed by Georgi Dimitrov, then internationally known as the hero of the Reichstag Fire Trial, but less known as a tireless henchman of Stalin. He was the head of the Communist International (not yet officially dissolved). In the spring of

1943 Rosa began the long journey to Moscow.

She was held up for three weeks at Alma-Ata. The public park was filled with people camping out while they waited for a train. But every train was full of soldiers. A girl soldier kept the crowd from even entering the station – until one night, when it rained, and the crowd rushed the building.

Rosa had brought with her a bag of unleavened bread (which does not go mouldy like ordinary bread). She saw a man looking at the bag hungrily, and then observed that he was too weak to walk. When she spoke to him he whispered that he was an army deserter, without money or a ration card. 'I wanted to steal your bread,' he confessed, 'but I hadn't the strength.' She gave him some. He could not get it down; his throat was too dry. She had to dip it in water to soften it for him. 'There are checks here all the time,' she told him. 'You must run away and hide.' 'I can't,' he said. 'I can't walk any further.' But he hid, for the time being, in the lavatory.

At about three the next morning, while Rosa sat on the station floor, her head on her knees, she was roused by a crash of jackboots. An official barked out: 'Dokumenty!' An old woman, holding a baby, clutched the baby closer and made the sign of the cross.

The terror that this official inspired in the people infuriated Rosa. She thought of the deserter, who, if still nearby, was bound to be shot. She thought of the innocent people whose suffering she had witnessed. She thought of the brutal contempt with which Russians treated Asiatic peoples. She answered the official back. 'We're not cattle,' she said. 'We're human beings. If you want to see our papers, why can't you ask politely? Why are you behaving like a fascist?'

Rosa, who had taken her first steps inside a prison, might well have taken her final steps in one. But the document signed by Dimitrov impressed the official. She came to no harm.

However, her money had almost run out. Then she remembered that Alma-Ata was the headquarters of International Red Aid, the body which had set up her boarding school. She appealed to them and was given more money, and a document so persuasive that it got her aboard a train.

This was a proper passenger train. It had bunks. The passengers, jammed together, worked out a twelve-hour rota. Everybody could lie down on a bunk for four hours, sit for four hours and stand for four hours. They could not keep exactly to this timetable, because at every station they had to get out and bargain with peasants, for food.

The train took eleven days to reach Moscow. Near the Aral Sea, Rosa bought a bucket of salt – scarce everywhere else in the Soviet Union. With salt, she bargained her way through the other stations, and arrived in Moscow with eggs and butter, such as nobody in the city had seen for months. She had a brief interview with Dimitrov. Then she went to work in a war factory. With a factory worker's ration card, it was possible to live; an office worker's rations meant starvation.

Yet there was something to cheer about. The Germans were in retreat. Kharkov was retaken; then Kiev. Cannonades and fireworks greeted the victories.

It was not until Rosa met the *Daily Worker* man in Moscow, John Gibbons, that she re-established contact with her parents. 'Bill's been looking for you for years,' John Gibbons told her. Then he asked her whether she wanted to stay in Moscow, or go to England.

'I want to go home,' said Rosa. She was quite clear that England was home, though she could not remember it, or speak a word of the language.

At the British Embassy an official asked whether she wanted to travel by way of Persia, or on one of the Murmansk convoys. 'Which is quicker?' she asked. She was told that the Murmansk way was quicker, but more dangerous. At eighteen,

9

Rosa thought nothing of danger. She chose Murmansk.

Convoy RA 57 sailed from Kola Inlet on 2 March 1944. Two days later a U-boat sank a merchant vessel, and the German planes came swooping down to strafe the lifeboats. Yet everybody was rescued. The captain's report ('All my crew behaved well') is in the Public Record Office. Cheerful because the escort carrier *Chaser* had sunk three U-boats, the sailors taught Rosa to play darts. The strangely named *Port Slave*, with Rosa aboard, docked safely at Leith.

Rosa became aware of a cloak-and-dagger atmosphere. She was asked to tie a white hanky round her sleeve, so that the Foreign Office men waiting for her at Edinburgh Station would recognise her. She recognised them at once. Never before had she seen men in bowler hats and pin-striped suits.

Rosa was so unaware of English ways that she did not think it odd there were no reporters about. It must have required the whole wartime apparatus of censorship to make sure of that. Stalin was our ally. The Foreign Office did not want to stress his habit of sending innocent people for six-week journeys on cattle trucks.

One of the Foreign Office men asked Rosa, in halting Russian: 'Only one suitcase?' They had brought two cars, expecting a lot of luggage. They had a hotel room booked for her, but a lady from the Women's Voluntary Services protested, in Russian, that Rosa would be lonely. The WVS lady took Rosa to her own home. She turned out to be a Russian refugee, longing to talk about the country she had not seen for over twenty years, and she treated Rosa with great kindness.Rosa asked what she should do in London, if she did not recognise her parents. She had not seen her mother for six years, her father for much longer. The WVS lady wrote a note in English, and told Rosa to give it to a policeman. 'Our policemen are wonderful,' said the lady – speaking, now, as a Briton.

Rosa's parents did in fact fail to recognise her. They had last seen her as a child; now she was nearly nineteen. However, they found each other. Rosa lived with her mother, who became concerned because the girl was obviously not well. For almost three years she had not had a period. A doctor said she needed only peace, quiet and proper food. That presented a problem in wartime London. But the British Government had set up agricultural camps where town-dwellers could have a cheap holiday and at the same time help the war effort by such simple farm work as picking peas. When the Communists switched from opposing the war to supporting it, in June 1941, they became super-patriots, and went to these agricultural camps with such enthusiasm as almost to take them over. Rosa went to one in Bedfordshire, where she was very happy. Because of her work in the collective farm, and then in the copper mine, she had developed such muscles that she could carry two sacks of peas while others carried one. She found it easy to earn enough to cover the very modest charges for board and lodging. The food was good, by wartime standards. After six weeks of this peaceful open-air life, Rosa blossomed into a beautiful young woman.

At the camp, too, she learned English. Her talent for music enabled her to catch intonations very quickly. People who met her afterwards did not always realise that she had lived in Russia. (Though a faint accent is perceptible to this day.)

She did not talk to English people about her journey in the cattle truck. At first she did not speak enough English. Then she settled down to this new life, where a policeman was a person who would help you find your parents. England began to seem the only reality. Her life in Russia became no more than a dream. Only many years later, when she met one of her surviving fellow-pupils, did these memories revive.

Rosa's mother remained a passionate Communist. She did not use the name of Rust, and most people who met her were unaware that she had ever been married to him. She rarely mentioned her daughter's experiences.

And certainly Bill Rust did not. This I can testify because I joined the *Daily Worker* editorial staff in the spring of 1944, just at the time Rosa Rust was returning to England. Not only did I not hear of this event; I did not know until 1991 that Bill Rust had a daughter.

Bill Rust was kind to Rosa; she has pictures of him beaming paternally at her twenty-first birthday party in 1946. He did not conceal her existence; he merely refrained from mentioning it to people who did not need to know.

Politically, he was ruthless to anyone who uttered the slightest criticism of the Soviet Union. Through every twist and turn of Stalin's policy, he was with Stalin. If anyone had described in our office one tenth of what Rosa had lived through, Bill Rust would have denounced such anti-Soviet lies and slanders.

But in this we were all his willing accomplices. Many things then happening inside Russia were kept from us. But the deportation of the Volga Germans had been publicly announced, and printed in English newspapers (though never in those of the Soviet Union). We knew about it, and we did not care. We had, by an act of will, decided not to care.

The rank-and-file comrades, the stooges like myself, were deceived because we wanted to be. Marxism gave life a pattern. During the 1930s it had explained the abject behaviour of British Conservatives, as Hitler gobbled one country after another. It explained the bumbling slowness of the Labour Party in the face of these events. We, with our pattern, understood what was going on. Whatever did not fit into our pattern we could, with an effort, ignore.

I joined the Communist Party early in 1939. Cecil

Day-Lewis had written: 'Why do we all, when we see a Communist, feel small?' It was a lousy poem but (I thought) a beautiful sentiment.

I was not quite 19. The comrade who signed me up was an old man of 31, Jack Selford, head of the play department at Unity Theatre. We got married, but not until some years later. After the war, when I was a deserted wife with a coffee-coloured baby, Jack fell in love with the baby. We settled down in flowery, well-wooded Muswell Hill.

I had a job I loved, as a sub-editor at the *Daily Worker*. Jack had a job he loved. On coming out of the army he had trained as a teacher, and had soon discovered his gift for teaching difficult children. Our working hours were complementary. Jack would be home by five, and would gladly take over the care of little Catherine, while I did the late shift. The disadvantage for him was that he could not carry out the first duty of a Communist – to work in his local branch. In his forties he minded this less and less. We used to meet the local Communists, but only in the parks. When we took Catherine to play, they would be out with their own toddlers. We would say more about our children than about our politics.

One thing we did learn about our local comrades. They were bedevilled by elections. Communist policy was not to put up a candidate where that would mean splitting the vote and letting the Tory in. We would support Labour, whether Labour liked it or not.

But not in our constituency, Hornsey. The Communist candidate, G. J. Jones, known as Jonah, got 10,000 votes in 1945. This ruined his life. Whatever he began to talk about, he would end by saying: 'I got 10,000 votes in 1945.' The obsession would have been merely sad, if Jonah had not been a very good-looking man, with an ecstatic female following. These girls backed him in his insistence on a Communist candidate in every local election. Those unaffected by Jonah's good looks would point out that he had got his big vote only because many people thought he was the Labour candidate. The local Labour Party was backing him until, at the last moment, Transport House put in an official Labour candidate. This made Jonah bitter about the Labour Party. 'If it hadn't been for Transport House, I would have been an MP.' (He wouldn't. The Conservative had more votes than Communists and Labour together.)

We heard enough of this to be glad that we had little to do with our local branch. Jack's Party work was to explain Marxist economics to a group of Communist businessmen. They met in surroundings of great splendour. A uniformed doorman said respectfully to Jack: 'The Marxist class, sir? Certainly, sir. This way.'

My own Party work was to speak at street corners, with nobody listening. The masses did not listen to us because the rubbishy papers they read kept them better informed than we were about the nature of Stalin.

Many things which could and should have shaken us did not. Only in 1947, when Russian women who had married Englishmen during the war were refused permission to join their husbands, did we fail to defend a Soviet decision.

Frank Lesser, who had succeeded John Gibbons as *Daily Worker* correspondent in Moscow, came back to London and said he had never heard a reasonable explanation of the Soviet attitude to these marriages. Bill Rust was annoyed with him for saying so, even at a private meeting of the editorial staff. Bill seemed very proud of the trouble he had had in getting Tamara to England. The trouble was caused mainly by the fact that he was still married to his British wife at the time, but this was another thing I did not know till 1991.

In the canteen I heard someone ask the assistant editor, Johnnie Campbell, what line he took when the Soviet decision came up at public meetings. Johnnie growled out: 'Not tae defend it.' He added that when he was in the Soviet Union, during the 1930s, he had taken up the cudgels for a Russian woman who wanted permission to leave the country with her English husband. He had confronted an official who said that the woman had been educated at state expense, and that the state therefore had a right to keep her working for it. 'I told him that was barbarous bloody nonsense,' Campbell said. 'The interpreter turned that into "rather barbarous".' Campbell got the woman out.

But nobody ever got the post-war Soviet brides out. Even those who, like Campbell, refused to say that the Soviet Government was right, stopped short of making any public protest. Either you were serious about wanting Socialism (we always spelt it with a capital S) or you weren't. If you were serious, you couldn't attack the one country which had achieved it. Well, then.

So 15 Russian women were compelled to divorce their husbands, without our having uttered one word in their defence. Hewlett Johnson, the red Dean of Canterbury, afterwards claimed that he had raised the matter with Stalin. But, as he also claimed that his efforts had been successful, his memory may be distrusted. On 21 March 1947 the Soviet Union formally forbade its citizens to marry foreigners.

Stalin's quarrel with Tito, in June 1948, was hotly debated at the *Daily Worker* office. (I did not then know that Rosa Rust was arguing with her father about his excessive readiness to take Stalin's side against Tito. She also told him that the *Daily Worker* was unreadable, as indeed it must have been to anyone who knew what the Soviet Union was like.)

Derek Kartun, the Foreign Editor, was indignant with Frank Lesser, who seemed insufficiently convinced of Tito's vileness. Derek pointed out that Tito had actually said: 'Members of the Soviet intelligence service attempted without consideration to recruit Yugoslavs.'

15

'But comrade!' said Frank Lesser. 'Aren't you glad that our comrades of the Soviet intelligence are showing a proper vigilance in Yugoslavia?' After this Frank Lesser did not last long at the *Daily Worker*.

It seemed simpler to throw ourselves into the world peace movement. Everybody wass in favour of peace... Except in China. We devoured the exciting news about the civil war there. Our boys were winning.

Our old colleague Alan Winnington came back on a visit from China. He had gone there when the Communists held only one big town, Harbin, and helped with the production of a newspaper. Learning Chinese as he went along, Winnington found out what it was like to work on a paper printed with hand-carved blocks of wood. When a character was missing, an old man would be summoned to carve one. From this place of legend and romance Winnington brought us news which we scarcely dared to believe. The Chinese Communists had already won. He was right; they had the whole mainland by the end of 1949. Even before that, the general secretary of the British Communist Party, Harry Pollitt, told us not to be discouraged because the British workers had given only 854 votes to John Mahon, our man at the St. Pancras North by-election. (The Labour man won with 16,185.) Pollitt said: 'We may not have won St. Pancras, but we've got China.'

Our enthusiasm for peace had one other exception.The British Peace Congress, organised by the British Peace Committee, issued press credentials to every newspaper and agency that asked for them, including the Yugoslav press agency, Tanjug. But when Milan Hoffman of Tanjug arrived at the hall he was turned away, because he was 'a representative of the Yugoslav Government'.

On 3 February 1949 Bill Rust died suddenly at 45. (It was, I now know, the day on which he had planned to meet his daughter's fianceé for the first time.) I did not go to his funeral, being at home with little Cathy, but 4,000 people did. The funeral orations were printed in full in the *Daily Worker*. If I had read them, I would have known of the existence of Bill Rust's daughter. Willie Gallacher, one of the two Communist MPs, expressed sympathy with her. But who reads funeral orations? Reading them in 1991, with hindsight, I observed that the first wife had become an unperson. That seemed ungrateful, in view of her continued devotion to the cause. Not until I found Rosa Rust in 1992 did I learn that the Party had asked the first wife to stay away from the funeral. Tamara was the official widow, and there was no room for another one. At the time, Rosa went to the House of Commons and protested to Gallacher. He trembled with rage. That was why he insisted on mentioning Rosa in his oration.

Later the *Daily Worker* building was called 'William Rust House', and a plaque unveiled in Bill Rust's memory. At that ceremony, too, Tamara had the leading role. Campbell asked Rosa to stay away. I would not, in those days, have believed this of Campbell; the events I shall describe, however, changed my mind.

Rosa got married, abandoned politics and lived happily ever after.

I did not, in those days, agree with people who thought Bill Rust an inhuman apparatchik. He had always treated me with kindness. But he was, to a degree which I found chilling, unmoved by the arts. Of Ted Willis (later Lord Willis) he once remarked: 'Queer chap. He sobs at plays.' (Queer did not mean what it came to mean later; nobody disputed Ted's interest in women.) I suggested to Bill Rust that people ought to sob at plays. 'Don't you ever sob at plays?' I asked reproachfully. He grunted.

Johnnie Campbell, who succeeded Rust as Editor, may not have done a great deal of sobbing at plays. He was a tough old Clydeside revolutionary. But he watched plays with enthusiasm. In his youth, he educated himself by helping out at a bookshop, and he developed a passionate interest in literature. He would look up from digesting some Blue Book full of statistics, to talk about Robert Browning's use of rhyme.

Besides working as a sub-editor, I began to review novels for the *Daily Worker*'s book page. Every reviewer has to face the question: should he be kind to books written by friends? Not, in my case, personal friends, but fellow-members of the Party. I maintained that my duty was to the readers. If a Party member had written a bad book, I ought not to con other Party members into spending their money on it. My view was hotly contested by the authors, and by the Cultural Committee of the Communist Party.

When such a dispute arose, Campbell would read the book. He would ask the people protesting on the author's behalf whether they would have preferred a review written by himself. In one case, he suggested, it would have begun: 'A story set in the least interesting period of French history, written in a style which is a curious mixture of Sir Walter Scott and *No Orchids for Miss Blandish*.'

Campbell was just as insistent that a good novel should get a good review, even if the author was regarded with disfavour by the Cultural Committee.Once a member of this committee denounced a novel, saying: 'The hero's nothing but an Uncle Tom.'

'Don't use that as a tairm o' abuse!' thundered Campbell. 'If ony o' oor so-called Socialist realists could write a book wi' one tenth o' the impact o' *Uncle Tom's Cabin*, then ye could talk.'

Campbell's respect for good writing was all the more remarkable, considering that he had got off to a bad start. His niche in history was that he had brought down the first Labour Government. In 1924 he was acting editor of the *Worker's*

Weekly, which published an editorial calling on soldiers to form soviets. He was charged with incitement to mutiny. Then the prosecution was dropped, largely because Campbell had lost a foot at Gallipoli, and had been awarded the Military Medal for rescuing a fellow-soldier under fire. The Conservatives, who wanted Campbell prosecuted, accused the Labour Prime Minister, Ramsay Macdonald, of Communist leanings. They moved a vote of censure, and the Liberals voted with them. On 9 October 1924 Macdonald, who had been in office less than nine months, was forced to resign. The General Election was fixed for October 29. On October 24 the Times published the text of a letter, supposed to be from the Soviet leader Grigori Zinoviev to British Communists, with instructions for revolution. The Soviet Government denounced it as a forgery. But it looked real, because it was on the same lines as the *Worker's Weekly* editorial, and the Conservatives had a landslide victory.

'Johnnie, what's your version of the famous Campbell case?' asked one of the reporters. Campbell replied: 'Ma vairsion o' the famous Campbell case is that a sentimental, hysterical article, which would make ony o' oor present-day comrades hoot wi' uncontrollable laughter, got me intae trouble.'

He was right about that article. The offending passage ran:

> Soldiers, Sailors, Airmen, flesh of our flesh, and bone of our bone, the Communist Party calls upon you to begin the task of not only organising passive resistance when war is declared, or when an industrial dispute involves you, but to definitely and categorically let it be known that, neither in the class war nor a military war, will you turn your guns on your fellow-workers, but instead will line up with your fellow-workers in an attack upon the exploiters and capitalists, and will use your arms on the side of your own class. Form committees in every barracks...

Did Campbell ever write as badly as that? Brian Pearce,

one of the living witnesses to these events, remembers hearing Campbell say that the article was by Harry Pollitt. But Campbell, as the editor, took the blame. By the time I knew him, certainly, Campbell was keeping his infinitives together and his sentences quite short. He liked to study the work of other journalists. Once I found him chuckling over an article in the *Spectator* by a witty Conservative. 'Do you know anything about this man?' he asked me.

'Oh yes!' I said. 'He's a Catholic, and he has a shocking habit of not quite seducing women. Just as the lady thinks that she's going to be seduced, he says this is mortal sin; they have to stop.'

Campbell said: 'I hope that some day some young woman, defending her dishonour, gives him a black eye.'

Such a phrase as 'defending her dishonour' would never get into the paper, which was extremely proper. Campbell's editorials were duller than that, and in a strange cramped handwriting, all aslope, to be read holding the paper up by one corner and peering sideways. The compositors put up with the handwriting; they loved Campbell.

Since then I have met several editors who put on matey airs. They imagine (as they lunch at the Savoy Grill) that the reporters lunching at the Wimpy Bar adore them. Campbell's matiness was real. He was interested in people. He would sit in the canteen we all used, and talk to compositors, tape boys or the latest recruit to the staff. Nobody could be better suited to keep the loyalty of a temperamental team, and hold it together amid external attacks.

We thought the attacks on us unjustified. We thought we had a good case, but were failing to put it across.

Campbell said on one occasion: 'We're no talking the same language as the workers. It's no just that we use Party jargon. It's what we say. I was at a meeting in a school and the chairman was telling the people that this Labour Government hasnae carried oot its promises. And I looked round at this fine school, just built, and this great new housing estate we were in, and I could see why the workers didnae believe us.'

To my husband I remarked what a vast improvement Campbell was on Bill Rust. 'Perhaps,' I said, 'when Stalin dies we shall all find we like the new chap much better.'

Jack was deeply shocked at the idea that anybody could be an improvement on Stalin. 'When you say things like that,' he said, 'you make me feel that you've never really understood anything.'

With hindsight, one can look through the *Daily Worker* for 1949, and see how Campbell was playing down the quarrel with Tito. Even Tito's acceptance of a loan from the United States was reported in a flat, factual way.

But the *Daily Worker* had to come off the fence in September 1949. Laszlo Rajk, formerly Minister of the Interior in Hungary, was tried for treason in Budapest, with seven other defendants. They all confessed to plotting with Tito to overthrow the Communist regime in Hungary.

This is often described as the first of Stalin's great political trials in Eastern Europe. It was not. An Albanian Communist leader, Kochi Xoxe, was tried in Tirana in May 1949 on similar charges. But that trial was not reported by the Albanian authorities, until it was over. On 11 June 1949 a brief announcement of it appeared in *The Times*. On June 14 an even briefer item carried the news that Xoxe had been shot. I cannot find Xoxe's name in the *Daily Worker* of those days.

While the Albanian trial was happening, our assistant editor, John Gollan, was at the Congress of the Czech Communist Party. He wrote enthusiastically of the welcome given to 'popular Rudolph Slansky, a Partisan leader during the war...'

Kartun was at the Rajk trial. So was a 22-year-old

reporter, who had joined the *Daily Worker* staff at the end of 1947, Peter Fryer. Both sincerely believed the confessions of the accused to be genuine. Derek Kartun, while still in Budapest, wrote a book based on the trial. It was rushed into print before the end of the year. We all paid half a crown for it, took it home, and neglected to read it. If a clever, cultivated, interesting man like Derek said that the trial was fair, that was good enough.

In Budapest Derek had a conversation to which he attached no importance at the time. Matyas Rakosi, Prime Minister of Hungary, came up to him at a reception and said: 'This Edith Bone – is she employed by the *Daily Worker*?'

Derek said: 'No; she just writes articles for us occasionally.' Rakosi nodded and turned away.

Edith Bone was a writer and translator, talented but not well known – until her disappearance made her so. Rakosi denied all knowledge of her whereabouts. She was a Hungarian-born Communist who had become naturalised in Britain.

I never knew Edith Bone, but my recollection is that nobody made any personal fuss. She was considered difficult and obstructive. Her abilities made her appreciated, not loved.

The other famous disappearance was of the Fields, two American brothers. They were loved, especially by the many refugees they had saved from Hitler. Noel Field disappeared in Prague on 12 May 1949. His brother Hermann Field was arrested while travelling from Warsaw to Prague on 22 August 1949. Herta Field, wife of Noel, disappeared in Prague on 26 August 1949. These dates and names were reiterated by the desperate wife of Hermann, Kate Field, who was living in London. Her protests were printed in the *New Statesman* and the *Manchester Guardian*, not in our paper.

In December 1949 the trial of the Bulgarian Communist leader Traicho Kostov opened in Sofia. He faced charges very similar to those against Rajk. But he pleaded not guilty, repudiating the 32,000-word statement he had signed in prison. The nine other Bulgarian defendants, and the one Yugoslav defendant, pleaded guilty. They got prison sentences; Traicho Kostov was executed.

By this time Stalin had told Tito to withdraw his ambassador from Moscow, since he was a spy. Russian troops were said to be massing on the Yugoslav border. And Campbell, my adored Campbell, told an editorial staff meeting that the Soviet Union, 'in defence of its legitimate interests', might have to invade Yugoslavia.

The General Election of February 1950 showed us how unpopular we were. In Hornsey somebody broke a window displaying one of Jonah's posters. Jonah sent a statement to the *Daily Worker*. The people who did this kind of thing, he said, would have jeered at Christ on his way to the cross. This was not printed. Jonah's vote was down to 1,100. The two Communist MPs lost their seats.

On the late shift, there was generally a slack time between the second and third editions. Early in 1950 I used this time with great profit to myself, by talking to our new copytaster, Brian Pearce.

The copytaster is the person who reads all the reports that come into a newspaper, and decides what is important. In case he is wrong, he does not throw away the unimportant items, but puts them on a spike. They can be retrieved for the paper's later editions. I was a copytaster for a week or two, but I was no good at it; I never could concentrate on what was politically important. I was too easily distracted by the items that amused me. 'Ye're no on the carpet,' Campbell said to me kindly, when he sent me back to subbing.

Brian Pearce was far better than I was at fitting everything into a coherent world outlook. But that was not what made his conversation delightful. He was a historian. Like a pig hunting out the truffles, he would go for the fact that everyone else had forgotten, the statistics meant to prove one thing which proved the opposite, the tasteless witticism which betrayed the real state of mind.

If I had a book to review with a background of which I knew nothing – India in 1850, or Greece in 1922 – I did not worry. Brian would tell me about it.

In those quiet moments, with everyone else at the pub, Brian and I shared the affliction of the Tass tape machine. There were three teleprinters rattling away: Reuters for foreign news, Press Association for British news and Tass for the only, the genuine, Soviet news.

Only it never gave us any news. Sometimes an excited employee of Tass would ring up, to tell us there was going to be some. 'We're just about to put over the May Day slogans.' The slogans were so long and boring that I wondered if they would be snappier in Russian. But Brian, who understood Russian, said not. Statistics of pig iron chattered out of the Tass machine. So did hectares and poods, and poods to the hectare, and cattle-feed. Hectares, poods, cattle-feed and slogans alike would end: 'Glory to the great Stalin!' None of this was usable in anything resembling a news story.

Yet there was news, if we had known how to decode it. Night after night, the machine would denounce frontier violations by 'the treacherous Synghman Rhee puppet clique'. As I slid into bed beside Jack at two in the morning, I murmured: 'What do you think of the treacherous Synghman Rhee puppet clique?' He said: 'I don't know, dear, but I'm against them if you are.'

On 25 June 1950 it ceased to be funny. Synghman Rhee was President of South Korea, and Communist North Korea attacked the South. We did not admit that; we maintained that the South had attacked the North. Against us, every man with battle experience could argue that North Korea must have been the aggressor, because only an aggressor could drive so fast into the opponent's territory. Campbell thought so too, though he was careful in what company he said it.

Yet we argued that, if Stalin had been planning for his ally, North Korea, to attack South Korea, he would not have chosen a moment when the Soviet Union was unrepresented at the United Nations. Six months earlier the Soviet delegate, Jacob Malik, had walked out because the Chinese chairman of the Security Council was Chiang Kai-shek's man, not Mao's. Unimpeded, therefore, by the Soviet veto, the United Nations was able to send arms and men to South Korea. This remains a mystery, explicable only by Stalin's madness.

That he was mad (though we could not see it then) appears from another episode of 1950. On April 30 a few British Communist scientists passed a resolution giving their support to Trofim Lysenko. This Soviet scientist, or pseudo-scientist, who claimed to have overthrown the whole of western genetics, was Stalin's favourite. The vast majority of British scientists considered him a charlatan. Stalin had a material interest, which we did not then admit, in keeping the friendship of British scientists. He was collecting the military secrets which they alone could provide. By insisting that they should support Lysenko, he was driving them out of the Communist Party.

The most distinguished victim of this policy was Professor J. B. S. Haldane. He was a dedicated experimenter. If an experiment was dangerous, he would try it on himself. His work on safety in submarines, after the sinking of *Thetis* in 1939, saved the lives of many sailors, but probably shortened his own.

In the late 1940s the girl who collected Haldane's Party dues found it a trying task, because his flat was full of white Persian cats, which stank. Haldane wanted to make sure that all white Persian cats with green eyes were deaf, and that all white Persian cats with blue eyes were blind. As a geneticist, he was prepared to put up with the smell. And, as a geneticist, he knew that Lysenko was talking nonsense.

We all knew the Russians were talking nonsense about our own subjects. As a journalist, I knew that they could not write a news story. I had been at an art school, long enough to know that Soviet art was awful. When I said so to Jack, he replied: 'That's an incorrect formulation.' And yet he knew that almost everything the Russians wrote about education was worthless. We met a British musician, just back from Russia, who told us that Soviet music had been stifled by worship of Tchaikovsky. Nevertheless we believed that in some general way the Soviet Union was all right.

Haldane seemed to share this attitude. His exit from the Communist Party was reluctant, slow and agonised. His articles, explaining science to the general reader in terms which can still be read with pleasure, continued to appear in the *Daily Worker* until 9 August 1950. Three months later a Sunday newspaper got hold of the fact that Haldane had left the Party. He issued an evasive statement and went into hiding.

The chief sub-editor, Allen Hutt, told me that the Communist leaders could not find Haldane. 'We should have been much firmer with him!' Hutt snapped.

Was Hutt, then, a ruthless apparatchik? He wanted to be one. In his youth he had attended the Lenin School in Moscow. Deeply sensible of the honour, he spent the rest of his life trying to be worthy of it.

But his nature was against him. Anyone who wants to know what Allen Hutt was like need only look at his son, a gynaecologist who in his spare time does a comic turn as Hank Wangford.

Hutt was a comedian. Veteran members of the National Union of Journalists remember him fondly, as the man who could make them laugh all the way from Blackpool to London.

Like all comedians, Hutt was given to repeating his

catch-phrases. When, battling against time and a chronic shortage of staff, he had succeeded in putting the second edition away, he would heave a sigh of relief and say: 'Well! I could do with a bottle of Burgundy and a black woman.' Once, when he had got as far as the bottle of Burgundy, he looked up and noticed the comrade from Nigeria, who was working with us on the subs' table to gain experience. Hutt let his sentence trail off in the air. He would never wantonly have hurt anybody's feelings.

This humane, civilised man, an excellent father (and for me an excellent father-figure) had contorted himself into a belief that Haldane ought to have betrayed his life's work, in order to stay on the Party line.

Later I came on Haldane by chance, in an underground train. We had met several times, but I reminded him who I was. I told him how much my little girl was enjoying his book: *My Friend Mr. Leakey.* Then I said: 'Your old friends wish that you would get in touch with them.'

Haldane gave me a look of absolute horror. I realised for the first time what he had been through. I also knew that nothing I said would persuade him that I was not a tail, set on him by the Party. I could do nothing but let him get off at the next station, and see for himself that I was not following him. I never saw him again.

There were still scientists who loved the Soviet Union. In October 1950 an atomic specialist, Bruno Pontecorvo, fled to Leningrad. Rebecca West wrote in the *Evening Standard* that the authorities should have known better than to trust a man with Communist relations. This caused hilarity in the office, where everybody knew that I was Rebecca West's niece. 'What's it worth to your aunt if we don't tell on her?' asked one of my fellow-subs.

We were more puzzled by the defection of the two diplomats, Guy Burgess and Donald Maclean, in 1951. We knew that the Soviet Union must have spies – but homosexual spies? Even the Soviet diplomats in London were shocked. One of them said to a *Daily Worker* man: 'But in our country this is a very serious offence. People go to prison for many, many years.'

Hutt said to me: 'You're too young to remember the frisson that went through Bloomsbury, when the Soviet Union made buggery a crime.'

Many of the older leaders felt no such frisson. Campbell had hated being in Pentonville prison, because he was surrounded by homosexuals. He was happier when they moved him to Brixton, among the burglars.

Pollitt was once asked by Stephen Spender (who was a Communist briefly, in the 1930s): 'What is the Party's attitude to legalising homosexuality?' Pollitt replied, in his robust north-country way: 'Ee! We'll have noon o' that filth and roobish, when we coom to power.'

Our feelings were tied up with our hatred of the public school system – felt most passionately by those who had been to public schools. Homosexuality was part of capitalist decadence... Tom Driberg, MP, was something of an embarrassment.

The alarm about Soviet spies, caused by the flight of Burgess and Maclean, had one happy result for us. An ex-Communist wrote, absurdly, that we got our orders from Moscow by way of the Tass teleprinter. 'What a lot of directives from Moscow I've put on the spike!' reflected Brian Pearce. Somebody believed this; the Tass teleprinter service was banned. In public we protested; in private we rejoiced.

On 6 February 1952 King George VI died. All the papers came out the next morning with thick black borders, except ours, which carried a few lines, headed: KING'S DEATH HALTS CENSURE DEBATE. I felt proud of working for a paper which kept a sense of proportion. He had died of being a heavy smoker, but nobody said so then.

That happened to be my night off. My colleague Florence Keyworth came to our house, to watch the new craze, television. It was catching on among the workers, but most intellectuals despised it. Jack, however, loved it all, even the clapped-out comics. Florence was disappointed. As a sign of national mourning, the BBC cancelled its programmes for the evening. There was no other channel. More than the hostility to homosexuals, more than the amity to heavy smokers, that blank screen shows how long ago this was.

At Easter 1952 the British Communist Party held a Congress, the first for three years. Its main business was to publicise the Party's new programme: *The British Road to Socialism*. This had some phrases which bewildered the faithful. The statement that our Party meant to break up the British Empire was described as 'a lie'. We had always thought it was true.

Another odd feature of that Congress was the attack by our leaders on Aneurin Bevan. Of all left-wing Labour men, he was the most popular, because he had brought in the National Health Service. Yet Campbell, reverting to the style of the old *Worker's Weekly*, declared: 'He continues to run along the coat-tails of their imperialist system.' This meant that Bevan had said a kind word for Tito.

Pollitt's speech to the Congress concluded in what was then the standard style: 'And we are led, guided and inspired by the greatest genius the international working class has ever produced, Comrade Joseph Stalin.' In one way this was an understatement. Stalin had not only inspired, but written, some of the odder phrases in *The British Road to Socialism*.

The *Manchester Guardian* commented that the speeches of the leaders had betrayed their desire to seize power and hold it by undemocratic means. John Gollan wrote to the *Guardian* denying that the Party intended to seize power for itself. It would have allies... In reply, one Leo R. Muray wrote about the way the Party treated its allies. He quoted a speech that, unbeknown to any of us, Matyas Rakosi had delivered in Hungary the previous February.

As that speech was to haunt us for years, I give it more space than the *Guardian* did. Rakosi was explaining his tactics after the 1945 elections, when the Smallholders' Party had 56 per cent of the votes and the Communists and Social Democrats 17 per cent each. That was not the moment, he said, to raise the problems of achieving the dictatorship of the proletariat. 'We did not bring them before the Party publicly because even the theoretical discussion of the dictatorship of the proletariat as an objective would have caused alarm among our companions in the coalition and would have made our endeavour to win over, not only the petty-bourgeoisie, but the majority of the mass of the workers more difficult.'

Rakosi went on to say how important it was for the Party to gain the Ministry of the Interior. This made possible the 'unmasking' and 'removal' of leaders of the Smallholders' Party. 'In those days this was called 'salami tactics', whereby we sliced off bit by bit reaction in the Smallholders' Party... We whittled away the strength of the enemy.'

One of the enemy, Bela Kovacs, was 'whittled away' to the Soviet Union for nine years. If we did not know that, it was because we were refusing to look at the evidence. The trials of peasant leaders in Eastern Europe in 1947 and 1948 were to us the mopping up of reactionaries.

How could the Communist Party stage these trials, when it was still a minority? Rakosi explained: 'There was a single position, the control of which was claimed by our Party from the first minute and where it was not inclined to consider any distribution of posts according to the strength of the parties in the coalition; and this was the State Security Authority... We kept this organisation in our hands from the first day of its establishment.'

What made this possible, Rakosi admitted, was the support of the Soviet Union.

The Hungarians were proud of this speech. They had it translated into English. But it was not what our leaders wanted us to read.

They had something else for us to read – or rather to buy, take home, and put on the shelf. *From Trotsky to Tito*, by James Klugmann, was a learned attempt to produce a coherent story linking the Rajk trial, the scanty information available on the Albanian trial and the trial of Traicho Kostov in Bulgaria. If any of us had read it, we might have noticed that Klugmann quoted at length from the written statement of Kostov, without ever mentioning that he had repudiated it in court.

In the summer of 1952 there was a crisis in the office. Freddie, who worked on the sports page, got the sack, and his friend Reg, the chief sub on the day shift, took offence. Were these two more prescient, politically, than the rest of us? Reg was an intelligent man. But I remember only one sign of intelligence in Freddie. He had worked out a theory that Peter Zinkin, our lobby correspondent, whom we all found intolerable as a person and ludicrous as a journalist, was the illegitimate son of Stalin. Freddie pointed out that Stalin had spent a few days in London, at approximately the right time. That would account for Zinkin being unsackable. This attractive theory was, alas, incorrect.

The main grievance of Freddie and Reg was that they were not paid enough.

It was our Party duty to mingle with people from Fleet Street. I used to do my mingling outside the Post Office at Mount Pleasant, waiting for the all-night tram. Cold as those waits were, they were entertaining; people would tell each other about the sub-editor on the news pages, handling a football story for the first time, who changed 'Sheffield Wednesday' to 'Sheffield, last night.' In 1952 the tram was replaced by a bus, which had not the same atmosphere. It did not announce its coming by a long romantic moan. And there wasn't the same friendliness aboard. Or were there, simply, fewer passengers? Late shift workers were becoming better off, and could go home by car.

Freddie and Reg used to meet the Fleet Street men more normally, in pubs. The trouble was that they could not afford to buy the drinks. The fiction was maintained that we were paid the Fleet Street rate, and that we voluntarily gave about half of it back to the paper.

No such arrangement was imposed on the production workers, most of whom were not Communists. Was it fair that it should be imposed on us? What about the rate for the job? Campbell insisted that we should stay on the Party rate, which was based on the working-class average. 'If I got what a Fleet Street man gets,' he said, 'then whenever I collected sixpence at a meeting, it would burrn ma fingers.' (Campbell did not tell us that he, like the other leaders, got ten shillings a week extra.)

Reg pursued his grievance by telling the wages department that he withdrew his consent to the voluntary contribution, and wanted his pay in full. He got it. If he had not, we should all have been expelled from the National Union of Journalists, and Hutt would no longer have been on its executive committee. If Campbell had sacked him, that would have been victimisation, with the same result.

There were tense moments while Reg sat about the office, doing very little work and, with what in the army is called dumb insolence, defying Campbell to sack him. I could take my turn on the day shift now, Cathy being at school, and more than once I felt I had brought out the first edition on my own. Finally Reg took a document produced by a colleague, and held it up to ridicule in a Fleet Street pub. Hutt was able to convince the union that this was unprofessional conduct, and that Reg could be sacked. Campbell was deeply hurt by the whole episode. Freddie and Reg could have brought their grievances to him, he said. 'I am no unapproachable.' And indeed he was not.

After that crisis I went on holiday to Eastbourne. To Jack and Cathy and me, it was Heaven on earth. The weather was perfect. I swam every day for three weeks. Funny, I thought. Then I fainted, and knew I was pregnant.

When I tried to work out when the baby was due, I could not remember any dates. My conscious mind had been engaged by the drama in the office. But I began to knit for April 1953.

The baby was not altogether good news. Modest as my wages were, we needed them. By his first wife (who died young) Jack had a son of whom we were both very proud. He had won a place at Oxford. He had to do his National Service first; it would be five years before he could begin to earn a living.

I continued to work full-time while pregnant. So I remember the excitement in the office, when the Communist Party of the Soviet Union announced its Nineteenth Congress. There had not been a Party Congress since before the war – a fact which the Yugoslavs acidly pointed out, when they were accused of running their Party in a dictatorial way.

Peter Fryer remembers Campbell's joy, when the Congress was announced. Peter thought he was glad for political reasons. But in fact he had a personal reason, which none of us knew then, to rejoice at any sign that the Soviet leaders were becoming approachable.

I began to take notes at editorial staff meetings. At first my notes were scrappy; they were meant not for posterity but for Jack. He was anxious to know what was going on inside the Soviet Union.

So I have notes about that Nineteenth Congress, dated 12 September 1952, though the Congress did not open until three weeks later. Somebody – the notes do not say who – was telling us about changes in the Soviet CP's rules, to be put before the Congress. Somebody was saying: 'There has never been more attention paid to criticism and self-criticism... Every party member has the right to criticise every other Party member, however high up...'

I remember this being said in that Scottish way which gives the wildest piffle the ring of common sense. Was the Scottish voice that of Campbell? The assistant editor, John Gollan, also a Scot, was about to be one of the British fraternal delegates to the Congress. Campbell was not. But my notes record the words: '*Pravda* published a letter asking for the collection of Party dues to be mentioned in the rules.' Campbell – but not Gollan – could read *Pravda*. So it must have been Campbell.

He admitted that discussion within the Soviet CP was being rationed. Wide discussions would be held, he said, only if such a discussion were wanted by several local Party organisations, on the scale of a region or a republic, or if there were not a sufficiently solid majority in the Central Committee, or if the Central Committee, though there were a solid majority, wanted to put the correctness of its policy to the membership. We were to learn later, in our own country, the meaning of such rules.

If my notes are right, Campbell had just been to the Soviet Union. His probable motive for the visit I did not guess until 1990.

After that Congress, Gollan gave us an imitation of Stalin. The genial Uncle Joe, whom we all knew from the photos, was beaming at the Congress when he discovered that some underling had failed to bring him something. Gollan conveyed the sudden dropping of the mask, when Stalin told his henchman off. Doubtless Gollan then made a serious report, but I have no notes of that.

In October Clement Attlee, leader of the Labour Party, accused the Bevanites of running a party within a party. Somebody in the office whispered to me that the real organiser of this left-wing group was our lobby correspondent, Peter Zinkin. 'That must be why it keeps falling apart,' I said. The whisper was intended to impress on me Peter Zinkin's political importance. He was being proposed as a member of the Party committee within the building.

We could not simply vote against him, because the committee was proposed en bloc; we had to vote for or against the lot. All we could do was tell the comrade responsible for the list, Fred Pateman, that Zinkin's name ought not to be on it.

Zinkin once said to me (while the whole office listened aghast) that he did not know the edition times of the paper, and did not see why he should. On another occasion he arrived in the office at three in the afternoon of a day when he was due to deliver his summary of a White Paper. He had not even read it. Fortunately a more competent person, Phil Bolsover, had read it for the feature page, and was able to produce a summary within an hour. Allen Hutt commented: 'Any other paper would have told Zinkin: "Sir! Here is your hat. There is the door." ' As for Zinkin's political expertise, he once wrote that the Chinese Communist armies were about to invade Hong Kong – a statement taken out of the paper at the last minute.

Somebody told Hutt something. Hutt dropped his opposition to Zinkin. Fred Pateman pleaded with us sub-editors to drop ours. 'You must remember,' he said, 'that Peter Zinkin finds it very difficult to construct a story of any kind.' None of us asked: 'In that case, why is he employed here?' We knew we were not going to get an answer to that. Zinkin became a member of the Party committee.

On 20 November 1952 the Slansky trial opened in

Prague. For the first time, the charge 'Zionism' was added to 'Trotskyism' and 'Titoism'. When I came home that night Jack asked me what on earth was going on.

I repeated what I had heard in the office. 'It's these American spies, the Fields,' I said. 'They keep letting out more and more information.'

If I were hoping to present myself as innocent, I would have to stop here. Did I really not know that the Fields were being tortured? In one part of my mind, of course I knew.

One of the defendants was André Simone, also known as Otto Katz. I subbed the report of his evidence, sent to us by our correspondent Sam Russell. Otto Katz confessed that he was an imperialist spy. So, he added, were Noël Coward, the Labour MP Konni Zilliacus, and Claud Cockburn.

Our old colleague Claud Cockburn had retired in 1948, pleading ill-health, and was living in Ireland.He had said some encouraging words to me, when he was a world-famous reporter and I was a beginner. But I had never known him well. I was shocked to find that people who did thought the accusation might be true.

I consulted Campbell. He told me to leave the name in. But, in the final edition, it was omitted.

A mysterious episode followed. Derek Kartun left the paper, apparently without any quarrel. Campbell appealed to us to rebut any suggestion that Derek was leaving because he was Jewish. (Sam Russell, who replaced him, was also Jewish.) Campbell then begged us not to ask Derek the real reason.

On 4 January 1953 the French Communists expelled André Marty, who to us was a hero. He had led a mutiny in 1919, to prevent the French fleet in the Black Sea from attacking the Bolsheviks.

The reasons for his expulsion were given in the French Communist paper *L'Humanité*. I came to work that evening

and found Campbell struggling through it. He asked me:
'What's this word – flagornerie?' I had to look it up.
'Sycophancy,' I reported. Campbell shook his head over the
allegation that Marty's admirers were sycophants. 'I hope this
convinces the French comrades,' he said, 'more than it
convinces me.'

I could not at first see what was upsetting Campbell.
Surely it was possible that Marty had exploited his prestige?
Hemingway said so, when he described Marty in *For Whom
the Bell Tolls*. But embedded in the French Party jargon was
the admission that the conflict was between those leaders who,
like Marty, had been in the Resistance, and those who, like
Maurice Thorez, had spent the war in Moscow. The Moscow
faction had won.

On January 13 the Russians announced the arrest of nine
doctors, six of them Jewish, accused of plotting to poison
Soviet leaders.

Now, at last, we were shaken. All but one tape boy, who
said, of the imperialist plotters: 'Gosh! They never give up, do
they?' I envied him his simple faith.

We went on struggling to keep our illusions. A Jewish
writer and his girl friend spent hours over a Chinese meal,
telling Jack and me that Stalin was anti-Semitic. Jack, Jewish
and a lifelong worshipper of Uncle Joe, insisted he was not. I
passionately backed him up. The girl was almost in tears at our
stupidity.

On 5 March 1953 Stalin died. But the image of Uncle Joe
took four terrible years to die.

II

Jack, who had seen the news on TV, called up the stairs in tragic tones: 'Alison! Stalin's dead.' We grieved together. The next morning Catherine, not quite seven, said: 'Our friend's dead.'

Grief pervaded the *Daily Worker* office. A Russian from Tass came in and Hutt wordlessly wrung his hand.

It was my last day; I was leaving to have the baby which I supposed to be due in April. Hutt said to me: 'Well! Joe's dead. You're leaving. And *Reynolds* has sacked Schaff.'

Reynolds News was the Sunday paper owned by the Co-ops; Schaff was Gordon Schaffer, a journalist who belonged to the Labour Party but had always been pro-Soviet. I was deeply flattered that Hutt should equate these three setbacks to our Party.

Campbell presented me with my colleagues' gift, a Pyrex bowl. I made a speech. I thanked everyone for being so kind to me during my pregnancy. It showed, I said, that, whatever our enemies might say, the Communists were the guardians of human values.

Harry Pollitt's piece on Stalin, published in the *Daily Worker* the next day, had a similar theme. 'Never... have I met anyone so kindly and considerate.'

On April 3 the Soviet Government, now run by Georgi Malenkov and Nikita Khrushchov, released the nine doctors.

But they weren't nine; they were 15. The Kremlin said: '...falsely accused...' and added that there had been '..the use of methods of investigation which are inadmissible and most strictly forbidden by Soviet law.' This was clear, even to us, as meaning that the doctors had been tortured.

Jack told me to ring up the Jewish couple with whom we had so passionately argued, less than six weeks before. 'Tell them they can come here and eat chicken,' Jack said. 'We'll eat humble pie.'

At the house of another friend someone bitterly attacked me, on hearing I was from the *Daily Worker*. 'How can you justify what they did?' he said. 'As soon as the doctors were accused, the *Daily Worker* wrote as if they were guilty.'

'I agree with you,' I said. 'The *Daily Worker* did wrong.'

A gasp went round the room at the sound of these words, coming from a Communist. I myself was taken aback. I had not known I thought this, until I said it.

A few days later a trade union official, Ben Smith, who had left the Party some years before, baited us about the release of the doctors. Jack said: 'Perhaps we'd all better keep quiet for a bit about our great leader.'

The baby was late. 'Nine months?' said the doctor at the ante-natal clinic. 'You've been coming here for nine months!' So I was 10 months pregnant. The doctor had a Jewish name and a huge hooked nose. Not once in those months had I heard any anti-Semitic remark from the other women. They talked only of how kind the doctor was, and how gently he examined them. I felt that my half-Jewish baby was going to be born in a friendly, tolerant place, very different from what we now suspected of the Soviet Union.

I was enormous – much too fat to begin with, and bursting with overdue baby. By May 19 even my face had swollen. Jack looked at me and said: 'I've never loved you more than I do now.'

Because he had said this, my labour pains were not painful. At 3.20 a.m. on May 20, before I could take my first whiff of gas and air, Ruth Stella got born so fast that the midwife had to field her.

She was Ruth because 'whither thou goest I will go', and Stella because I wanted a name like a peal of bells, to show my delight in having her. I was light-headed with happiness. True, we were rather poor. But, before the baby was a month old, that problem was solved. I became the *Daily Worker* television critic. This is probably the only form of journalism that can be combined with breast feeding. As it was a part-time job the pay was only £4 a week, but it made a great difference to us then.

And the job was politically important. The television era began in earnest when Queen Elizabeth II was crowned, on 2 June 1953. Proud of not being sectarian, we invited some of Jack's fellow-teachers to watch the Coronation. That was the last time anybody came to our house for the television. By the end of 1953, every family had its own.

For two or three years more, indignant comrades kept writing to the *Daily Worker*, asking why it gave space to television. The masses couldn't possibly afford it. But the masses had made up their minds that, whatever else they could not afford, they were going to afford that.

There were also comrades who argued that we were encouraging a passive, receptive attitude. Why didn't we tell the workers to make their own entertainment, for example by learning to play the mandoline? I replied that, when I went to meetings of the Co-op Women's Guild, I never heard anyone say: 'The thought struck me when I was practising my mandoline...' Political arguments always began: 'Did you see on the telly last night...?'

Because of my new baby, I was not present on 14 June 1953, when a huge demonstration outside the American

Embassy demanded the reprieve of Ethel and Julius Rosenberg. The Rosenbergs had been found guilty of passing atomic secrets to the Soviet Union. I still think they ought to have been reprieved. Alive, they could have been called to give evidence at the trial of Peter and Helen Kroger, who were convicted of spying in London eight years later. The Krogers were said at their trial to be part of the same spy ring as the Rosenbergs.

Two days before the execution of the Rosenbergs, a rather timid lady, Ray Waterman, stood up in the Strangers' Gallery and shouted to the House of Commons: 'The Rosenbergs are innocent!' She was seized and taken down to the crypt by two policemen. Her husband, Alec Waterman, followed, crying: 'Don't you hurt her!' One of the policemen was nice and one nasty; Ray felt she had read about that somewhere. They explained to her that she would have to stay in custody until the House rose. It might be an all-night sitting. Ray said she didn't mind; what was that to the fate of the Rosenbergs? A policewoman had to be called to sit with her. Ray apologised to the policewoman for making her do extra work. The policewoman was kind and said it was quite all right. The House rose at 1 a.m. and Ray was released into the arms of her husband. By being imprisoned for several hours (and without a trial, too!) Ray became a legend. She does not now like to be called a heroine, but there are still old Party stalwarts who think of her as one.

Why did we feel so much for the Rosenbergs, and so little for the workers of East Berlin, whose rising was put down by Soviet tanks on 17 June 1953? It was not that we could not see what was happening. This was the first great event in Eastern Europe shown to the western world on TV.

Brian Pearce had by this time left the *Daily Worker*, because his competence as a translator of Russian made him indispensable to the Society for Cultural Relations with the

Soviet Union. He remembers his boss, Andrew Rothstein, saying of the events in East Berlin: 'It shows the Russians didn't kill enough Germans in 1945.'

Did we really not care what happened, so long as it happened to Germans? The war had been over eight years. But the wartime hardships were not over yet. We still ate stews, not roast beef, because stewing meat made the ration go further. (The new baby's ration book was a great help.) You had to buy the meat from the butcher where you were registered. If you became convinced that another butcher was better, you could change, but that meant some bureaucratic formalities. A shop was a place where you queued up to be served. I used to do my knitting while I stood at the Co-op counter. Rationing did not end until the middle of 1954.

With our wartime habits we kept a wartime mentality. The Germans were still the enemy. We had seen the pictures of Hitler's concentration camps, and we had not seen any pictures of Stalin's.

The Russians announced the arrest of Lavrenti Beria on 10 July 1953. It had in fact taken place a month earlier. Since Beria had been head of the security police, he could be blamed, and blamed alone, for the torture of innocent people.

Who was to be blamed for the Korean War? It ended four months after Stalin died, in July 1953. On the other hand negotiations had begun in Stalin's lifetime. Once, while the talks were dragging on, Campbell said: 'I wish this thing could be ended on almost any terms.' Winning or losing, that war was a curse to us. By taking the North Korean side, we had antagonised British people. Our comrade Alan Winnington could not return to England; his passport had been withdrawn and he was threatened with prosecution for treason.

We were far from ready to admit that all this had been Stalin's fault. Inside Russia, and in Russia's relations with the world, something was going on which everyone called 'the

42

thaw'. We saw this gladly, and yet we could not admit that what was thawing was ice.

On Christmas Eve 1953 the *Daily Worker* came out with its usual strapline: 'A merry Christmas to all our readers.' Well down the page was the headline: BERIA SHOT. This was the official Soviet announcement that Beria and six other NKVD men had been shot after a secret trial. It had happened on December 16.

The day this news was in the Soviet press, Brian Pearce was on a long railway journey from Moscow to the Caucasus. Everyone on the train was reading *Pravda* with interest – an unusual spectacle. Brian went up and down the train, trying to find someone willing to talk about Beria's execution. He failed. Nobody knew yet how much it was safe to say.

Brian returned to London in January 1954. He brought with him a despatch from the *Daily Worker* man in Moscow, Ralph Parker, and gave it to the foreign editor, Sam Russell. 'Ralph thinks this ought to be the splash,' Brian said. Sam read it and exclaimed: 'The bloody fool! We can't even mention it.'

Ralph Parker's news was that the Soviet Union had abolished the 'Special Conference', the procedure which had enabled the NKVD to imprison, deport and shoot people without trial. This was, of course, good news. The trouble was that the *Daily Worker* had always denied that any such procedure existed.

I knew nothing of this conversation at the time, since I was working peacefully at home. Or, sometimes, not peacefully. Once I found fault with Wilfred Pickles, for inviting on to his programme a man with a performing dog.

I referred to the dog's look of misery, as it slowly went through its pointless tricks. Little did I know that this was a Marxist dog. 'Let me tell you the dog Mij is highly respected up here in the north,' wrote a reader from Durham. 'You will be surprised to know this same dog has earned some good money for the *Daily Worker* at socials etc., and its master is a Party member, so I'm afraid you owe some apology.'

Among the other letters was one enclosing a picture of the dog about to do the trick which always brought the house down at *Daily Worker* bazaars. It was presented with an array of newspapers, and unerringly put its paw on the Daily Worker. 'A trick which, I think you will agree, has some point.'

Another letter assured me that the dog's owner, Robert Gummerson, was 'a gentle and sympathetic person.'

There was a letter of congratulations, though, from the Performing and Captive Animals' Defence League.

> Never having heard of Robert Gummerson I went to the Home Office this morning to look him up in the Performing Animals Register of Trainers and Exhibitors. I drew a blank. Now, if Mij is a performing animal (i.e., one that does its trick on demand) it follows that, as its exhibitor, Robert Gummerson has been making a practice of contravening the law of the land. According to the Performing Animals (Regulation) Act, 1925, there is a fine of £50... the BBC who also are not on the P.A. Register have been acting illegally and should be fined another £50... So thank you, Sir, and Alison Macleod! And now for Yorkshire's Chief Constable.'

At this point I stopped trying to reply to these correspondents, and left Mij, his owner, his admirers and the Chief Constable of Yorkshire to sort things out for themselves.

That year, 1954, was the one that put an end to Senator McCarthy's power in the United States. Because of television, the whole world had been able to watch McCarthy bullying professors and civil servants. That the anti-Communist cause should be represented by a brutal, ignorant loudmouth was marvellous for us. Anybody accused of spying, justly or not, could be called a victim of McCarthyism. 'McCarthy's the best friend we've ever had,' a Soviet diplomat said to Sam Russell.

In February 1954 McCarthy began to accuse the US Army of harbouring Communists. By the end of the year he was finished. The careers he had wrecked stayed wrecked, but the people were still alive.

Brian Pearce was becoming aware how many of Stalin's victims were not. He wrote part of a pamphlet about a Soviet Republic, Northern Ossetia, published under the title: *A People Reborn*. In his first draft he mentioned that, after World War Two, Northern Ossetia's territory had been enlarged by the annexation of part of the Chechen-Ingush Republic – 'whose inhabitants,' wrote Brian, 'were deported.'

When Andréw Rothstein saw this he asked Brian to accompany him to the Soviet Embassy for a talk with the Cultural Counsellor there. The Russian asked Brian to remove all mention of deportation and annexation. Brian's conscience as a historian was aroused. If it were not mentioned that Northern Ossetia had grown bigger, the comparative statistics given elsewhere in the pamphlet would not be comparing like with like, and would give a false impression.

The Russian saw the force of Brian's argument. Only, he stipulated, the pamphlet must not use the word 'deported'. The official formula was that the Chechens and Ingushes 'were given an opportunity to develop elsewhere in the USSR'. To this day, Brian cannot forgive himself for putting his name to those words. He did not know then, but discovered afterwards, that two-thirds of those deported had died on the journey.

At the beginning of 1955, Khrushchov emerged as the winner from the obscure power struggle in Moscow. This had unexpected results. Hitler's pilot, Hans Bauer, a prisoner of the Russians for over ten years, was released and allowed to say that Hitler and Eva Braun really had died in their bunker. In 1945 the Russians had tried to throw doubt on it, suggesting that the western allies had allowed Hitler to escape. Simply by abandoning this lie, Khrushchov did more for peace than the

'World Peace Movement' had ever done.

At the end of May Khrushchov was in Belgrade, admitting that there were 'different roads to Socialism'. On June 2 he signed a pact with Tito. 'He must be a traitor!' I exclaimed. Jack told me not to be so silly. This was long overdue... But if Khrushchov was not a traitor, and Tito was not, then Rajk's confession, and the confessions of those in the dock beside him, were false and had been extorted by torture. In that case Derek Kartun and Peter Fryer, when they reported the Rajk trial, had acted as accomplices to murder.

Nobody felt this more keenly than they did. But both were still disciplined Party members; they did not talk about their anguish outside the Party. Derek Kartun was not ready to talk, even inside the Party, about the real reason why he had left the *Daily Worker*.

What little he said to the comrades in his local branch was not well received. They did not want to hear anything which might undermine their faith. 'I discovered that I had been taking part in a religious movement,' he said later.

Peter Fryer tried to talk to James Klugmann, the man who had written the book: *From Trotsky to Tito*. Klugmann was the tutor at a Party school on philosophy, which Fryer was attending. 'What's all this about Tito?' Fryer said. Klugmann flippantly replied: 'I haven't had a postcard, you know.'

Back at the office, Peter Fryer passionately argued with a colleague, who said: 'I don't know why the Russians had to go and get drunk with Tito. I've been through all those Comintern documents again, and I say they were right to expel Tito. And I've been through the Rajk trial again, and Rajk was guilty.'

At the beginning of 1956 I went to a meeting for 'cultural comrades' at the Holborn Hall. We were harangued by Harry Pollitt and the art critic John Berger. I cannot remember one word said by either; I remember only that we had no opportunity for questions or discussion. It must have been the last time Pollitt got away with that.

I walked to King's Cross with Brian Pearce. I thought he, if anyone, would know what was going on in the Soviet Union. 'Is anything known,' I said, 'about... about the harm Beria did, for example?'

Why didn't I say: 'About the harm Stalin did?' Why didn't Brian tell me about his railway journey, or the abolition of the 'Special Conference', or the deportations? Nobody was going to send us to Siberia. What were we afraid of? Of losing our illusions, nothing else. But this fear was so powerful that we had lost the habit of frankness.

Brian said cautiously: 'Well, they've just made abortion legal. That's a sign of something. You know abortion was made illegal in 1936?'

I remembered that controversy from my schooldays. 'They had a nation-wide discussion first,' I said.

Brian said: 'Yes, they had a discussion, and there was an overwhelming majority in favour of keeping it legal, and then they made it illegal.'

That was news to me. Brian went on: 'Look out for something important being said at the Party Congress in February.'

That Congress was heralded by a big introductory article from Sam Russell in Moscow. It was the splash in the *Daily Worker* on Saturday, February 11: THE AGE OF PLENTY DAWNS. There followed the usual ecstatic account of the Soviet economy.

On the same day, Burgess and Maclean appeared before the cameras, at last admitting that they were in Moscow. Until then, Khrushchov had denied it. Were all the other denials to be denied? We looked forward to a new beginning, a time of openness.

III

Alec Waterman and his wife Ray (the comrade who shouted in the House of Commons) were becoming disturbed by the reports of anti-Semitism in the Soviet Union. Alec was general manager of Collet's Bookshops. His job took him frequently to Eastern Europe. He was also a member of the National Jewish Committee, a body set up by the British Communists in 1941, when Stalin set up the Jewish Anti-Fascist Committee. Nobody yet knew for certain what Stalin had done with the members of his committee. Alec was still trying not to believe the rumours about that, when the Twentieth Congress of the Communist Party of the Soviet Union opened on 14 February 1956.

In a six-hour speech, Khrushchov promised more consumer goods and a seven-hour working day. (We thought they had that already.) Embedded in the gludge was one telling phrase. 'Making a particular leader a hero and miracle worker,' according to Khrushchov, had minimised the role of collective leadership.

The following day Ekaterina Furtseva, First Secretary of the Moscow City Committee, said that work was to be restarted on the Palace of Soviets interrupted by the war. But the war had been over 11 years. What was she trying to tell us?

On February 16, Khrushchov asked the delegates not to

applaud as the Party leaders filed on to the platform. Mikhail Suslov, regarded as a theoretician, said that the theory and practice of the cult of the individual which existed before the Nineteenth Congress was alien to Leninism.

We remembered that the Nineteenth Congress took place five months before Stalin's death. The 'cult of the individual' reigned supreme before, during and after it. This juggling with dates made us less inclined to believe Suslov's assurance that the collective principle was being restored.

Much more impressive was a speech on the same day by the First Deputy Premier, Anastas Mikoyan. He was 'the twenty-seventh commissar', who, in obscure circumstances, was merely imprisoned when 26 commissars of the Baku Bolshevik Government were executed during the Civil War.

Mikoyan declared that there had been mistakes in Soviet foreign policy. 'We, too, were to blame for increasing tension... The Yugoslav question is a case in point. Since then steps have been taken to rectify the position, and such steps could only have been taken by Leninists. The abolition of the military base in Finland and the treaty with Austria likewise show the boldness of our policy and how it takes into account the realities of the situation.'

Mikoyan then uttered three sentences which landed on the front pages of the world's newspapers (and the back page of the *Daily Worker*):

> The principle of collective leadership is elementary for a party of the Lenin type. Yet for 20 years we did not have collective leadership but the cult of the individual. This had a harmful effect.

Mikoyan denounced the falsification of history. This was the speech where the rehabilitations began. The first names mentioned were Stanislav Kossior and Vladimir Antonov-Ovseyenko.

Not everything had changed. The day Mikoyan spoke, two Jews were sent to prison in Moscow for 'distributing Zionist literature.'

The Congress went on for a fortnight. As in a war, long stretches of boredom alternated with moments too exciting for anybody's health. Georgi Malenkov, former Premier and now Minister of Power Stations, spoke on Friday February 17. What he said scarcely mattered; what mattered was to see on the platform, alive and well, a man who had fallen from power.

Saturday was for fraternal speeches by foreign delegations. Harry Pollitt said: 'The workers welcome and salute the brilliant achievements and plans of the Soviet Union.' Then he said it again, at length.

On Monday February 20 the President of the Soviet Union, Kliment Voroshilov, announced a new draft of the penal code. On Tuesday the Soviet President, Nikolai Bulganin, promised an abundance of consumer goods. On Wednesday a member of the Presidium, Mikhail Pervukhin, denounced *The Times* for saying that consumer goods took second place to heavy industry. And on Thursday the Deputy Premier, Alexei Kosygin, promised the population 50 yards of cloth a head in 1960.

Trying to follow all this from a distance, I was most interested in Maria Kovrigina, Minister of Public Health, who spoke on Friday February 24. She said that the infant mortality rate was 'far too high'. So she knew what it was. Why were the rest of us not allowed to know?

A ghost from the past addressed the Congress that day – Trofim Lysenko, Stalin's pet scientist. It was his last moment in the limelight.

The same day, the *Daily Worker* published an article on the Congress by Harry Pollitt: 'The weather is very cold in Moscow, but there is a hot wind of enthusiasm blowing through this great and glorious land.'

It was felt in the office that this kind of thing would no longer meet the case. Campbell had been sending urgent messages to the British delegation, asking for an explanation of Mikoyan's remarks. Pollitt said he was too busy to write this. Palme Dutt, editor of *Labour Monthly*, felt busy too. Both turned to the youngest member of the delegation, the assistant general secretary, George Matthews.

He is the only one still alive. He remembers being asked to write the article, and doing his best to comply. 'I'm not very proud of it now,' he said in 1990.

It appeared under the headline: IT'S NOT A SIGN OF WEAKNESS TO ADMIT MISTAKES. 'Has it weakened the Party and the country to admit the lack of collective leadership which existed for many years up to the Nineteenth Congress?'

> ...the admission of this most serious mistake has been followed by the most far-reaching measures to strengthen collective leadership... The cult of the individual, the lack of collective leadership, the activities of Beria and his group – all these did harm. But the vital thing is that the mistakes have been recognised and the wrong policies put right.

In its way, the article was a masterpiece. It managed to mix half-admissions, half-apologies and whole reassurances, without once naming Stalin.

George Matthews was unlucky, though, in his date. His article appeared on 25 February 1956. In the early hours of that morning, at a closed session prolonged from the previous evening, Khrushchov made his four-hour secret speech on the mass murderer, Stalin.

At the time, George Matthews knew only that the Congress was going into closed session, which meant that the fraternal delegates would not be admitted. Other amusements were found for them. The British were told that the workers of the Caoutchouc factory were longing to hear them make speeches. Five thousand workers duly cheered when Harry Pollitt said that he had visited the Soviet Union 50 times since 1921. (Those words were quoted against him, when people began to ask whether, in 50 visits, he had really noticed nothing.) The *Daily Worker*, which reported this visit, recorded all three of the British as being there. George Matthews remembers that he was there with Pollitt, but cannot recall the presence of Dutt.

Who was where on which day is important, because it was afterwards rumoured that one of the British delegates was given a copy of the secret speech, and concealed it from the other two.

Clearly, the one who got the speech was not Matthews. As the youngest, he was the least likely to have Moscow's confidence. Matthews himself cannot believe it of Pollitt. If it happened at all (which he does not regard as proved) the man who got the speech, and hid it, would be Dutt.

Rajani Palme Dutt was, to the capitalist press, 'the mystery man of British Communism'. I used to hail him by this title when I met him pottering round the shops of Muswell Hill. In the *Daily Worker* office, where he seldom set foot, he was regarded with derision. One night he rang up several times, leaving messages about something important which had happened in China. It should, he said, be the splash. That day Vyshinsky, then Soviet Foreign Minister, had made a speech, and Campbell had decided that this would be the splash. Allen Hutt, always on the wing between the editorial office and the composing room, was told of Dutt's urgent messages and merely grunted. At last Dutt got through when Hutt was at his desk. Hutt picked up the phone and shouted: 'You want us to splash on China. Well, we're splashing on Vyshinsky.' Then he slammed the phone down. Dutt's political guidance always counted for about as much as that.

His views on culture counted for even less. He once protested because a production of *Timon of Athens* was reviewed with the remark that this was far from being Shakespeare's best play. Dutt said that the reviewer should have been more respectful to a play 'beloved by Marx'. The features editor replied that he knew as well as Dutt did the quotation from *Timon of Athens* used in the first chapter of *Capital*. Could Dutt show him any other indication that Marx thought highly of the play? Campbell murmured happily: 'Old Raji's exposed himself as a literary and dramatic critic.'

So Dutt was not an awe-inspiring leader. Nor was he, as another legend had it, a political automaton without a private life. He looked ascetic, being tall and lean, with hollow cheeks and visionary eyes. But he had a wife, an Estonian lady, whom he had romantically courted while her presence in Britain was illegal. (She had come as an agent of the Comintern.)

There may have been some truth in another legend – that he was the man the Russians trusted. Dutt had twice insisted on maintaining Stalin's line, against all such unworthy considerations as common sense.

In 1928 the tiny Communist Party of Great Britain was debating whether the Labour Party was a workers' party or 'a third capitalist party.'

Campbell argued that the Labour Party was based on the trade unions, and that the Communist Party should continue to seek affiliation with it.

Dutt argued for a change of line. The Labour leaders were no better than 'social fascists'. The Soviet leaders declared that Dutt was the only British Communist who understood the situation. Pollitt replaced Albert Inkpin as general secretary of the Party in 1929 because he supported Dutt.

The results for the Party were disastrous. There had been a strong alliance between Communists and left-wing Labour people. The most effective expression of this alliance was the

Minority Movement in the trade unions, presided over by a much respected veteran, Tom Mann.

One day in 1931 Jack, going into the Party's London district office, met Tom Mann coming out. In a fury, Mann cried: 'They've dissolved the Minority Movement, without telling me.'

After Hitler's rise to power the 'social fascist' line was replaced by the 'popular front' line, with which Dutt never seemed entirely happy. In 1939, the Communist leaders supported Britain's entry into the war, while demanding that the politicians of appeasement should be removed from the Government. (If they had persisted in this, they could have claimed a political victory in May 1940.)

Unity Theatre put on, almost overnight, a topical revue: 'Sandbag Follies'. One of the songs went: 'If we can't win the war with Chamberlain's permission, we'll just have to win it without.'

Harry Pollitt rang up the theatre about that song. Jack was called to the phone to talk to him. Pollitt said: 'My wife Marjorie was at your show last night. That song... Well, she felt that if people's sons are killed, you know, they might not like it...' Here a throb of deep sincerity came into Pollitt's voice. 'So if you could take it out, or tone it down...'

What was behind that phone call became apparent a few days later, when the Party line changed. Dutt had been trying to persuade the other Party leaders that they were wrong to support the war. It was an imperialist war. Look at India... (Dutt's father was Indian and he regarded himself as an expert on India, which he first visited many years later, long after writing a book about it.) Campbell and Pollitt were ridiculing Dutt's arguments. Then Douglas Frank Springhall, a Party organiser, arrived from Moscow. He explained that, according to Stalin, it was an imperialist war.

Campbell said (according to Dutt): 'It's the same line as

Dutt's, but Dutt's arguments are better.'

Why Campbell and Pollitt, after holding out for several days, accepted the new line, I shall discuss later. Pollitt must have been preparing to accept it, when he rang Unity Theatre.

In 1956, secure in the knowledge that Stalin had twice backed him, Dutt could ignore the antagonism of other leaders. But to go to Moscow, and find Stalin's memory under attack, threw him completely. 'Khrushchov put his foot right in it at the closed session. He treated Stalin as if he had been an absolute idiot, an incompetent. This kind of treatment by a little fellow like Khrushchov simply gave an impression of spitefulness.'

To whom did Dutt say this? Why, to the capitalist press.The interview was printed in the *Sunday Times* colour supplement on 30 August 1970. Dutt had by then forgotten his insistence (which I shall come to later) that a Communist must never talk to a capitalist newspaper.

All this throws only a glancing light on the question – was Dutt given a copy of the secret speech at the time? Other clues have emerged – but no proof.

On March 1 J. B. S. Haldane unbecame an unperson. His picture appeared on the front page of the *Daily Worker*, and his words were quoted with approval. This was part of a roundup of scientists' views on civil defence in a nuclear war.

Our office was packed for the staff meeting on Monday morning, March 5, when George Matthews gave us his report back. He cannot remember the occasion. Nor should I, perhaps, if I had not taken notes.

The best words to describe Matthews might be: 'typically English'. Not very colourful, not very eloquent, he gave the impression of earnest honesty. The impression was correct; throughout the ensuing months, Matthews believed that he was doing right.

He told us that at the Twentieth Congress there had been

'sharp exposures of weaknesses and shortcomings'. This turned out to mean that Bulganin had denounced the wasteful use of timber. That sort of thing could be denounced in Stalin's day.

Matthews mentioned that the work of economists and historians had been too dogmatic. 'The references to Gandhi in the Great Soviet Encyclopaedia were all wrong.' He added that Mikhail Sholokhov (who wrote *And Quiet Flows the Don*) had denounced his fellow-leaders of the Writers' Union, for never going near the factories. Sholokhov's slogan: 'Send Fadeyev to Magnitogorsk!' was thought by some delegates to be too personal. (Fadeyev shot himself later, on May 13.)

Matthews assured us: 'There was nothing said that hasn't been published. I've got no inside information.' Then came the reassurance: 'That there is now a collective leadership couldn't be doubted by anyone at the Congress.'

Matthews added: 'The lack of collective leadership doesn't mean that everything done was wrong, only that the progress might have been greater than it was. After all, the war was won.'

And the 20 years? His personal opinion, said Matthews, was that this was the period since the rise of fascism. The Soviet Union had spent most of those 20 years in war, or the threat of war. The supreme need, when the Soviet Union was fighting for its life, was the unity of the Party.

A reporter, Leon Griffiths, asked: 'Didn't the delegates want to know more?'

'They weren't so surprised as us,' Matthews replied. He found that the delegates had already been discussing the cult of the individual in their own branches. 'Some delegates mentioned how it had weakened work in their area, with local dictators setting themselves up.'

Phil Bolsover, who had been foreign editor since Sam Russell went to Moscow, felt uneasy about what he had been

writing. He asked: 'Did anyone criticise Khrushchov?'
Matthews said nobody had asked Khrushchov why he had
not criticised Stalin in Stalin's lifetime.

And Beria? 'Nothing new,' said Matthews cautiously.
'Delegates from Armenia, Georgia and Leningrad spoke about
the unjust accusations against good Party comrades, and the
efforts they were making to put things right.'

The meeting was adjourned. People had to start
producing the next day's paper. We agreed to continue the
discussion on the following Monday, March 12.

That week, Jack went to a report-back meeting for
London comrades, addressed by Pollitt. I suggested: 'Ask
Pollitt what he would have said if Beria had won.'

Jack did not have to. Someone shouted: 'If Beria had
won, you'd be coming here to tell us that Beria was OK.'

Pollitt shouted back at his hecklers: 'Defending the
Soviet Union gives you a headache? You think *I* don't know
that? All right – if it gives you a headache, take an aspirin.'

We were still such disciplined comrades that, when Jack
reported this, he reported it with approval.

Dutt had a simpler way with his meetings. He told them
the Soviet output of pig-iron. 'And after all,' said Jack, 'the
pig-iron is the answer.' He meant that the economic triumphs
of Socialism showed the system to be basically good.

On Sunday March 11 the Executive Committee of the
Communist Party met to hear and discuss the reports of the
Twentieth Congress. On March 12 nine letters appeared in our
paper, asking for explanations about Stalin. After them came an
announcement that this correspondence was now closed, and
that there would be a summing-up by the editor. (Matthews
thinks the Party leadership forced Campbell to write this.)

We still knew nothing of the secret speech when we
resumed our *Daily Worker* staff meeting. Matthews was not
there. Mick Bennett, who had replaced John Gollan as

assistant editor, presided. Mick, in the 1930s, had lived in Russia, and had felt honoured when he was allowed to help in the digging of the Moscow Metro. However, his only qualification for talking about the Twentieth Congress was that he belonged to the British Communist Party's executive committee, and had been at its meeting the previous day.

The first to speak was the features editor, Malcolm MacEwen. He had built up a considerable head of steam, during his efforts to keep the features page literate, with interesting letters. That morning's announcement that the correspondence was closed was to him an outrage. He demanded explanations.

'We in this country have suffered from the ignorance and stupidity of the Tass news agency, for example. And that hasn't been the only cause for embarrassment. Next time we have a Soviet election, will we have an article explaining that one candidate is the most democratic system?'

Malcolm asked what was meant by 'the cult of the individual' and 'no collective leadership'. He commented: 'What appears to be meant is that Stalin established a personal dictatorship, kept going by Beria.'

Malcolm added some details, which, he said, he had heard from Andréw Rothstein. (Rothstein, still alive in 1990, confirmed that he was in Russia just after the Twentieth Congress, but did not answer my request for more information.)

Hundreds of innocent comrades were returning from Siberia, Malcolm said. The Soviet leaders were explaining in private that Beria couldn't be removed without removing Stalin. They had all been so busy with reconstruction that, when Beria said: 'I've had some more people shot', everyone said: 'We've got complete confidence in you.'

Malcolm demanded that we should give up 'our chocolate-box picture' of the Soviet Union. 'Let's show the bad side as well as the good side!' He pointed out that many people refused to join the Party 'because of our identification with a police state'. He asked why there had not been a proper discussion of the Russian reconciliation with Yugoslavia. Finally: 'If people get the idea that we've got to go through Beria to get Socialism, they won't want Socialism. I'm not sure I should, either.'

Here I must, alas, admit my own part in the discussion. I said that workers couldn't criticise the shop steward when the boss was listening. In the same way, we couldn't criticise a country ruled by the working class, while the capitalist press was listening. History would be very simple, I argued, if the leaders of progressive causes were good through and through. It would have been much nicer if Oliver Cromwell hadn't massacred the Irish, if Calvin hadn't burned his friend Servetus at the stake, if Peter the Great hadn't tortured his son to death with his own hands. Stalin (I suggested) couldn't have been so bad, if he hadn't been so good; people put power into his hands because he was such a good leader.

A sub-editor, George MacDougall, agreed that workers did not criticise the shop steward when the boss was listening. However, our application of this principle meant that the workers were getting explanations only from *Tribune* and the *Observer*. The George Matthews article was useless. (He did not mean the article on February 25, but a fresh one, in the paper that morning. This was the first one over again, except that, this time, it did mention Stalin.)

Robin Jardine, our librarian, said that Stalin was not the all-important question of the Congress. 'The fact that the Soviet Union is actually building Communism is all-important.'

May Hill, one of the stenographers, had made her views known in a letter to the paper. 'I believe we should continue to place Stalin among the truly great.' Now she seemed to be in two minds:

For 20 years people have been saying: 'Stalin is a dictator', and I've been saying: 'No; he's subject to Party discipline.' Because all I know about collective leadership I've learned from the works of Stalin.

Eric Scott, who acted as Hutt's second-in-command, declared: 'The cult of the individual does not mean a personal dictatorship of Stalin.' Then he added: 'I have felt nothing but relief about what has been said. The rigidity in Soviet thought was leading to an impasse. Our Party was wrong to hold up discussion on this for so long.'

Llew Gardner, a reporter, said: 'We have been guilty of double or treble think, in defending what we think was meant by the Soviet leaders... It is not "full and frank criticism of past mistakes" to say that there were past mistakes.'

Pat Devine, before he came to the production side of the *Daily Worker*, had been in charge of *Russia Today*. He had developed shock absorbers. 'The reason this came up,' he explained, 'is that the Soviet Union is going forward into Communism. It is precisely because of Stalin that people did feel confidence in their own ability to carry on after the death of Lenin, and through the war.'

Gabriel, our cartoonist, whose real name was James Friell, asked incredulously: 'This was not the most important thing in the Congress? For us it is! And we needed a quicker reaction from King Street.' (The Communist Party headquarters.)

Mick Bennett put in: 'Not as quick as Ulbricht!' The East German leader Walter Ulbricht had already declared that Stalin could not be considered a classic Marxist author. (In May 1953 Ulbricht said: 'Comrade Stalin, in his work of genius on dialectical materialism, has creatively developed the teachings of Marx, Engels and Lenin.')

The reporter Leon Griffiths objected to my mentioning great leaders of the past. 'They don't excuse us,' he said, 'because we set up to be a Party of a new type. It's no answer to the people who say: "There you are, power corrupts your leaders like it's corrupted other leaders." '

Then Leon reminded us all of the Soviet brides. 'What Party speaker could ever defend it?'

Mick Bennett put in: 'Stalin didn't defend it, but he was overruled by the Soviet Parliament.' I am sure Mick believed these words while he was uttering them.

'Well, they still didn't get here,' Leon rejoined. 'And we defended that in our paper.'

Mick insisted: 'The cult of the individual does not mean that there has been a personal dictatorship of Stalin, upheld by Beria.'

Nor, he argued, had the British leaders been subservient. 'The political committee of the British Communist Party had sharp differences with the Soviet comrades about the first draft of their economics textbook, and over hydrogen bomb tests. But must we say all this in the paper?'

He argued that Stalin's example had not extended downwards. 'There was no absence of collective leadership in the lower organs of the Soviet Communist Party.'

Several people reminded Mick that delegates to the Congress had complained of little local dictators. Mick swept on: 'After Lenin's death, and the crises that followed, Stalin was, at first, the necessary symbol of collective leadership. Distortions followed. There was a tendency merely to quote what Stalin said as the end of any argument on any subject. This is the cult of the individual... Beria was not just the instrument of Stalin's personal rule.'

We knew that Mick had been no nearer the Twentieth Congress than we had. Somebody laughed derisively. Mick was rattled. He suddenly blurted out: 'In the last three years of Stalin's life he wasn't altogether normal. Beria could do what he liked with him. Why, Stalin even thought that

Voroshilov was a British spy. And Voroshilov was kept out of every meeting for the last seven or eight months of Stalin's life.'

Somebody asked for the evidence that Beria was an imperialist agent.

'Objectively he was, at least,' Mick said. 'How did Churchill know there was conflict inside the Kremlin?'

As we still seemed unconvinced, Mick blundered on: 'Hundreds of comrades were shot by Beria. The whole Leningrad leadership was framed and shot. It happened in Georgia, too...'

But Mick still saw the bright side: 'Perhaps the development of Siberia has been due to the banishment of leading comrades there. Many people were not sent to concentration camps, but to factories.'

Besides, he felt sure it wouldn't happen again. 'The Party will never again be in a position where one person has to be used as a rallying symbol.'

To show how liberal our own leaders were becoming, Mick added: 'The political committee has decided not to lay down a line on art, science, music or literature. When deputations of the two sides argued about painless childbirth, the political committee said it hadn't got a line.'

We scarcely had time to savour the thought that, if Stalin had lived longer, our leaders might have ordered us to have babies painlessly. Mick was denouncing Ulbricht for speaking with indecent haste: 'A little more modesty would have been becoming from those whose failure to resist Hitler led to the whole situation in which collective leadership went by the board.'

Mick concluded with a rousing defence of Stalin as a thinker. 'Can anyone rewrite his *Dialectical and Historical Materialism?* Or *Marxism and the National and Colonial Question?*'

After the meeting Phil Bolsover baited me about the great leaders of the past. 'And I suppose it was all right when Ivan the Terrible hung a corpse from every tree within 10 miles of Moscow?'

I scarcely replied. I was too deeply shaken by Mick's indiscretions.

That same day, Pollitt told a public meeting: 'The security organisation was under the control of traitors.'

On March 15 the promised summing-up by Campbell appeared in the *Daily Worker*. By this time Campbell certainly knew as much as Mick had blurted out to us. That he also knew the contents of the secret speech is possible. But no hint of that appeared in his article. He said that in the readers' letters there had been 'no exaggerated denigration of Stalin'. He then admitted: 'While not throwing the baby out with the bathwater, nevertheless a lot of the bathwater has got to go.'

It went. The following day the correspondence, which Campbell had declared closed, broke out afresh, with five more letters.

That was a Friday. I was watching television, since it was my job, but as the programmes promised nothing special I was also knitting. I had come to the last bit of a polo neck sweater – the neck itself. It seemed endless. I kept measuring, unable to believe that it was growing so slowly.

Chris Chataway appeared on the screen, looking dazed. He said: 'The most extraordinary story has just come in from Bonn. It seems that at the Soviet Communist Party Congress last month Khrushchov made a secret speech…'

When he got to Stalin thinking that Voroshilov was a British spy, I said: 'That bit's true.' Jack said grimly: 'It's all true.'

Not quite. Chris Chataway said: 'Even children were tortured.' That wasn't in the speech as it was published later.

I continued, mechanically, to measure my knitting. Jack said: 'You've just heard that the hero of your life is a torturer of little children, and all you can think of is your knitting.'

In fact I was thinking what Jack was thinking. First: this is true. Then: as we turned a blind eye to these crimes, we are guilty too.

IV

Jean Pronteau, who in those days was on the central committee of the French Communist Party, has described his efforts to make Maurice Thorez, the Party leader, admit that the secret speech had been made:

> Without turning a hair, Thorez said: 'There is no secret report.' I started to get worked up, and took out of my briefcase the notes I had made in Poland. At that point Thorez said to me: 'Oh! So you've got it. You should have said so straight away.' And he added in a pontifical manner: 'Anyway, just remember one thing. This report doesn't exist. Besides, soon it will never have existed. We must pay no attention to it.' *(Socialist Register*, 1976.)

According to Pronteau, the Orwellian words: 'Soon it will never have existed' meant that Thorez was expecting Molotov, Malenkov and Kaganovich to overthrow Khrushchov. They had already drafted a resolution declaring him to be 'an enemy of the people', on account of the secret speech. It was a near thing; they had a majority in the Presidium. Marshal Georgi Zhukov, however, backed Khrushchov, not so much with arguments as with tanks. The western correspondents then in Moscow reported that the army liked Khrushchov, because he had blamed Stalin for the unprepared state of the Soviet Union when Hitler invaded. That put the generals in the clear.

The Thorez line was evident at the time, from the stolid Stalinism of *L'Humanité*. Sam Russell, the *Daily Worker* man in Moscow, knew how Thorez first heard of the speech. The French delegation was given a copy in Russian, and a comrade who spoke Russian translated the salient points for Thorez immediately. If Pronteau is right, Thorez must then have met the Russians who were trying to overthrow Khrushchov.

If he did, he was acting in pursuit of a rational plan. He had some reason to hope that the whole thing could be hushed up, for good.

But what rhyme or reason was there in the behaviour of the British leaders? Pollitt knew that there was a secret speech, while it was being made. Sam Russell, on his way to see Pollitt in Moscow on the evening of 24 February 1956, met a Russian journalist. Sam remarked: 'I suppose they've gone into closed session just to elect the leaders?' The Russian said: 'No, I understand that Khrushchov is going to dot the Is and cross the Ts of the cult of the individual.' Sam repeated this to Pollitt, who raised his eyebrows. The Russian official who was looking after Pollitt then indicated that he was not pleased with Sam. The conversation turned to other matters. Is it conceivable that Pollitt never tried to find out more? True, if the speech had been handed to him in Russian, as it was to Thorez, he would have been obliged to find a translator. His 50 visits to Russia had left him unable to say more than 'Da' and 'Nyet'.

Later Pollitt said that he had first heard of the existence of the speech on March 11, which was not true. But the date is interesting. It was the day of the executive committee meeting, at which the three British comrades who had been to Moscow made their formal report back. What did Pollitt hear on that day, which he was unable afterwards to deny? What did Mick Bennett hear, which enabled him to tell us the next day that Stalin had thought Voroshilov a British spy? The one member of the British delegation who did read Russian (though he seldom attempted to speak it) was Palme Dutt.

Once the story had broken, on the evening of March 16, the British Communist leaders ought to have known that there was no hope of denying it. The murders, tortures and frame-ups filled the newspapers on Saturday March 17. The *Daily Worker*, in its final edition, had a single-column piece headed: 'Stalin: a strange story'. This mentioned Stalin's rudeness to Lenin's widow and a few other points:

> The story alleged that there had been extensive 'purges' in the years 1936-38, and that 5,000 officers had been killed. It also declared that Stalin had ignored warnings from Britain of the Nazi attack... It was stated that Stalin was conceited and was fond of seeing films and pictures of himself in favourable circumstances. The Bonn report follows a less detailed story quoted earlier in the day from the *New York Times*, written by Harrison Salisbury. Up to the time of going to press, no confirmation had been received of either story by the *Daily Worker* correspondent in Moscow.

This was not for want of trying. Campbell had repeatedly phoned Sam Russell at his hotel. The Russians on the switchboard denied that he was there. (He was.)

Most comrades could not believe what they were reading. On Sunday morning, March 18, Sheila Lynd came to her job on the features page, laughing at the ridiculous things they believed in Bonn. How Sheila Lynd could be so naive I never understood. Ever since her work for the Left Book Club in the 1930s, she had known all the Party leaders personally, and she had few illusions about them. Why did she still think that what they had been telling her, all these years, was true? She had missed the staff meeting with Mick Bennett.

Sheila was pointing out how impossible the whole thing was, when Frank Gullett, the news editor, said to her: 'Fraid it's all true, dear.'

How did he know? Because Sam Russell, in touch at last, had sent the paper a six-page summary of the secret speech. He had written down what he was told by Dennis Ogden, a British comrade who worked at the Foreign Languages Publishing House in Moscow and consequently had to belong to a branch of the Soviet Communist Party. Every Party branch, throughout the Soviet Union, heard the speech read aloud within a fortnight of its being made. There was rioting in Tbilisi on March 8, because the Party members there were incensed at this attack on Georgia's most famous son. Years later a Georgian lady explained to me: 'They thought Stalin must be good, because he'd killed so many Russians. They forgot he'd killed a lot of Georgians too.'

A speech which was causing riots could not be kept a secret. Though nobody at any of the Party meetings was allowed to take a note, the main points of the speech were universally remembered and passed on. It was impossible to keep them from western pressmen in Moscow. But everything the journalists tried to tell their papers about it was censored. In Stalin's day the censorship had applied to Communist correspondents too, but by this time Sam Russell was free to put over what he liked.

He was, however, such a disciplined Party member that, after hearing Dennis Ogden's account, he wasted several days in trying to get some official confirmation. Everywhere he met blank denials that there ever had been such a speech. He thought the Russians' behaviour incomprehensible. But it made good sense if Jean Pronteau was right, and everyone was expecting Khrushchov to be overthrown. If the speech had become an unspeech, any official who confirmed it would have become an unofficial.

Sam in vain tried to convince the Russians that the next pressman who left the Soviet Union would send the story to his paper. It was, as it happened, the Reuters man who got out first. He persuaded Reuters to attribute the story to non-existent Communists in Bonn. This concealed the fact that it came from Stockholm – which, in those days, was everybody's first stop after Russia.

On March 18, before Sam put over his summary of the speech, he told the stenographer that this was for Campbell and the Party leadership only. The *Daily Worker* stenographers listened through earphones, which left both hands free. They took down what the reporter said straight on to the typewriter, using abbreviations which the subs and compositors understood. This meant that anybody looking over the stenographer's shoulder could read the story. Peter Fryer tried to read it; the stenographer told him to go away. Then Malcolm MacEwen read the first page. He rushed through the office waving it and crying: 'Look what Sam's sending over!' Campbell snatched the page from him and told him to shut up. But the whole of Sam's despatch was very soon common knowledge in the office.

If Campbell had printed Sam's six pages as they stood, the rest of 1956 would have turned out differently. Instead, he told Sam to send over another story, admitting that the speech existed, and that it had been discussed all over the Soviet Union, but giving few details of what it contained. This was the splash on Monday March 19.

Under it was Campbell's leading article, which declared: 'Truth and fiction are inextricably mingled in the capitalist press accounts of the speech.' This was a lie. With Sam's summary before him, Campbell knew that there was scarcely any fiction in the capitalist press accounts.

The New York *Daily Worker* also described the nationwide discussion in the Soviet Union, but it did so in the words of a capitalist pressman, Henry Shapiro of United Press:

Floodgates of discussion and criticism have been opened as

never before, so that every Soviet citizen is beginning to enjoy the feeling of freedom from fear.

We had some floodgates to open inside the *Daily Worker* office. Malcolm MacEwen has said of Campbell: 'He ran a very democratic paper, on which the tape boys could, and did, criticise the editor at staff conferences.' (*The Listener*, 16 December 1976.) This is true. But what is also true is that for several years 'criticism' had meant what it meant in the Communist countries. Dora Scarlett has described this in her book, *Window onto Hungary*:

> The situation was that you could, and indeed must, criticise anything which the Government had already marked out for criticism... Bureaucracy, inefficiency, or mechanical, heartless and unfeeling behaviour on the part of minor officials were accepted targets for criticism. But there were some things you could not say, and here are a few of them. You could not say that the general direction... of the Five Year Plan was mistaken; after the Government had said it was mistaken you could not then say it was right. You could not say anything against Rakosi, or anyone in the higher ranks of the Party; you could not criticise them for cutting themselves off from the people or riding about in cars with the curtains drawn. You could not say that you thought Laszlo Rajk, or anyone else condemned on a political charge, was innocent; until May, 1955, you could not say anything favourable to Tito; you could not criticise any action of the Soviet Union...

Dora was in Hungary, where people had every reason to fear what might happen to them if they spoke out of turn. We had nothing to fear but the loss of our illusions. Yet the effect had been remarkably similar.

Now, at last, we were demanding a proper explanation from Campbell. At the editorial staff meeting on Friday, March 23, Campbell seemed willing to give it. He took us through the history of the Soviet Union: 'Trotsky's idea was that without a revolution in Germany the situation was hopeless. Bukharin believed that Socialism could be built only "at a snail's pace". And some of the difficulties he pointed out actually materialised... Stalin's alternative was to combine a great drive for collectivisation with a great drive for industrialisation... It was at this time that Stalin came forward as an outstanding leader...'

Campbell appealed to us to think 'dialectically', not like primitive Methodists. We should say neither: 'Poor old Joe' nor 'bloody old Joe'. He argued: 'A man can be a great historical figure and then a menace.' And he asked us to remember that, in the drive for collectivisation, 'force was used, not only against the capitalists, but also against the peasants'.

During the rise of fascism in Europe, 'we tolerated the building of Stalin's personal power, which we now ought not to defend'.

He insisted that the Soviet people had improved their conditions: 'The ground gained was never lost. But despotic power was a handicap to further development, to science, to living Marxism. Were we never embarrassed – by the Russian brides, for example? The Soviet Union is now rid of its suspicious mania. We ought to feel that our burden has rolled away. Why don't we? Because we defended the indefensible. We know that. But we also defended the Socialist achievements...'

Campbell took a swipe at Ulbricht. 'He reminded me of the Nicean Council, deciding which books of the Bible were sacred. It's not for him to say who is a classic writer and who isn't.'

He concluded by asking us to look at the 'positive sides' of Soviet achievements – for example the steel output.

Malcolm MacEwen said that this was the best contribution we'd heard so far from any Party leader. We all applauded. But Malcolm pointed out that we did not yet know the full text of the Khrushchov speech.

Phil Bolsover was incensed because Pollitt was still making speeches about Stalin's 'mistakes'. Phil said: 'Mass murder is not just a mistake.' As for Campbell's plea to look at the positive achievements, Phil asked: 'What's the use of a good house, if you may be snatched out of it?' Then he asked when the present Soviet leaders were going to criticise themselves.

Frank Gullett, the news editor, said: 'We don't have to think that every inhabitant of the Soviet Union has been going to bed every night in fear of the 3 a.m. knock.' (I was becoming aware that we did have to think that.)

Robin Jardine of the library took comfort from the fact that the present leaders had not conducted purges against Stalinists. Then his assistant, Claire Madden, threw a spanner in the works.

Claire was an Irish Catholic. She had shown great ingenuity in arguing, in the columns of the paper, that one could be both a Catholic and a Communist. (The Pope had said one couldn't, but he hadn't said it under the seal of infallibility.)

Now she was using her ingenuity in a way which was to make life uncomfortable for everyone around her. She said: 'There is not a single person in the Party who would not have been glad to have personal leadership replaced by collective leadership. We would all have been glad to see the end of "Roma locuta est; causa finita est".' Some of the less erudite comrades put in: 'End of what? ' Claire translated: 'Rome has spoken; the case is concluded.' Then she went on: 'That's not what is causing the confusion. It's the report from Bonn. Our first reaction was to deny the lot. Then the editorial said it was an "inextricable mixture". And have there really been no purges against Stalinists? Then what about Beria and the other Georgians?'

Claire was not the first person to remark that to try Beria and his men in secret, and to announce their executions after the event, was an odd way to introduce the rule of law. But she was the first to challenge Campbell with that question at a meeting. 'Radek and the others were tried in public,' she reminded him. Campbell made no comment.

Peter Zinkin said of the Khrushchov speech: 'Don't let's pretend that it was not a shock.'

'A relief,' said Eric Scott.

'To me a shock,' insisted Zinkin. 'I spent the winter of 1931 in Moscow, living mainly on poor rice and sour bread – oh, yes, and caviare. There was no butter, no milk, no eggs – but enthusiasm inside the factories, and completely free expression of opinions. When we see how conditions have changed in the Soviet Union, we can see how the cult of Stalin arose.'

Campbell defended his treatment of the news from Bonn. 'Sam's report on Monday was ahead of any other Communist paper in the world.' (It was ahead of *L'Humanité*, certainly.) 'Don't demand a complete explanation in five minutes. Phil says a good house is no use without personal liberty. What's the good of personal liberty in a mud hut, working 18 hours a day?'

Jack, when I showed him my notes of this meeting, pointed out the phoniness of Campbell's argument about personal liberty and mud huts. We had always argued that if the worker had personal liberty he would be better able to struggle out of the mud hut.

On March 27 the *Daily Worker* gave great prominence to a speech by Willie Gallacher (who from 1935 until 1950 had been the Communist MP for West Fife). He declared: 'When the tumult and dust subsides, make no doubt about it, the balance will be heavy on the side of Stalin.' The same day, the

Polish paper *Trybuna Ludu* published a summary of the secret speech – the first such press report in any Communist country. Over 30 years were to pass before the speech was published in the Soviet Union.

On March 29 Rakosi admitted that Rajk and his co-defendants had been framed. He admitted it late, reluctantly and half-heartedly – which was natural, since he was declaring himself a murderer. Still, it was rehabilitation. When the news arrived in the *Daily Worker* office, Walter Holmes put it on the spike.

Walter Holmes was the copytaster, who also wrote a daily column: 'A Worker's Notebook'. (Because of the shortage of staff, almost everybody on the paper did two jobs.) He prided himself on his rock-solid adherence, through thick and thin, to the Party line.

This time, though, the Party line had left him behind. Khrushchov had, after all, not been overthrown. So the line was that Tito had been unjustly accused, and, that, therefore, so had Rajk. Malcolm MacEwen and others hauled the news off the spike, took it to Campbell and got him to agree that it should be published. It appeared on the front page of the final edition on Saturday, March 31. Walter Holmes defended himself by saying: 'Who the hell cares about Rajk?'

Peter Fryer did, for a start. He read about the rehabilitation on the morning of Easter Saturday, as he was on his way to the Congress of the British Communist Party. When he arrived at Battersea Town Hall he saw, among the people distributing leaflets outside, a short, square man, with a head too big for his body and a deeply entrenched scar slanting across his brow. This was pointed out to him as the notorious Trotskyist, Gerry Healy. The Trotskyist evidently knew Campbell; he cried out to him: 'Hey Johnnie! What about that book, eh? *From Trotsky to Tito.*' Campbell pointed to the gutter and made a gesture, as if pulling a lavatory chain.

ALISON MACLEOD

Peter Fryer was at the Congress as a reporter, not as a delegate, but he was determined to speak. When the Congress went into secret session, the following day, he got his chance.

The purpose of the British secret session was to criticise the Russian secret session. Why had foreign delegates not been allowed in to hear the Khrushchov speech? To set an example, the British let foreign delegates in. The French one was deeply shocked to see the British pass a resolution which (however mildly) criticised the Soviet leaders for not issuing a public statement on Stalin.

This was the first chance the British Communists had to call their own leaders to account. While the Congress was in open session, with the capitalist press listening, the delegates criticised the leaders for isolating them from the Labour movement and for failing to oppose conscription (then still in force in Britain). But in the secret session they could demand explanations about Stalin.

Pollitt said that he regretted the reaction of many Party members. Of the letters received at Party headquarters, over 300 had been about Stalin, and only 50 about other issues. He was, he said, worried about a gap between intellectuals and workers on this issue. (There was, as we shall see later, no such gap, though the intellectuals may have written longer letters.) Pollitt then said that he had not, while in Moscow, known that there was a closed session.

A liar needs a good memory. Pollitt forgot that the fact of the closed session had been mentioned at the time in the *Daily Worker*. (Which said that it was for the purpose of electing the Party leaders.) We have already seen that he knew Khrushchov was making a speech.

It was at this point that Pollitt said he had first heard of the secret speech on March 11. Not until March 18, he went on, did he know what it contained. That was the day of Sam's six-page summary. So many people now knew of its existence

75

that it ended the period of deniability.

Pollitt then declared that the British Communists had no copy of the speech, though the Russians said they had sent one. It must have been mislaid in the post.

This was the remark which led many people to believe that either Pollitt or Dutt had been given the speech, and had concealed it. The reference to the post was not taken seriously; important Russian documents were always handed personally to trusted comrades.

Willie Gallacher, the former MP, said: 'I haven't yet succeeded in adjusting myself.' He spoke of Stalin as he had known him in the 1920s – quiet, unassuming and kindly. Some doctors, he said, were convinced that Stalin had had strokes before the one that killed him; that might have disturbed his balance towards the end. 'I'm satisfied,' Gallacher conceded, 'that things were wrong.' But he thought some of the more critical comrades were being 'irresponsible'.

This was a word we were to hear again, often. Sheila Lynd later told an old Stalinist: 'I can't think of anything you can do with facts more irresponsible than to ignore them.'

At the Congress Peter Fryer had no right to speak, as he was not a delegate. But Campbell, who was in the chair, knew what he was feeling, and called his name. 'I had to practically fight my way on to the platform,' Peter later recalled, 'because I had no delegate's credentials.'

Peter told the Congress: 'It is a painful process to have our fancies and illusions swept away. But it is a healthy process.' He quoted Friedrich Engels: 'Sacrifice every idealist fancy which cannot be brought into harmony with the facts.' Consequently,

It is not right for us to accept uncritically, unthinkingly, unquestioningly, what we are told on these matters either by the Soviet Party leaders or by the leaders of our own Party... I think we have not the right but the duty to press for honest and straightforward answers to certain questions...

One: What were the present Soviet leadership doing to allow the development of the cult of the individual and the substitution of arbitrary one-man rule and ultimately tyranny for collective leadership in the period between 1934 and 1953?

Two: Why does the self-criticism of the Soviet leaders not apparently extend to a critical reassessment of their own weaknesses and shortcomings during that period?

Three: What solid guarantees are there that such a combination of circumstances so grievously harmful to the interests of the working-class movement shall never happen again?

If I press this third question it is because I feel a particular personal anguish in the fact that I helped to report the trial of Laszlo Rajk for the *Daily Worker*, and therefore shared, however unwittingly, in the responsibility for deceiving thousands of British workers about the character of that trial and the character of Rajk himself.

Palme Dutt made no comment on this, but attacked Gallacher's statement as 'a diversion'. Gallacher hadn't brought out Stalin's 'positive role'. The British Communists' attitude to Stalin, Dutt said, had not been one of servility but of 'international solidarity'.

Then a rank-and-file Party member, Alan Wilson, outdid even Dutt. 'If another Russian brides issue came up, my place would be on the soapbox justifying it.'

Campbell urged people not to minimise the great injustices done to good revolutionary socialists. 'If Gallacher had been one of those unjustly condemned,' he said, 'I hope we'd have shed some tears for him.' Few people then knew what personal reason Campbell had had for tears.

Even Campbell, though, told the delegates: 'Don't swing too far the other way!'

Andrew Rothstein pointed out that the Extraordinary Commission (better known as the Cheka) had arrested and executed people without a public trial in Lenin's day. True, and some of us were beginning to think about that.

Pollitt, replying to the debate, did not reply to any of Peter's questions. He did, however, apologise for having said, less than a month earlier: 'Defending the Soviet Union gives you a headache? Take an aspirin!' This was, he now admitted, 'an irresponsible and stupid statement'.

The only leading Communist who congratulated Peter Fryer on his speech was Maurice Cornforth, known as a Marxist philosopher. Peter heard later that after his speech Isabel Brown had turned to somebody near her and remarked: 'That lad won't last long in the Party.'

Who was Isabel Brown? From one point of view, a fat old granny, whom Jack and I saw sitting peacefully in Alexandra Park on a Sunday, knitting for her grandchildren, with her placid husband Ernie Brown beside her.

From another point of view, she was one of the Party's leading orators, who used to wax particularly eloquent on the need for mothers to demand peace. 'I have held my son's young body in my arms...' she would cry, while the son, a grown man, would shrivel with embarrassment at the back of the hall.

Her long-standing *amitié amoureuse* with Campbell was not concealed by either, though they continued to live with their respective spouses. Once, when Allen Hutt was gossiping about this, I remarked on Isabel Brown's lack of any obvious physical attraction. 'Still,' I added, 'people might say that about me.' Hutt cried: 'I'd rather sleep with you than I would with Isabel Brown!' I repeated this to my husband, proudly. It was the best back-handed compliment of my life.

On the Friday after that Congress, April 6, Campbell reported back to the staff. He admitted: 'In the past our line was to defend the Soviet Union, warts and all. It will take a long time to break down the 20-year cult, and it won't be done by substituting the name of Lenin for the name of Stalin.' He expressed his disquiet at a recent article in *Pravda*, containing repeated references to 'the great Lenin'.

As for the suggestion, which was then gaining ground, that we should dissolve ourselves and apply for individual membership of the Labour Party, Campbell argued: 'The Labour Party is not standing for any transition to Socialism, only for a reformed capitalism. We remain the Communist Party because that's the only way forward out of capitalism.'

Malcolm MacEwen commented that there was a great difference between Campbell's line and that of Pollitt and Dutt in the closed session. 'They seemed not to have changed their line at all. We can point out the warts in Soviet housing, for example, but never in current Soviet policy... Why is there still no statement, still no discussion on Yugoslavia? Why are we not apologising to Zilliacus?' (The Labour MP who had been called a British agent in the Slansky trial.)

Eric Scott recalled what he had been told by German refugees 20 years earlier. 'Many people who worked for Moscow Radio ended in prison. People were arrested because someone had a grudge against them. Yet the comrades who knew this remained in the Communist Party, because they believed Socialism was the only way forward.'

Walter Holmes (who had put Rajk's rehabilitation on the spike) said: 'I remember Stalin's splendid speeches to collective farmers in the early 1930s. They were enthusiastically received. And yet force was being applied all the time. Trainloads of kulaks were being taken away to Siberia. I defended this then on the ground that these were the class enemy.'

Frank Patterson, who like Holmes was a copytaster, asked: 'What explanation is there for Rajk's confession?'

'Nobody has any explanation,' Campbell said. 'Rajk may have agreed to confess in the interests of the state, but we don't know.'

I had been re-reading all the documents issued at the time of the quarrel with Tito. 'It looks to me,' I said, 'as if both sides had a cult of the individual, but they were culting different individuals.'

'I'm inclined to agree,' said Campbell. 'Nowhere has it been stated that the Yugoslavs were right. What has been said is that Stalin handled it in such a way that it led to a breach with the Yugoslavs, which was unnecessary. It was unnecessary to call Tito a fascist... We are not making any statement on the Yugoslavs until an appropriate moment.'

Before the appropriate moment came, another shock hit the Party. The Polish Communists, longing to escape Soviet domination, were the first to tell Jean Pronteau about the Khrushchov speech, the first to publish a summary of it and (shortly afterwards) the first to give the complete text to the American State Department. They were also the first to allow their tame Yiddish-language paper, *Folks-sztyme*, to publish an account of Stalin's anti-Semitism.

This came out in Warsaw on April 4. A few days later it landed on the mat of Alec Waterman, who had been born in Poland and whose first language was Yiddish. Ray, who had been seeing him off to work from the first floor, heard him cry out in the hall below. She looked down and saw him reel back against the wall, very pale. Holding the paper in his hand, he exclaimed: 'So it's true!'

He had seen other headlines in other languages, on the fate of Russian Jews. That every member of the Jewish Anti-Fascist Committee was framed and shot in 1948, that this began five years of terrible persecution, that the arrest and torture of the Jewish doctors would have led to still worse horrors if Stalin had lived longer – this he had been told. But now the headlines were in Yiddish. Now he could see they were true.

V

Alec Waterman was a disciplined Party member. He took the Yiddish paper to the Party leaders, who concealed it from the rest of us. Alec and Ray Waterman and some other comrades signed a letter to the *Daily Worker*, demanding that the article from *Folks-sztyme* should be published. They did not even get an acknowledgement.

But the New York *Daily Worker* published the news on April 11, and some further details two days later. Several articles followed – one by the novelist Howard Fast – demanding an explanation from the Soviet Government.

The New York Daily Worker was not completely controlled by the US Communist Party. The editor, John Gates, was waging a fight against Stalinism which was all the more to his credit as he was also fighting the authorities. On March 28 four US Treasury officials seized his office for non-payment of taxes. John Gates very reasonably contended that the paper could not owe any taxes, as it was operating at a loss. By legal action, he got the office back a week later. Not once, during that week, had the paper failed to come out. On April 2 it published an editorial on the rehabilitation of Rajk, demanding that Hungary and the Soviet Union should explain themselves. In our own *Daily Worker*, at the same time, Malcolm MacEwen had the same idea. But the article he wrote was rejected by Campbell.

On April 2 Steve Nelson, an American Communist, was released from prison. The Supreme Court ruled that the State of Pennsylvania had no right to sentence anyone to 20 years in prison for conspiring to advocate the violent overthrow of the Federal Government. Only a federal court could do that. In theory, the United States could have continued to put Communists in prison for being Communists, by prosecuting them through the federal courts. But in fact the release of Steve Nelson ended the practice. This event, which ought to have made headlines in our own *Daily Worker*, was reported weeks later, very briefly.

What made Steve Nelson an ex-hero? He had fallen out with the American Stalinist leaders. And his first public act, after his release, was to congratulate the New York *Daily Worker* on its editorial about Rajk.

I write as if I had known all this at the time. In fact I caught up with the American events later. What I did know was that the Poles were setting the pace. On April 6 Wladislaw Gomulka, accused of Titoism in 1949 but never tried, was released from prison. So were several other leading Polish Communists, and 20 army officers. The paper *Zycie Warszawy* mentioned that Professor Haldane had been forced out of the Communist Party by Stalinist interference in science.

Not everyone in Poland was delighted at such frankness. Edward Ochab said: 'Some comrades seem to be losing their sense of balance or proportion.' Ochab was first secretary of the Communist Party, a title which, in a Communist country, normally meant the boss. But Ochab came second to Marshal Rokossovsky, the Soviet brass hat who had remembered his Polish origins when Stalin wanted someone to run Poland.

In Prague the Stalinists put up a stubborn resistance. For several days the Czechoslovak Government would not confirm the release of Artur London, who had been on trial with Slansky in 1952. On April 12 the paper *Rude Pravo* said that

Slansky himself had been to blame for the excesses of the secret police. On April 14 the Czech Prime Minister, Siroky, admitted that Artur London and two other survivors of the Slansky trial had been released. But he said that the death sentences on Slansky and Clementis were justified. He acknowledged that it had been 'a mistake' to introduce charges of Titoism – 'a secondary issue' – and to bring in an anti-Semitic element. The same day, Molotov and Mikoyan went to the Israeli Embassy in Moscow to join in the celebrations of Israel's Independence Day.

On April 11 the Dutch Communist Party expressed regret that it had defended Stalin's erroneous policies, and urged the present Soviet leaders to abolish the death penalty for political offences. On April 13 Marshal Blucher and other military leaders, sentenced with Tukhachevsky in 1937, were rehabilitated.

'But isn't Blucher dead?' asked Malcolm MacEwen. Gabriel said: 'In the Soviet Union, comrade, they have some very good taxidermists.'

On April 14 Traicho Kostov was rehabilitated, and on April 16 Vulko Chervenkov, Prime Minister of Bulgaria and responsible for framing Kostov, was forced to resign.

On April 17 Dmitri Shepilov, editor of *Pravda*, announced the end of the Cominform. It had never done anything, except denounce Tito, and publish a paper: *For a Lasting Peace, For a People's Democracy*. The title could not be changed; it had been written by the famous purple pencil with which Stalin captured his thoughts. Even in Stalin's lifetime, Hutt remarked that this wasn't his brightest thought. Some British seamen who had gone too near the Chinese coastline were imprisoned, briefly. On being released they said that they had not been exactly tortured – only made to read a paper called *For a Lasting Peace, For a People's Democracy*.

On April 18 Khrushchov and Marshal Nikolai Bulganin

arrived in Britain on an official visit. They quarrelled with Labour Party leaders over human rights, but got on splendidly with the Conservative Prime Minister, Anthony Eden. Khrushchov declared that if he were British he would vote Tory.

On April 19 the Soviet Government repealed two laws... but what laws? The Soviet apologist D. N. Pritt mentioned the matter coyly in *Labour Monthly*, the following July. He said only that the laws were 'draconic' and that they had been passed on 1 December 1934 and 14 September 1937. In a western country the dates would identify them, but some of the laws passed during Stalin's purges were kept secret for a long time. The laws now repealed did not include the one inflicting the death penalty on children of 12, or the one providing that, if a Soviet soldier deserted, his relations would be sent to Siberia. Pritt had always done his utmost to conceal that any such laws existed.

We were expecting, from the leaders of our own Party, something like the apology the Dutch Communists had made. Things moved slowly. On April 21 Harry Pollitt, in the Party's weekly paper *World News*, formally withdrew Klugmann's book, *From Trotsky to Tito*. (Since the Russian apology to Tito, 11 months had gone by.)

Pollitt wrote: 'The enemies of the Communist Party are trying to pretend that... everything that they have said about the Soviet Union was correct, and everything we said was wrong.'

Well, yes. But Pollitt had his answer. 'Despite the faults, weaknesses and mistakes, all the basic Marxist principles have been proven correct, and confirmed again and again, above all in the indestructible Socialist system...'

When Pollitt wrote this he knew, not only what we all knew – the main horrors of the Khrushchov speech – but also what hardly any of us knew, the anti-Semitic outrages revealed in the Yiddish paper. Alec Waterman was making sure that Pollitt knew everything. So was Professor Hyman Levy.

Levy, like Waterman, had grown up speaking Yiddish. This was to prove important. More important still was his talent for getting things done.

When the First World War became suddenly imminent, Levy was doing post-graduate work at Göttingen University, where a few pioneers had launched the new science of aerodynamics. He got out of Germany just in time to avoid internment, and brought with him several other British people, who had thought they were stranded. They agreed that it was Levy who talked them past the frontiers. It was a feat he made light of, when I asked him about it 25 years later, in 1939. But it made a lasting impression on his grateful fellow-travellers.

Levy's eloquence was not always put to such good use. While the Party was insisting that the Second World War was an imperialist war, Levy defended this line with great ingenuity and wit, using to the full the Edinburgh accent which made everything sound sensible. The late Louis Simmonds (who until the end of 1993 worked in his wonderful bookshop in Fleet Street) attended a public meeting addressed by Levy in Welwyn Garden City in the winter of 1940/41. Simmonds was dazzled by Levy's brilliance in demolishing every questioner. Afterwards Simmonds went up to him and said quietly: 'Tell me, as one Jew to another, how can you talk such piffle?' Levy looked round cautiously and then said: 'Between you and me – this line can't last much longer.'

Like the rest of us, Levy went on defending the Soviet Union, long after it had become clear to everyone outside the Party what was going on. We had, at least, the excuse that we could not go to Russia. It was closed to tourists for years after the Second World War. But Levy was there several times by invitation.

An enchanting talker, and a lecturer of genius (though

rather a dull writer) Levy had done a great deal to mislead the young. He now began to pay for all his sins, in his long, agonising struggle to make the British Communist leaders face the facts about Soviet anti-Semitism.

On April 24 the Poles announced that they were releasing 30,000 people, including members of the Polish Home Army – the partisans responsible for most of the resistance to the Germans. The Communists had imprisoned them for being loyal to the exiled Polish Government in London. The Polish Prime Minister said compensation would be paid to them.

Though the Czechs were slow to admit the frame-ups, it was a Czech paper, *Prace*, which declared on April 26 that innocent people had suffered *because they were Jews*. Or, it added, because they had served in western forces during the Second World War, or were related to people who had been arrested.

This was on the front page of the *Daily Worker* on April 27 – in the first edition. It vanished from the second and third editions. That would suggest a row inside the office. I heard nothing of it at the time. I was working at home, and did not attend another staff meeting until the beginning of June. The odd thing is that none of the *Daily Worker* people still alive in 1990 could remember anything about it.

If political pressure was exerted to take this item out, it did not come from Pollitt. He had a haemorrhage behind the eyes on April 25. Two days later, though, he was well enough to attend a reception for Khrushchov and Bulganin on the eve of their departure from Britain.

Peter Fryer met him there. Pollitt was, not for the first time, drunk. 'I'm going blind, you know,' he confided to Fryer. Then his bitterness against the Russian leaders burst out. 'You think *you're* having a hard time; those two buggers have spoken to everybody here, except a lad called Pollitt.'

On April 30 Pollitt was interviewed by Frank Owen on

television. Frank Owen was a former editor of the *Evening Standard*, and a former Communist. He owed Pollitt a favour. When Frank Owen was arrested for driving while drunk, all the other Fleet Street editors ganged up to keep the case out of the papers. Frank Owen's one anxiety was that the *Daily Worker* might mention it. He appealed to Pollitt as an old friend, and Pollitt kept it out of the *Daily Worker*. (After all that, Owen was found not guilty.)

So Pollitt got his chance of publicity on TV, with the sort of heckling he knew how to handle. I reported this interview for the *Daily Worker*.

Frank Owen asked Pollitt about the visit of Khrushchov and Bulganin – 'your two big brothers'.

'They're not my big brothers; they're my dearest and oldest comrades,' declared the man they had been refusing to speak to, three days before.

Frank Owen asked him about the reassessment of Stalin. 'We don't need to have our mistakes pointed out,' Pollitt said. 'Stalin was a very great leader. But as you yourself, Frank Owen, have pointed out, in your own book on Lloyd George – and I make no charge for advertising it here – all great men make mistakes.'

Frank Owen said that the reason the Communist Party had not made more headway in Britain was its subservience to Moscow. 'Look at yourself! In 1939 you walked down the aisle – '

'I never walked down the aisle,' protested Pollitt. 'I walked into the registry office.'

'You walked down the aisle as a penitent,' Frank Owen reminded him.

'I've never been a penitent, and I'm not penitent now,' Pollitt said. 'In 1939 I thought it was an anti-fascist war. I thought it then and I think it now. But I was outvoted by the majority of our Party, and being a democrat I advocated the policy of the majority of our Party.' (That majority consisted of Dutt and Stalin.)

Frank Owen asked about the one-party state, and the lack of free trade unions in Russia. 'When Socialism has been established,' Pollitt explained, 'there's no room for two parties. The Russian trade unions are the freest in the world. Why, the trade unions are the architects of all that has been done.' He went on to speak of the 'miraculous achievements of Soviet democracy'.

Frank Owen asked: 'Why did nobody challenge Stalin?'

Pollitt said: 'The essence of the situation in the Soviet Union, in view of the circumstances prevailing, was at all costs to preserve the unity of the Party. If they hadn't done that, neither you nor I would have been here on TV, with some detergent following to wash the air afterwards. I'm not going to join all your gang in attacking the Soviet Union.'

That remained Pollitt's line. His second article for *World News*, on May 5, declared: 'It is vital that we should not be thrown off balance.' This was a phrase much used from then onwards. It meant: 'We must not say we are sorry.'

However, Pollitt went on: 'We are all deeply shocked to learn that many of those who were represented as traitors to the people's cause were in fact devoted Communists.'

Dutt would not admit even to being shocked. In the May issue of *Labour Monthly* he wrote:

What are the essential themes of the Great Debate? Not about Stalin. That there should be spots on the sun would only startle an inveterate Mithra-worshipper. Not about the now recognised abuses of the security organs in a period of heroic ordeal and achievement of the Soviet Union. To imagine that a great revolution can develop without a million cross-currents, hardships, injustices and excesses would be a delusion fit only for ivory-tower dwellers in fairyland who have still to learn that the thorny path of human advancement moves forward, not only through unexampled heroism, but also with accompanying baseness, with tears and blood. The Great Debate that has opened is about larger issues...

Neither Dutt nor Pollitt knew what was going to hit them. On May 13 Pollitt was replaced, as general secretary, by John Gollan. This was presented as an amicable resignation. Pollitt was nearly 65, and his eye trouble had made him unable to read. He recovered sufficiently to take part in the next delegation to Moscow.

The executive committee meeting which accepted Pollitt's resignation also ordered Palme Dutt to apologise for his 'spots on the sun' article. It published a resolution:

> It is clear now that on the basis of false information we, in all good faith, made a number of mistakes, as in our support for the accusation against the Yugoslav Communist leaders as traitors, and our condemnation of a number of those falsely convicted... There is, in the future, bound to be a more critical examination of policies, from whatever quarter they come...

We hoped they meant that. It was not a good sign, though, that the *Daily Worker* failed to carry a report of the press conference Artur London gave in Prague. He said that his confession at the Slansky trial had been extorted by torture.

During May I went to Leicester to see my brother, who was lecturing in the university there. What I read on the train was Derek Kartun's book, *Tito's plot against Europe*, which had been in our house for six and a half years. It described, in a racy, readable style, plots hatched by traitorous Party members who had been police spies since the 1930s... Because people like myself had been prepared to believe all this, innocent men had been hanged. I was met at Leicester by my brother, always kind and good to me. 'How pale you look!' he said. I felt pale, and I could not tell him why. My brother was not in the Party.

In Hungary Dora Scarlett, whom I did not know then, had read the same book with the same feelings. She was a convinced Communist when she first went to Hungary, just before Stalin's death, to work on the English-language broadcasts of Radio Budapest. Every day, as she walked to the radio building, she passed within a few yards of Edith Bone. Neither knew the other was there. Edith Bone was in solitary confinement, held so secretly that she had no prison number, and therefore could not be allocated warm clothing for the winter.

I had great hopes of our new leader, John Gollan. He had been much loved in our office, when he was assistant editor. His gentle Edinburgh voice purred in counterpoint to Campbell's Clydeside growl. Only once did I see Gollan angry – when he learned that someone had neglected a sick comrade.

That many of us became Communists in order to defy our parents, or for other neurotic reasons, is probable. But Gollan learned his politics where Levy learned his, in the slums of Edinburgh. If you see your brothers and sisters struck down by diseases which appear to miss the better parts of town, it is natural to ask why. 'Capitalist exploitation' may be the wrong answer, but it used to look very reasonable from the Old Town. The great killer of the poor in Scotland was lung tuberculosis. Gollan talked to me once about its ravages in his family. They were rehoused, but too late to save his sister's life. Gollan himself always looked as if one puff of wind would blow him away.

We had hoped that Gollan would expound the new Party line to us. But he was getting ready for a vital journey to Moscow. It was Campbell who called us together on June 2, a Saturday. We came into the office on our day off, so that nobody could tell us it was time to stop talking and start work.

Campbell drew our attention to the resolution which promised that the British leaders would be more critical of policies 'from whatever quarter they come'. He said: 'That is a clear indication that we are not accepting the voice of authority.'

The Party's policy, *The British Road to Socialism*, was being rewritten, he said. 'We need to find out how to guarantee civil liberties... Some of the liberties which the bourgeoisie gained were not bourgeois gains; they were human gains.'

And he declared: 'The debunking of Stalin was not a side issue, diverting us from constructive work. It may be the most constructive thing the Twentieth Congress has done.'

With evident pleasure, Campbell gave us his opinion of Dutt. On Dutt's phrase 'an inveterate Mithras-worshipper', Campbell asked: 'Who were the bloody high priests of Mithras, anyway?' Dutt's reference to 'ivory-tower dwellers' had given offence to Communists in the universities. 'Our members in academic circles are not living in ivory towers,' Campbell said. Many of them had suffered professionally for their politics.

As for the trials of 'Zionists' in Russia, reported by the *Manchester Guardian*, the Party was trying to get more information. 'The Polish Jewish statement is to be published in the *Jewish Clarion*.' (The Party paper for Jews.)

Like the vast majority of Party members, I did not then know what was in the *Folks-sztyme*. If I had known, I would have asked Campbell how it could be a matter only for a Jewish paper. We used to argue that, if a government was anti-Semitic, it must have so many other things wrong with it that it was the duty of every citizen to work for its overthrow. (I still think so.) To do him justice, Campbell showed later that he did not think anti-Semitism a matter only for Jews.

Gabriel asked: 'Are we really taking things more critically? Our statement is very careful not to criticise the USSR any more than it has already criticised itself... The

American *Daily Worker* has been much more forthright, honest and human.'

Both Gabriel and Malcolm MacEwen were amazed that the Party's new education officer was James Klugmann, author of: *From Trotsky to Tito*.

Campbell told them not to re-introduce the Stalinist method of the scapegoat. 'Klugmann wrote the book on the Party's instructions.' He added that Klugmann was one of the most energetic comrades pressing for change. 'We are not at the end of changes; we are at the beginning of them.'

Because Gabriel had commended the New York *Daily Worker*, I went into the library to read it. That was how I first learned what Alec Waterman had learned some seven or eight weeks earlier.

In the library, Claire Madden pointed out to me that four of Beria's men had just been shot in Azerbaijan for torturing prisoners. 'And, again, it's without a public trial.' There was a rumour about the reason why the indictment against Beria had never been published. It was said to accuse him of friendship with Tito. Khrushchov made friends with Tito eighteen months after having Beria shot.

On June 10 the *Observer* printed the full text of the Khrushchov speech. Jack and I could talk of nothing else. Catherine, who was 10, attempted a judicious summing up. 'Stalin was good and bad.' Stella, who was three, said as she took the shell off her boiled egg: 'He was bad, because he shot people.'

That Sunday Bert Ramelson, the Party's full-time Yorkshire District Secretary, was about to join Gollan and Pollitt on a delegation to Moscow. At the last minute the *Observer* was thrust into his hand, with the instruction: 'Find out if that's the real text!'

Some of the Party leaders already knew that it was. An American veteran of those days, Maurice Isserman, has written in the *Socialist Review* that at the end of April the American Communist leaders got a full text from the British Communists.

In a statement printed on the front page of the *Daily Worker* on June 22, our leaders admitted that the *Observer* text was authentic. They also called on the Russians to abolish the death penalty.

This was timely; the people who had not been shot were being set free. Hermann Field was released from a Hungarian prison; Noel Field from one in Poland. Both were exonerated in the course of a six-hour speech in Prague by Antonin Novotny (who, however, went on refusing to rehabilitate Slansky). In Hungary Rakosi had already announced the release of 20,000 people. But he could not release Edith Bone, because he had so often denied that she was there.

Palme Dutt's apology in the June issue of *Labour Monthly* seemed scarcely apologetic enough.

'It was essential to carry through the drastic review, the reassessment in relation to the role of Stalin in his later period...'

According to Khrushchov, this 'later period' was from 1934 to 1953.

Dutt declared:

> There was here no parallel with the traditional forms of one-man rule, with Bonapartism or the Fuehrerprinzip or fascist dictatorship... nothing was changed in the nature of class power, the socialist soviet power of the working people... This was the very period when the Webbs were describing the 'multiform democracy' of the Soviet Union as the widest participation of the largest numbers of ordinary men and women in the administration of their affairs that had ever been evolved. And it was true... Throughout this period, despite all the evils, the masses of the people were continuing to enjoy and exercise self-rule in running their affairs to a degree unknown

in any capitalist democracy and continuing to justify Lenin's description of Soviet democracy as the highest form of democracy.

Dutt recalled how sad it was, shortly after the revolution, to see the leaders at odds.

It was no less pain and anguish during the thirties to see so many dear friends and comrades, some of whom, like Bela Kun, have now been cleared of their sentences, revealed and proclaimed as traitors and enemy agents... And if now the Twentieth Congress has revealed that the party was not seething with traitors and agents, that it was, on the contrary, the security organs that had got out of hand and gone wrong, that many of these dear friends and comrades were not traitors and agents, that although they suffered cruel and unjust deaths their revolutionary honour stands high, then some younger comrades must forgive the 'callousness' of some of us longer in the movement if this feels, not like the end of the world, not like 'the god that failed', but like the sunrise breaking through the clouds at the dawn of a new day.

One of Palme Dutt's puzzled readers wrote to ask what he meant about Bela Kun. (Leader of the short-lived Hungarian Soviet Republic in 1919, believed to have been shot by Stalin in 1937, reviled as a traitor by Rakosi in December 1955, and the subject of an admiring article by Eugene Varga in *Pravda* in February 1956.) What, the reader asked Dutt, was this 'sentence' against him? When was it made public? When was he 'cleared'? Dutt replied that he knew nothing beyond 'the official statement'. There never had been an official statement; only the words in *Pravda*: 'Bright memories of Bela Kun will remain for ever in the hearts of the Hungarian people...'

What were my own articles like at the time? I did not have to comment on political events, though I reported them when (like Pollitt's interview) they happened on TV. My main task was to write, twice a week, chatty articles of a mildly cultural character. Modern TV critics get previews of programmes, but in those days almost everything went out live, and sometimes unrehearsed. If you didn't watch incessantly, you might miss Gilbert Harding bursting into tears, or Brendan Behan collapsing into alcoholic stupor. At any moment, the producer's plans might go disastrously, but entertainingly, wrong.

So there was always something to write about, and I wrote about everything, except what was most on my mind. Fritz Hochwalder's play, 'The Strong are Lonely', gave me the excuse to write about the Jesuits in eighteenth-century Paraguay. On the whole, I thought they were a good thing. Brian Pearce wrote in fierce disagreement, quoting Voltaire. I was delighted to hear from him; here was someone whom Jack and I could consult about what was happening in Russia.

Now, at last, we were talking frankly. Now Brian told us about the Chechens and Ingushes, 'given an opportunity to develop elsewhere in the USSR'. As we lost our beliefs, we gained the ability to open our hearts to our friends.

Dora Scarlett, in Budapest, spoke Hungarian and could take part in the new freedom of speech. The writers' club, the Petöfi Circle, held a meeting which spilled out into the streets. Julia Rajk spoke of the false accusations against her husband. 'How could it happen that they believed it? The way we were taught to look everywhere for enemies and spies is also responsible for what happened…'

Gabriel drew a cartoon, with two worried people reading the Khrushchov speech. Behind them loomed two symbolic figures, labelled 'humanity' and 'justice'. The caption was: 'Whatever road we take we must never leave them behind.'

This brought some furious letters from our readers. One of them called the cartoon '…the most disgusting example of the non-Marxist, anti-working class outbursts…' which, it seemed, he was detecting elsewhere in the paper. Another reader rejoined: 'Does he imply that Marx and the working class favour inhumanity and injustice?' We were soon to learn how many Party members did believe that.

Gollan, after his visit to Moscow, still did not come to the *Daily Worker* office to tell us about it. Instead, everything was relayed to us at second hand by Allen Hutt, who was a member of the Executive Committee.

He said that the Soviet leaders wanted to arrange their relations with other Communist Parties 'on a new basis'. Voroshilov was particularly keen on this.

Allen Hutt was regarded as a great newspaper designer, but not as a great political thinker. Several people became disrespectful about his tacit admission that in the past we had done whatever the Russians told us. (And that, if we were going to be less obedient, it would be because the Russians gave us permission.) Hutt severely told us that we had been 'in a flat spin' ever since the Twentieth Congress, and that we must now get out of it.

Nevertheless, we asked him about the Khrushchov speech. Why hadn't Khrushchov sent a copy to the British Party?

'He did,' said Hutt. 'But it went astray.'

There was a general gasp. Someone asked: 'Was that the copy the State Department got hold of?'

'Oh no!' said Hutt. 'Not went astray like that. Just... went astray.'

We could get no more out of him. Sheila Lynd and I, talking it over in the canteen, conjectured that 'astray' meant 'into Harry Pollitt's wardrobe'. Why didn't we think of Dutt's wardrobe? By this time Dutt was, to us, such a figure of fun that we forgot how important he might seem to the Russians.

And we had other things to find out, such as what, exactly, had happened in Poznan.

VI

POZNAN RIOTERS HAD BEEN DRILLED IN MURDER (*Daily Worker*, 3 July 1956, first edition).

POZNAN WORKERS SPEAK OUT ON GRIEVANCES (*Daily Worker*, 3 July 1956, second and third editions).

The confusion about those riots had been going on for days. Martial law was declared in Poznan on June 29. The following day the *Daily Worker* told its readers that the riots there were 'organised by secret agents'. That was a Saturday. The following Monday morning the *Daily Worker* was admitting that the riots began with a peaceful demonstration, and that the workers had genuine grievances.

All the despatches from Poland were written by the same man, Gordon Cruickshank. He was an honest reporter, when he was describing what he saw and heard. But he also had to report what the Polish Government told him. Hence the contradictions from edition to edition – indeed, from hour to hour.

On the day martial law was declared in Poznan, June 29, the Petöfi Circle held its fourth great meeting in Budapest. Six thousand people packed three halls from 7 p.m. to 3 a.m. Then Rakosi's government closed the Petöfi Circle down, and the Hungarian Communist Party passed a resolution condemning its proceedings. Dora Scarlett afterwards wrote:

The meeting at the Radio in which this resolution was discussed was a long and bitter one. Some people started their contributions with the customary acceptance of a Party resolution, and then went on to make reservations; others more boldly said outright that they disagreed with it. It was especially noticeable that the majority of those who had been at the Petöfi Circle, including Communists of long standing, opposed the resolution. When some who had not been present started to talk about 'impermissible expressions' and 'anti-Party, demagogic statements' made there, they were roundly told that they did not know what they were talking about. In the course of the discussion one could feel the majority hardening against the resolution, and hear people more and more plucking up their courage to express their thoughts frankly; this was the first time that the Party as such had been opposed... The same kind of thing was going on at other work-places all over the country, and the ultimate result was that the resolution was withdrawn.

Budapest Radio described the Poznan riots as the work of foreign agents. Later, like the *Daily Worker*, it had second thoughts.

On July 16 the *Daily Worker* readers were given yet another explanation of Stalinism by George Matthews. 'The abuses of the 1934-53 period were not in the nature of the Socialist system, but in conflict with it.'

The same day, John Gollan was interviewed on television by Robin Day, who proved a tougher questioner than Frank Owen had been to Pollitt. 'You say,' said Robin Day, 'it is not true that these injustices and crimes arose from the nature of the Soviet social system. Then what did they arise from?'

Gollan said it all happened because of the threat of attack from outside.

Also on July 16, Peter Fryer arrived in Budapest. So did Mikoyan. What Mikoyan was doing there soon became apparent; Rakosi resigned on July 18. He was replaced, however, by another old Stalinist, Ernö Gerö. Fryer's optimistic account of these events was the splash in the *Daily Worker* on July 19. The readers were given the impression that whatever had been wrong in Hungary was now being put right. General Mihaly Farkas, the secret police chief who had framed Rajk, was expelled from the Communist Party on July 22. Two days later, under the headline: HUNGARY TO HAVE A NEW PENAL CODE, the *Daily Worker* published Peter Fryer's article about the rehabilitation of 474 people, including Rajk.

On July 26 Gamal Abdel Nasser, President of Egypt, nationalised the Suez Canal. 'Why don't you discuss that?' asked some of the comrades who thought that we had been discussing Stalin for too long. About Suez, though, there was nothing to say. We were not in any doubt that the Egyptians were entitled to nationalise the canal if they liked, and that the warlike noises which our own government now began to make were infamous. Jack and I were happy to demonstrate against the Tory Prime Minister, Anthony Eden. But nothing Eden did could cause us the intimate, family-row anguish, the gut-twisting mixture of anger and shame, we felt when Campbell wrote about 'the excesses of the last years of Stalin'. (*Daily Worker*, 28 July 1956.) Nineteen is a lot of last years. We expected this nonsense from Dutt, but Campbell knew better.

In Hungary, Peter Fryer was determined to find out the truth about the trial he had so naively reported, seven years before. How had Rajk been made to confess?

> First he was tortured by Farkas' son. Then, when the softening-up process had made him suitably receptive, a Soviet Communist – 'a Beria man', I was told – put it to him that the Soviet Union needed his confession as a weapon against Tito. If he agreed to do this important political job he would (though officially dead) be well looked after in the Soviet Union for the rest of his life, and his child would be given a good education.

He agreed. When they came to take him to the execution, which his wife Julia was made to witness, they put a gag – a piece of wood – in his mouth to prevent his revealing to the soldiers how he had been betrayed. His last words were: 'What are you doing to me?' (*Hungarian Tragedy*, by Peter Fryer; New Park Publications, 1986.)

According to Sandor Kopacsi, who during the Rajk trial was in the civilian (as distinct from the secret) police force, the Soviet Communist who made the offer to Rajk was General Bielkin of the NKVD. The immediate superior of Kopacsi told him about the offer at the time, and added: 'It's all a lie. Bielkin has had scaffolds erected, coffins readied, and quicklime piled up in a cellar.' (*In the Name of the Working Class*, by Sandor Kopacsi; Fontana/Collins, 1989.)

While Peter Fryer was hearing about this in July 1956, he did not know where Edith Bone was. Still in prison, still incommunicado, she was, at least, alive. She too, in Rakosi's time, had received offers of an easy life, if only she would do her Party duty, and confess to being a British spy. What saved her was that difficult, awkward nature, which had so much irritated her British comrades. Kept in a cell where one wall was solid ice, tormented by arthritis, her guts ravaged by the prison food, ragged and barefoot, she laughed in the faces of her interrogators. Recounting her experiences (*Seven Years Solitary*, by Edith Bone; Hamish Hamilton, 1957) she scrupulously recorded that those who gave in had probably been treated worse than she was. And she added that she had no children who could be used to torment her. Julia Rajk's baby was taken away from her; even when she was released, in 1955, the authorities would not tell her where he was.

On August 5 Peter Fryer talked to Miklos Gimes, who had been expelled from the Hungarian Communist Party for demanding the rehabilitation of Rajk. Gimes told him that, if there were free elections in Hungary, with no foreign troops, the Party would get 10 or 12 per cent of the votes. The only Communist leader who would be trusted by the people was Imre Nagy (who had been Prime Minister from the summer of 1953 until early in 1955, when Rakosi made a comeback). But, as the Communist Party had so little support, Nagy would have to come in as the head of a people's front government, with genuine representatives of other parties.

Peter Fryer came back from that visit to Hungary sickened by what he had discovered. And yet everything that appeared in the *Daily Worker* under his name carried the message with which we were now becoming familiar. Things had been terrible, but everything would be all right from now on.

Peter himself no longer believed this. He told Campbell that he must leave the paper. Face to face with Peter, Campbell said that he had been in Moscow during the purges of the 1930s; he had known what was going on. But what could he do? How could he say anything in public, when the war was coming and the Soviet Union was going to be attacked?

This might have been some excuse for silence. However, Campbell was not silent in the 1930s. He wrote a book: *Soviet Policy and its Critics*, which was published by Gollancz in 1939. In this he defended every action of Stalin and argued that the purge trials were genuine.

In 1956 he never admitted in public that those trials were frame-ups. To Peter, though, he admitted a great deal. When Peter insisted on going, Campbell said: 'You must give me a year!' So from then onwards Peter was working out his notice.

I did not see Peter on his return from Hungary. I did, however, notice a very short letter, which appeared in the paper on August 3. It was signed by Alec Waterman, Ray Waterman, Hyman Levy and Alf Holland (another Yiddish-speaking comrade), and asked about the information published in the Yiddish paper *four months earlier*. Campbell appended a note saying that the information seemed to be correct, though he had not been able to get official confirmation. He assured the readers that everything had been put right – without specifying what there was to put right.

Six days later the paper published a letter of protest from Vera Leff. 'The Editor's reply to the letter concerning the fate of Jews in the USSR... typifies the complacent attitude which I believe is even now preventing the British Communist Party from gaining sympathy and support. If, as the Editor says, "in spite of very considerable efforts" definite facts concerning the executions have not been obtained, what guarantee is there that such things could not happen again?'

Perhaps the *Daily Worker* would not have printed even this much, if its hand had not been forced by a smudgy, duplicated publication: *The Reasoner.*

To look at this paper after 40 years is to remember what hell it was to type stencils. If you made a mistake, you had to cover it with a substance resembling nail varnish, and wait until it dried. To place the stencil on the duplicator without crinkling it required neat fingers and a steady nerve. Then the duplicator would go wrong, covering you with black ink so thick and sticky that nothing would ever quite get it out of your clothes. The cost of the whole process was, in real terms, about four times the cost of making perfect copies by the methods of today. Only very determined people would use this method of putting across their views.

The editors of *The Reasoner*, John Saville and E.P. Thompson, were not only determined but angry. These two university lecturers in Yorkshire had been arguing with George Matthews through the columns of *World News*. George Matthews wrote that Thompson had 'unconsciously echoed all the most familiar anti-Communist jibes and sneers of the enemy press – that Communists repeat dogma like Holy Church, have little regard for morality, are un-British, not much concerned with democracy, and so on.'

Thompson replied: 'He is quite wrong. I was consciously and openly suggesting that our party, and especially our leadership, has – from time to time – laid us open to these very serious accusations.' He went on to give examples. (For the dogma, he had only to quote Dutt.) *World News* refused to print the letter. So Saville and Thompson produced their own paper, defying Party discipline.

In their first issue they quoted words that the Soviet writer Fadeyev uttered shortly before his suicide. 'For us writers ideology should have been a helpmate and an inspiration. By our excesses and our stiffness we made her a cross-grained shrew.'

Perhaps, if Thompson and Saville had quoted only what was said in Russia, the leadership would have taken no disciplinary action. But they also quoted, from the New York *Daily Worker*, its editorial on Rajk, and Steve Nelson's letter of congratulation. Moreover, they quoted the American Communist paper *Jewish Life*, which humbly apologised to its readers for misleading them, and for not making more enquiries into Soviet anti-Semitism. *Jewish Life* demanded that the Czech Government should come clean about the Slansky trial. And it asked: 'Why has no word on this terrible series of events come from the Soviet Union itself?'

On August 24 the *Daily Worker* printed a letter signed only 'MD', which was the first indication ever given to our readers that Russian anti-Semitism was still going on. The letter quoted the National Guardian of New York, which had interviewed Yelena Furtseva, a minister in the Soviet Government.

'She said that some years back talk of anti-Semitism was stirred as a result of misinterpretation of certain Government actions. The Government had found in some of its departments a heavy concentration of Jewish people, upward of 50 per cent of the staff. Steps were taken to transfer them to other enterprises, giving them equally good positions and without jeopardising their rights...'

Furtseva's version was not true, as we then suspected and later knew. Jews had been thrown out of the civil service on to the street. What shook us, though, was Furtseva's bland assumption that nobody could possibly object to a quota system for Jews. We knew all about the quota. When Jack's grandparents and thousands of others left Russia, it was not entirely because they were beaten on the head by Cossacks. There was also the Tsar's quota system, which made it hard for a Jew to get an education, and harder still, if he was educated, to get work.

On holiday, Jack and I found Weymouth rainy and cold. Before the end of August it was rendered grimmer still. Troops, tanks and weapons began to pour through the town to the harbour. For the first time, we realised that Eden meant what he had been saying. There was going to be a war over the Suez Canal.

At that time there was one small incident which many people remember more vividly than Suez or Hungary. Nina Panomareva, a Russian discus thrower, was charged with stealing five hats, total value £1.12s.11d, from the C&A in Oxford Street. On August 30 she failed to appear before the Marlborough Street Magistrates. She was believed to be hiding in the Soviet Embassy. After issuing a statement in old-fashioned Cold War language, describing the charge as 'a provocation', the Soviet team withdrew from the White City games as a protest.

On September 1, the day we came home from Weymouth, Campbell's editorial had words we were glad to see. 'The decision of the Soviet athletic team to withdraw from the White City games is in every way regrettable.'

This was the first time a *Daily Worker* editorial had ever

criticised any Soviet action. The impact was all the greater because it appeared on a Saturday. Not one of the letters about Stalin, not one hint that the Russians might not be perfect, had ever appeared on the day set aside for our comrades to go out and sell the paper to the masses. The masses were not supposed to be aware of our growing reservations about the Soviet Union. But we had to comment on the White City games, because the scratching of a team from a sporting event was one thing the masses thoroughly disliked.

There were other odd conventions about the days of the week. 'I see we've got some good french letter ads,' Campbell once remarked on a Sunday evening. 'That's a' reet on a Monday.' (Monday was the day of the fewest readers, and therefore of the fewest casual readers, who might be Catholics.) The theatre column appeared on a Monday too. But films were for the masses; therefore the film reviews appeared on Saturday. My own TV column appeared on Tuesdays and Fridays, because nobody could yet believe quite how much the masses loved TV.

One of the stalwarts who went out and sold the paper on Saturdays, a factory shop steward, told Campbell how grateful he was for that editorial. 'If we'd crawled to the Russians just once more,' he said, 'I wouldn't have been able to take the paper out and sell it.'

Letters of congratulation poured in. So did letters of protest from shocked Stalinists. Then the Bolshoi Ballet threatened to cancel its visit to London because of Nina and the hats. Gabriel drew a cartoon, captioned 'Corpse de Ballet'. It showed two stubborn male dancers, with arms folded, allowing a ballerina to fall on her bottom. One of the male dancers was the British Foreign Office; the other was the Soviet Union. This was the first time a *Daily Worker* cartoon had suggested that the Soviet Union was acting unreasonably. Three days later the Bolshoi Ballet decided to come after all.

The *Daily Worker* printed four letters about Gabriel's cartoon; two for and two against. The two for were Ray Waterman and Brian Pearce.

The end of the Nina story came as an anti-climax. She appeared at the magistrate's court, was found guilty of stealing the hats, and was then given an absolute discharge. This could have been predicted from the start, since she was a first offender. But every comment made by the Russians on the case indicated that they still clung to their fantasies about British life. We had always found those fantasies embarrassing. After the 1950 General Election Derek Kartun got a message from a Communist country, demanding that he should immediately explain the methods by which the votes were falsified, to make it look as if the Communists had little support. Even after Stalin's death, Soviet economists produced a textbook, and sent a draft copy to British Communist leaders. Campbell was disgusted to read in this that British miners had more accidents than before the war. (After the coal mines were nationalised in 1945, small accidents began to be properly reported for the first time.) But we on the *Daily Worker* had always tried to keep such absurdities from our readers.

On the day of Nina's discharge, she sailed for home on the Russian ship which was then called *Molotov*, but was soon to be rechristened *Baltika*.

That was on October 12. But before that a great many things had happened.

Some of the Poznan rioters had been brought to trial. Their defence lawyers, given a freedom of speech which (as Gordon Cruickshank was allowed to report in the *Daily Worker*) came as a complete novelty to Communist Poland, pointed out that they had been beaten to make them confess. The prisoners said so, in court. On October 8 three of the accused – all in their teens – were sentenced to four years in prison. On the following day Hilary Minc, the Polish vice-premier, resigned. On October 11 all further trials of Poznan rioters were shelved.

In Britain a second issue of *The Reasoner* appeared. This persistent defiance of their decrees outraged the Party leaders. By this time Pollitt had recovered his eyesight and was back at his desk. His desk? Yes; although John Gollan was now general secretary, a new post had been created for Pollitt. He was Party chairman. He insisted that the Party's headed notepaper should have his name above Gollan's. Above them both, in the Party headquarters at 16 King Street, Covent Garden, hung the old pictures of Stalin.

So there was not likely to be much toleration for the editors of *The Reasoner*. Their second issue contained a cartoon by Gabriel and an article by Levy; more to the point, it had another American contribution. This one was from the *Monthly Review*, which said of the Stalinist state: 'It embodied a gigantic contradiction: in its aims and achievements it can fairly be described as superhuman; in its methods and attitude towards the rights and dignity of the individual it was subhuman.'

However dissident we were, we were still so much impressed by lying statistics that we thought the Soviet economy had superhuman achievements to its credit.

Derek Kartun was now helping the editors of *The Reasoner*. Though still a Party member, he had begun to talk more freely. I asked him why he had left the *Daily Worker*, and he told me that it all arose from that moment in the Slansky trial when Otto Katz (André Simone) had named Claud Cockburn as a British agent. Derek, who was a particular friend of Claud's, and had stayed with him in Ireland, went to Harry Pollitt and asked him if he thought this would make things awkward with the Russians. Perhaps (Derek suggested) he would no longer be persona grata in Eastern Europe, and ought to move to some other job in the

Daily Worker. Pollitt consulted somebody, and, a few days later, told Derek he would have to leave the paper altogether. Whom did Pollitt consult? Not, of course, the Executive Committee, the body which formally controlled the Party, but which in fact met only once in two months. Nor was it the body (unmentioned in the rules) which was supposed really to control the Party – the Political Committee, a small group consisting entirely of full-time officials. Derek knew at the time that the Political Committee had not been told the truth, because he happened to meet Palme Dutt, who was a member of it. Dutt said: 'That was very quixotic of you – insisting on resigning from the *Daily Worker.* Quite unnecessary, you know.'

Derek said to Isabel Brown: 'I suppose Harry went and consulted the Russians.'

'I suppose he did,' said Isabel.

We had always denied that our leaders took their orders from Moscow. But, once I had heard Derek's story, I knew there could be no other explanation.

'If we'd been in power,' commented Derek, 'they'd have had my head.'

The countries where 'we' were in power had taken off heads for much less. On October 4 the *Daily Worker* mentioned that there was going to be a reburial, with full military honours, of Rajk and his fellow-victims: General Palffy, Tibor Szonyi and Andras Szalai. But it did not, for a whole week, report the event, which took place on October 6.

Imre Nagy (himself an unperson, till Rakosi's fall in July) was present. So were either 200,000 or 300,000 people – accounts differ. At the graveside Gyula Oszko, who had been found guilty with Rajk, said: 'Why did we sign false confessions? To say that we suffered physical and mental tortures does not provide adequate reply... We adopted a false theory according to which there exists political necessity that is opposed to the truth. We believed that if we told the truth we should serve the imperialists, and by lying we would serve the cause of socialism.'

In the cemetery Dora Scarlett met Miklos Gimes, who remarked: 'People are saying that this is not enough; the same men who killed Rajk are still up there.' Later Dora wrote:

> More astonishing than the ceremony itself was the newsreel which was shown in the cinemas during the following week... It brought together a number of shots of Rajk – working, speaking at a dinner of veterans of the Spanish Civil War, (he had fought in Spain) and the camera caught him in the most appealing mood and circumstances – he looked young, unassuming, dedicated, earnest.

> Then came a shot of the *Cominform* journal of June, 1948, which had published the condemnation of Tito; then, in rapid succession, the front pages of Hungarian newspapers published during the Rajk trial, screaming abuse of Tito, clamouring for the blood of Rajk; the printing presses pouring out more papers and still more; then a mass meeting with the audience on its feet performing that mechanical, rhythmic clapping which had been customary at the names of Rakosi and Stalin. Then, finally, the scene in the Kerepesi Cemetery the previous Saturday, with its falling leaves and storm-tossed banners, and the silent, never-ending files of the people of Budapest passing the coffins.

> This was the climax of the journey towards truth which had been made throughout 1956.

> When people saw that it was possible to sweep away this great lie, they believed that far more was within their grasp. The moment was ripe for the great demonstration, the first demonstration in Hungary for eight years which was really supported by the people, of their own free will and for their own demands.

VII

A *Daily Worker* editorial on October 16, ten days after the event, made the first reference to the size of the crowd at the Rajk reburial. Its estimate was 200,000. (The other facts of the reburial had been on the back page on October 15.) The editorial, headed: NO VENGEANCE, argued that '...it would be distressing to Hungary's friends... if new trials were to disturb the life of the Hungarian people...'

In 1990 Peter Fryer had a nasty feeling that he wrote this, though of course at Campbell's direction.

Two days later a reader's letter asked why it should disturb the friends of Hungary if the men responsible for the Rajk frame-up were brought to trial.

Campbell defended that editorial at our next big Saturday morning meeting, on October 20. He had more than this to explain. On October 19 Khrushchov, Molotov, Mikoyan, Kaganovich and Marshal Konev, commander-in-chief of the Warsaw Pact forces, had flown to Warsaw, apparently to prevent Gomulka from coming to power.

Wladislaw Gomulka had been accused of Titoism in 1949, and imprisoned in July 1951. After the Slansky trial in Prague, Stalin's men were probably preparing for a show trial in Warsaw. Stalin's death prevented that, but did not open the prison doors. Gomulka was released three years later, on 6 April 1956. By October he was a hero to the Poles, and to us.

Still irrationally hopeful, we did not guess what a bad ruler Gomulka would turn out to be. Nor did we imagine that he would prove as ready as any other bad ruler of Poland to put the blame on the Jews. Our anxiety, on 20 October 1956, was that the Russians would invade Poland, and that this would precipitate the Third World War.

Campbell, on Eastern Europe, said: 'In these countries there is a peasant majority which is either indifferent to Socialism, or hostile to it.' Hence the ruling Party must not get 'into a state of incoherence'. We must not be guilty of 'naive democratism', or forget the existence of hostile forces.

Why had he called for no vengeance? 'The pursuit of a policy of vengeance could lead to a resistance to change in those countries where it is necessary.' He apparently meant that the old Stalinists who ought to resign would refuse to do so if it put their lives in danger. 'Just as we condemn the policy of repression under Stalin, we don't want counter-repression.'

The *Daily Worker*, he argued, must not go over to saying: 'Everything in the garden is lousy.' He pointed to the article by Gordon Cruickshank, in that day's paper, as an example of the way to show 'the positive side'. (True to the tradition of the Saturday paper, the article explained that the Poznan rioters were not typical of Poland's young people. Far more important were those enjoying new educational opportunities.)

Campbell warned us against 'cuddling up to the Labour Party – running back to mother'. Yet he was for unity on a local basis with the Labour Party. 'Our Party exists to make an impact on the wider working-class movement. To do that it must speak with one voice. We cannot have six different policies... If Socialist governments exist in one third of the world, whatever evils there are in our methods of organisation, there must be some virtues in it as well.'

He admitted that the leadership might get out of touch.

'There are two extreme views emerging. The first is that things went wrong because centralism was stressed, and democracy allowed to become moribund. Also that comrades were condemned for mistakes once made... The other idea is that democratic centralism is an idea made only for foreign countries in revolutionary conditions. I believe in the first...'

The problem, as he saw it, was 'how to avoid the leadership degenerating, the Party splitting into "we" and "they"... how to enlarge the area of discussion within the Party, without disrupting the Party as a disciplined force...'

He admitted: 'We could have had more discussion on *The British Road to Socialism*.' Then he added: 'The circulation of *World News* has not increased since we started this wide discussion, so the people who want more discussion are not prepared to spend sixpence a week for it.'

Campbell was juggling with figures. All Party papers had lost circulation, because the membership had been falling since the Khrushchov speech. If *World News* had kept its circulation steady, it showed that those remaining in the Party did want more discussion.

'We have made some impact on the Labour Movement,' Campbell pointed out. 'I came into this movement when it was a congeries of competing sects, very good at tripping each other up, but not good at leading the masses. We don't want to go back to that... It took a long struggle to get working-class papers controlled by their parties. The Social Democratic Federation paper was financed and controlled by Hyndman. The *Herald* was an attempt to break away from that, but it failed. We are the first to succeed.'

Succeed? We were rumoured once to have sold 150,000 copies, not on a weekday but during one of the all-out Saturday efforts. The daily sale at this time must have been less than 60,000. Yet I knew what Campbell meant. We were sitting in our airy, spacious newsroom. Our building, which the Party had picked up cheap after the bombing, had been transformed by a Party architect to house our editorial floors, our fine modern composing room and the great rotary press which in 1945 had been the very latest. We could have printed a million copies a day, if anybody had wanted them. And we, on the editorial staff, were a team. If times changed, if our line became popular, we were capable of producing a much bigger paper. Whereas, if we split up, what could bring us together again? We saw the danger, and listened quietly to Campbell, even when he began to attack *The Reasoner*.

'The comrades of *The Reasoner* are having the best of both worlds; they claim their full rights as Party members, and send in long statements to the Party commissions...' (They had been invited to do so, in the Executive Committee statement which instructed them to stop issuing *The Reasoner*.)

Campbell asked: 'Is Party discipline only for the mugs? There are two comrades that could run for a trade union position in London at the moment; one of them must stand down.'

None of us had yet denied the need for discipline. The question was who imposed it. Whose policy were we to carry out?

'There is a view,' said Campbell, 'that the Soviet Union is practically a dead loss, and that we have no relation with that firm across the street. That's the American Communist Party view. The other view is that the Russian and Chinese revolutions are the great events of our time...'

If we threw out our Marxist-Leninist theory, Campbell argued: 'It does not mean that we are making an impact on the outside world, but that it is making an impact on us.'

The first to challenge him was Gabriel, who wanted us to be honest about the past. 'I showed great concern for the Rosenbergs; none for Rajk and Kostov. Are these things past and done? I support the Soviet Union. But if my leg's broken I don't say how well the rest of my body is.'

Gabriel quoted the speech of Gyula Oszko at the graveside of Rajk. 'We adopted a false theory according to which there exists political necessity that is opposed to the truth.' Then he asked why our leaders were not trying to ascertain the truth. 'Beria – agent of imperialism! Where are the facts?'

He recalled the promise of the leaders, five months before, to be more critical – a promise they had failed to carry out. 'I might have felt my position an intolerable one, if it had not been for my personal regard for the Editor.'

He denounced the attempt to stifle discussion after the Khrushchov speech. 'That flourishing correspondence in *World News* did not flourish until the appearance of *The Reasoner*... The EC is as much to blame for *The Reasoner* as Thompson and Saville. We publish nothing from the US Party. The Polish Party statements were not published. Not our job? Then whose job is it?... Stalin got away with it because there was no free press. The way the Party is behaving here shows how they would behave if they were in power.'

Malcolm MacEwen was indignant because, while the Party leaders were discussing *The Reasoner* with Thompson and Saville, they had imposed a ban on all mention of the matter in the Party press. Thus the ordinary Party members did not know, except by word of mouth, that *The Reasoner* existed. At meetings where Malcolm had tried to protest at this ban, he had been ruled out of order. Malcolm continued:

Two months ago we asked the EC to find out about the reported heavy sentences on Zionists in the Soviet Union. The Labour Movement is watching us. The comrades don't know the position of Zionism in the Soviet Union; they don't know and don't find out; but they are quite sure that democratic centralism is operating in the Soviet Union...

What did Lenin say about it? He said that democratic centralism was essential. He also said at a different time that a party in a democratic country should operate in the fullest publicity...

Comrade Campbell shows that Eastern Europe is in such a morass that we have to start all over again without vengeance... Those who think that there is no great change to be made just don't know what's hit them. They can sit on their basis of monolithic unity until they get corns on it.

Eric Scott admitted: 'We could have published the things now appearing, rather earlier than we did.' But he added: 'Every party has the right to tell its members not to publish rival papers.'

Llew Gardner said: 'The Editor talks very expertly now about what is happening in the People's Democracies. So he did before... Yesterday Mick [Bennett] got very annoyed when I suggested that the Soviet leaders had gone to Warsaw to put the Poles on the line. He then showed that he thought that was what they had gone there for. But he thought they were right, and he was sure they have collective leadership. *I* thought they had under Joe.'

I had come to the meeting to oppose the suggestion, first made by Pollitt the previous April, and now taken up by his admirers, that these debates were of no interest to the workers, that only intellectuals cared about such 'theoretical questions' as liberty and a free press. During the war I had been a shop steward in a shipyard; I heard mocking voices in my memory... An old labourer declaring, as he turned his back on a Communist meeting: 'We wants our old free England, like we always been used to...' A woman telling me, before she slammed the door: 'They ain't got no freedom in Russia...' Now a letter just published in *World News* claimed that the workers in a rail depot cared only about the bread-and-butter issues. I said that anyone who insulted the workers, by saying that they cared nothing for their own freedom, ought to be shot.

'Alison is wrong in wanting to shoot the comrade in the rail depot,' said Fred Pateman, 'because what he says is true.'

Pateman went on to ask rhetorically: 'What sort of Party do we want? One which will lead the working class to power in this country.'

George MacDougall, a sub-editor, pointed out the remoteness of this aim. 'We have no MPs, and our local councillors could be numbered on the fingers of four people's hands... People come to us for help in economic struggles... But Socialism is more than bread and butter; it is the spirit of the thing... There is not sufficient evidence to show that this all-round Socialism does exist in the Soviet Union... We have got to criticise things that we think they are doing wrongly.'

MacDougall then spoke of a question which had been rumbling on in our correspondence columns: the Soviet atom bomb tests. 'The Soviet Union should stop them,' he declared.

A reporter, Bob Leeson, spoke of the Party's continuing support for conscription, which infuriated the Young Communist League. The Party called for the reduction of the two-year call-up to one year, not for its abolition. This was purely because the leaders thought it would look bad to support conscription in Russia and oppose it in Britain. 'We considered how it would strike other people in the country,' Bob Leeson said, 'instead of going into the principle.'

He added that there had been a cult of the individual in the British Communist Party. 'One comrade was discussing the leadership. "Look at our leaders; they have done their best. So let's be careful how we handle them." I don't think they will break... Another comrade said that when he got a statement from the leadership which he could not immediately grasp or agree with, he thought it was the product of their experience, and that tided him over until he could work it out for himself.'

Bob Leeson added that a 'middle cadre' – a leading comrade not quite in the top flight – had come to his branch and said: 'This has been an excellent discussion. I don't think there was any need for me to come down here.' Leeson commented: 'It never occurred to him that he might learn something.'

May Hill, the stenographer who had written that Stalin was among the truly great, complained: 'My own branch is nearly driving me dotty. The EC has got to come to the branches and rehabilitate itself.'

Campbell laughed, but she insisted: 'Yes, it is as bad as that.'

The hardliner Pat Devine asked indignantly: 'Is Gabriel for *one* Reasoner, or is he for any other Reasoners which anybody wants to start? We are told about this wonderful article by Professor Levy. Who is Professor Levy, anyway?'

At this there was such a chorus of derision that Pat Devine backtracked. 'I mean, he has always been seen as someone who has a contribution to make. But there is room in the Party journals for all discussion. *The Reasoner* is a menace.'

On the alleged divergence between workers and intellectuals, Phil Bolsover pointed out that the Party branch at Briggs Bodies (a large car factory) had passed a resolution supporting *The Reasoner*. 'I was one of the people in this office who wrote a letter to *World News* about *The Reasoner*, which was not published because there can be no discussion until the whole thing is over.'

Mick Bennett unexpectedly agreed with me about the importance of moral issues to the working class. 'The Raleigh comrades are faced with one of the greatest moral problems of all time.' (Raleigh Industries had introduced a profit-sharing scheme; the moral problem was whether to take the money on the basis the management suggested. The workers can't have found the problem as tricky as Mick thought; they took the money in good time for Christmas.) Mick went on: 'Imagine the workers there seeking guidance and finding that all the Party thinkers are engaged in abstract thought.'

So he was, after all, going to denounce *The Reasoner*. 'It is not what is contained in *The Reasoner* which is the important thing. If it has merit it could have appeared in *World News*.'

Malcolm and others interrupted him, to point out that *The Reasoner* arose from the rejection of an article by *World News*. Mick replied: 'The issue is that *The Reasoner* has got to stop now!' (Afterwards, in conversation, Mick admitted that he had not read *The Reasoner*.)

There was one thing Mick might truthfully have said, which would have made us respect him. During the Slansky trial he had realised that one of the defendants whom he knew personally, Otto Sling, was innocent. He had tried to convince Pollitt and Gollan, without result.

Mick told me this in 1990. He could not say it in 1956. He was then a loyal member of the Executive Committee, and it was unthinkable for him to tell us rank-and-file members how badly Pollitt and Gollan had behaved.

Because he hadn't read *The Reasoner*, Mick was still, on 20 October 1956, denying that there was anti-Semitism in the Soviet Union. He now produced for the first time what he was later to repeat – his own, original defence of Stalin's memory. 'You mustn't say that Stalin stifled Jewish culture. Stalin stifled *all* culture.'

Mick explained why he had disagreed with Llew Gardner about the Soviet leaders in Warsaw. 'We had heard some unofficial information that the Polish CP was discussing whether to let in the Soviet leaders.'

Mick's unofficial information was dead right. The Poles had kept the Soviet plane circling, while they debated whether to let it land. To Mick this was deeply shocking. 'Any break between Poland and the Soviet Union would be the biggest disaster since the Second World War.'

I cannot now remember why I had to rush away, and miss Campbell's reply to the discussion. I was in the office again the next day, Sunday, to take Malcolm a last-minute article. I heard then that Campbell had said blaming the EC for the appearance of *The Reasoner* was like blaming a man for having been hit on the chin. Malcolm commented: 'But if I hit people I always feel it's their fault.'

I said to him (because the affairs of Poland were still in the balance): 'I hope to Christ the Russians don't do anything silly.'

'You say that,' said Malcolm, 'and yet Johnnie Campbell...'

I went to look at the New York *Daily Worker* in the library. Claire Madden said to me: 'It's no use *The Reasoner* bringing all this up again, because it's obvious that we, here, can't do anything about it. We all know that Stalin's had a raw deal.'

I said: 'Uh?'

Claire showed me the file she'd collected to prove Khrushchov a liar. He'd said Burgess and Maclean weren't in the Soviet Union, a few weeks before admitting that they were.

Claire had looked up everyone whose name was mentioned in the Khrushchov speech, as having been shot. Eikhe, for example, was a particularly unpleasant police chief, who had shot a lot of innocent people, before he got shot in his turn. And look what Khrushchov himself said in 1935! (She was quoting from the denunciation of Enukidze for not shooting enough people, printed as a footnote to the *Manchester Guardian* edition of the Khrushchov speech.)

And how (asked Claire) did Khrushchov come to hear Stalin say: 'I will shake my little finger – and there will be no

Kossior'? Khrushchov should not have been in Moscow at the time; he was supposed to be working in the Ukraine, under Kossior himself. It seemed obvious – didn't it? – that Khrushchov had come to Moscow to tell tales to Stalin about his own chief.

I said that, from the context, it didn't seem to me that Khrushchov was claiming actually to have heard Stalin say this about Kossior. He had heard him say it about Tito, and thought it typical of the way Stalin talked about people he meant to destroy.

Claire thought I was very slow in not seeing that Khrushchov had himself carried out the worst of the purges. I agreed that he probably had, else he would not be alive; but this was no advertisement for Stalin's rule.

Claire said it was clear to her that Khrushchov had bumped off Stalin, and then he'd had to bump off Beria, because Beria *knew*. I said I thought Khrushchov probably had bumped off Stalin. That, I argued, wasn't the real horror of the situation; the horror was that there had been no other way of getting Stalin out.

Claire brushed this aside; her mind wasn't running along such lines. She showed me the cuttings she had accumulated, about police chiefs who had been shot as 'Beria men' since the death of Stalin. The announcements had been made in twos and threes, but it added up to something over 20. 'And all without a trial!'

As for the deportations of the Chechens, the Ingushes and the Crimean Tartars, Stalin had good military reasons for the way he treated them, Claire said. I said: 'Not half such good military reasons as Cromwell had, when he massacred the garrisons at Drogheda and Wexford.'

As Claire was Irish, that made her walk away in a huff. Her boss, the gentle Robin Jardine, who had been silent all this time, burst out: 'Oh, if only she'd stop!'

Claire met her match, I heard later, at the CP historians' group. She pointed out to them that Khrushchov had carried out the purges in the Ukraine. 'And where was Beria all this time? Living quietly and harmlessly in the Caucasus. We never heard of any purges *there*.' Brian Pearce (who else?) told her about the purges in the Caucasus.

That Sunday the Poles, defying the Soviet leaders, put Gomulka in power. Marshal Rokossovsky stayed in the government, as Defence Minister, but he was no longer in the leadership of the Polish Communist Party. These events formed the splash in the *Daily Worker* on Monday, October 22. The headline was: POLAND'S FATEFUL WEEKEND.

Brian Pearce said that this reminded him of what schoolboys do, when they can't remember whether a French accent has to slope forward or back. They put it straight up in the air. The *Daily Worker* did not yet know whether the Soviet tanks were going into Poland.

On October 22, too, a meeting of students in Budapest demanded the return of Imre Nagy to the government. And on Tuesday, October 23, Hungarians began to demonstrate their support for the Poles.

Dora Scarlett, who was in the thick of the first demonstration, kept the duplicated leaflet a student gave her, headed: OUR SLOGANS.

1. Poland sets the example; we want the Hungarian way!
2. New leadership, a new direction, require new leaders!
3. Children of Father Bem and Father Kossuth [Hungarians and Poles] let us go hand in hand!
4. Children of workers and peasants, we go along with you!
5. We demand a new leadership; we trust Imre Nagy!
6. We shall not stop half way; we shall destroy Stalinism!
7. Independence! Freedom!

8. Long live the Polish people!
9. Long live the Polish Workers' Party!
10. Worker-peasant power!
11. Long live the People's Army! [The Hungarian Army, as distinct from the Russian one.]

These were the slogans the vast peaceful demonstration did in fact shout. The officers and soldiers of the Hungarian Army cheered on the people; the people cheered the soldiers. Once Imre Nagy had appeared and spoken to them, the people in front of Parliament quietly dispersed. But in the meantime Ernö Gerö had made a disastrous broadcast, calling the demonstrators 'hostile elements'. Then men of the AVH, the secret police, fired on a crowd which had gathered outside the radio building. The crowd invaded the radio building and killed three AVH men.

Charles Coutts, English editor of *World Youth*, who had lived in Budapest for three years, sent the *Daily Worker* a despatch: 'The quiet and orderly behaviour of the marchers was impressive.' This was published on October 24. But, even as we read it, we knew that Russian troops were fighting demonstrators in the streets of Budapest. The rumble of the Russian tanks had woken Dora Scarlett at 5 a.m. That was the first Soviet intervention. Who had asked for it? Ernö Gerö, or Imre Nagy, who had become Prime Minister during the night? (It is now known that nobody invited the Russians in. After the event, the Russians drew up an invitation and told Imre Nagy to sign it. He refused. But one of his ministers, Andras Hegedus, did sign. At the time, we knew only that the Russians claimed to bein Hunfgary by invitation.) The phones were down; the reports on the radio contradictory. Campbell told Peter Fryer to go to Hungary at once.

Campbell himself was needed at his post. But this was the very moment when he had to leave it. All through the summer the row had rumbled on: should the British Communist Party send a delegation to the Soviet Union to find out about anti-Semitism? Dutt was against it, but there was a reason why Dutt's opinion on this matter counted for even less than usual.

Just before Stalin's death, when the Jewish doctors were arrested, Dutt asked Hyman Levy to write an article explaining why they were guilty. Levy objected. They hadn't, after all, been tried. Dutt then turned to another prominent Jewish comrade, Chimen Abramsky. He refused for the same reason. So Dutt asked Andrew Rothstein, who hastened to oblige. There was some delay in the printing of *Labour Monthly* for March 1953. It came out, complete with Rothstein's article taking the doctors' guilt for granted, just after they had been released and cleared.

So in 1956 Campbell got his way against Dutt. A delegation was formed including Levy, Campbell, the historian A. L. Morton and some of those industrial comrades who were supposed to be indifferent to moral issues. If Campbell had pulled out of it at the last moment, he would have left the delegation without that political weight which was needed in all dealings with the Russians.

Campbell arrived in Moscow late on the evening of October 25. That morning the *Daily Worker* carried reports on 'counter-revolutionary forces' and the 'shooting of shop stewards, Socialists and Communists by armed detachments of terrorists'.

Socialists? Their party had long been banned in Hungary. As for shop stewards, any worker who honestly tried to fulfil the functions of a shop steward in a Hungarian factory would have been shot by Rakosi, long before. But none of this was as clear to us in London as it was to the Poles in Warsaw. They were already demonstrating in support of the Hungarians. They were also voicing their own slogans: 'Rokossovsky to Moscow!' and 'Katyn, Katyn, Katyn!' (It was not until 33 years later that the Russians acknowledged their guilt for the murder of 4,000 Polish officers in Katyn Forest.)

We still thought the demonstrators might be fascists. On October 25, the *Daily Worker* carried a historical piece by Peter Fryer, THE HELL THAT WAS HORTHY'S, on Hungary's fascist past.

Peter himself was doing his utmost to get there. At the Hungarian Legation in London he was given a visa, 'issued on the personal instructions of Comrade Imre Nagy' and assured that Budapest knew he was coming. It was all arranged…

And, in the past, it always had been. The finances of the *Daily Worker* are a murky subject, but one subsidy at least was undisguised. Any *Daily Worker* reporter who went to a Communist country went as an honoured guest. A car met him at the airport; a guide was at his disposal; all doors were open and all expenses were paid by the government of the country he was in.

In 1989 one of the men who founded *The Independent* told me that it would cost any British newspaper a quarter of a million pounds a year to keep a man in Moscow. In real terms it must have been much the same then. To have a Moscow correspondent free of charge was a subsidy indeed. There were smaller subsidies, too, such as holidays in Eastern Europe for the *Daily Worker* staff. (I was offered one in Romania, but without my children, and what was a holiday to me without them?) Peter Fryer's month in Hungary, that summer, had also been subsidised.

Now, for the first time, Peter found himself on a level with other reporters. There were no planes to Budapest. In Vienna there was no transport to the frontier. Reporters were hiring (or even buying) cars, but Peter, having expected to visit Hungary on the usual basis, had only about £10. He got a lift to the frontier. Having a visa, he could walk across to the first frontier post. And that, for a whole night, was as far as he got.

In London, I went to a buffet lunch for the press, given by a Czech millionaire who made scenery for commercial TV. 'The smoked salmon *kills* the caviare,' a Fleet Street man was complaining. Such gatherings provided the one luxury of my job, and I always enjoyed them. Since weaning Stella I had pulled myself together – or pulled my outlines together, by dieting – and bought a presentable dress. So I could face my fellow-journalists, and other hirelings of the capitalist class. Once a girl from the BBC asked me: 'Are you a Communist? A real Communist?' And she touched me, to make sure.

On another occasion I found that Tom Driberg MP (who is nowadays said to have hated women so much that he could not bear to shake hands with one) would shake hands willingly enough with anybody from the *Daily Worker*. True, he was drunk at the time. He was celebrating his world scoop – an interview with Guy Burgess in Moscow. 'All these years in journalism, and at last I've hit the jackpot.' He was sober enough, however, to tell me that he had met Khrushchov, and formed an 'extremely favourable' impression.

The Czech millionaire's buffet was not such an important occasion as that. I remember it only because it was the last time I felt proud of representing the *Daily Worker*.

My fellow-journalists went for me, about Hungary. What sort of a Communist government was it, that had to bring in foreign troops against its own people? As far as I recollect, I said that Imre Nagy was a real Communist and would soon have everything under control. I had a confused impression that there were two demonstrations, one good and one bad, and that the Soviet troops were suppressing the bad one.

Arguing on my side was one of those journalists who worked for a capitalist paper because he needed the money, but was far more sentimental about our cause than we were. He described the great work of reconstruction that the Communists had been doing while he was in Budapest, at the very beginning of the Rakosi regime.

Not until I went to a staff meeting on Monday, October 29, did I understand the horror aroused in our own Party by the Soviet intervention.

VIII

That was the day the *Daily Worker* carried the following announcement:

> Unlike other newspapers who want to see only the destruction of Socialism, the *Daily Worker* is interested only in facts. Not in rumour or counter-rumour. Nor in idle speculation. To improve our news service from this vital centre we have sent Peter Fryer to Hungary. *Daily Worker* readers know Fryer's reputation as an experienced and skilled reporter. No-one is better qualified for such an assignment.

None of us knew then that Peter Fryer had been in Hungary since the previous Friday night, and was desperately trying to get to Budapest, to find a phone that worked, and to put over the story of a lifetime.

Mick Bennett told us to study the speech Gomulka made on coming to power, in order to get a balanced picture of events in Poland. 'One does not get the impression of a Polish patriot fighting Russia.'

That speech was a landmark on my way to total disillusionment. Gomulka took the official statistics, accepted them as true, and then showed what low productivity and miserable standards they reflected. He proved that the small, backward peasant holdings of Poland were more productive, per acre and per man, than the collective farms. So, throughout

127

the countries where 'we' were in power, peasants had been rounded up and forced into a *less* efficient method of farming. It would be nice to think that, after that speech, I gave up talking about the economic triumphs of Socialism. Unfortunately my notes prove that I went on spouting that particular kind of rubbish for months.

Mick, after reading Gomulka's speech, saw only 'difficulties and mismanagement' which were 'not the fault of the Russians, but of the Poles'. He went on to explain: 'The situation in Poland is that the great mass of the people have never been completely won. Catholic education in the schools has had to be accepted.'

As for Hungary: 'There is a great contradiction between what we say today and what we said last Thursday.' There was indeed. The editorial on Thursday, October 25, began: 'Counter-revolution in Hungary staged an uprising in the hours of darkness on Tuesday night.' The editorial on Monday October 29 declared: 'It is now clear, despite the confused and incomplete picture, that counter-revolutionary actions and the just demands of the people were both factors in the situation.'

Mick explained:

We were misinformed. The trouble with Hungary was that for a long time there had been the airing of grievances by students and others. But the government and the Party were not at the same time putting things right, so that the airing of grievances just made the situation more explosive... It was right to rehabilitate Rajk, but nothing else was done...There is some difficulty in deciding whether it is a counter-revolution or a desire for a progressive movement of the working class. It is *not* a national liberation movement... It is a counter-revolution too. There is a powerful counter-revolutionary movement which has been working underground for a long time. The fact that there are workers who are helping them does not make it progressive. Were the Finns progressive?

Mick was referring to the war between Finland and the Soviet Union which began at the end of November 1939 and ended in March 1940. To Mick (though no longer to others) it was self-evident that the Finns could not have been progressive, since they were fighting the Soviet Union.

Mick then brought up another episode which most of us were now looking at afresh. 'The June 1953 uprising in East Berlin was the fault of the German Democratic Republic, but they were rescued by the Soviet troops.' Mick thought this so obviously right that it would reconcile us to the Soviet intervention of October 24 in Hungary. 'We can't allow ourselves to join an anti-Soviet camp.'

The copytaster Frank Patterson challenged Mick's arguments. Frank came from that industrial working class which was supposed not to care about freedom. His father was a Scottish miner. When on strike, father fed the family by going out at night and dynamiting trout. (The dynamite came from a quarry.) 'I know it was hard on the trout,' Frank said to me once, 'but we had to eat.' Father kept his dynamite under the bed. Once the police came in and searched the house, because father was one of the leaders of the strike. 'Och, there's nothing but rubbish here,' reported a policeman, giving the dynamite a hearty kick.

Now Frank, whose whole life had been spent in poverty and struggle, told Mick to face the real horror of Eastern Europe. 'Stalin's personal apparatus was working in all these countries, and how do we know the extent of it? If the same proportion of people had been unjustly imprisoned here as in Poland, 280,000 people would have had to be rehabilitated... Imagine that number of people hating the governmental guts!' And Frank reminded Mick what Julia Rajk had been through.

'Mick says we were misinformed!' exclaimed Malcolm MacEwen. 'But there were members of this staff begging and pleading and fighting for a more realistic line... Should a

People's Government which has so far forfeited the respect of its own people that it dare not call on its own army have the right to maintain itself by Soviet troops?'

Malcolm spoke of the Congress of the Young Communist League, which had taken place the previous weekend. I now learned for the first time (it had not been reported in our paper) that a resolution condemning the use of Soviet troops in Hungary had been defeated only after an all-out appeal by John Gollan.

Malcolm said: 'Gollan's speech had certain expressions in it which could not go out to the people of this country. He referred to the Hungarian Government 'supported by the workers'... I suggest that there should be a leader in this paper apologising to our readers... We should reconsider our six-pager on Saturday.'

We had been advertising, for Saturday November 3, a six-page paper to celebrate the 39th anniversary of the Bolshevik Revolution.

'We are still in the cult of the individual,' said George MacDougall. 'The cult of the one nation, the USSR...We don't have to be told what to do by the USSR, but we are like the British journalist in the rhyme.

'You cannot hope to bribe or twist,
Thank God, the British journalist.
But seeing what the man will do
Unbribed, there's no occasion to.'

Phil Bolsover was particularly distressed. He had written the splash on October 25. It began: 'Workers in Budapest factories yesterday formed armed groups to protect the factories and the country against counter-revolutionary formations that had attacked buildings, murdered civilians and tried to start a civil war.'

All this came from Budapest Radio, which went on

130

calling the demonstrators 'fascist, reactionary elements' until Saturday, October 27, when it abruptly changed its line. All the newspapers had been on the side of the demonstrators from the first, but Hungarian newspapers were not reaching London, and few people could have understood them if they had.

Now Phil Bolsover asked: 'Why are the majority of the Hungarian people fighting against the 'People's Government'? The basis of all this was an intense demand for independence. The Hungarians do not want the Soviet Army in the country, and to say this is not being anti-Soviet; it is recognising facts.'

He ridiculed 'the line that this is just a counter-revolution financed by the Americans'. He attacked Gollan for telling the YCL Congress to 'look at Eden'.

'To compare our government with the Hungarian Government is in itself an insult to the Government of Hungary... If you get huge demonstrations taking place, isn't it obvious that a number of these are Party members? What has been the policy of the leaders, which put them apart from the Party members? The explanation I wrote was completely wrong.'

Gabriel asked: 'How could the *Daily Worker* keep talking about a counter-revolution when they have to call in Soviet troops? Can you defend the right of a government to exist with the help of Soviet troops? Gomulka said that a government which has lost the confidence of the people has no right to govern.'

On Gollan's speech to the YCL, Gabriel said: 'When we start talking about "Kenya, Cyprus and Malaya" I know we have no case.'

And he criticised Campbell (who was in Moscow) for writing about the 'irresponsibility' of the Polish press. 'What does he know about the Polish press? *Pravda* said it was irresponsible, so that was enough for the editor.' (Several people in the office could read Russian, but nobody could read

131

Polish.) 'No matter what the intentions of the editorial comrades, they have got us into one hell of a mess.'

Eric Scott said: 'There is every kind of element mixed up in the present revolt, so it is a little sweeping to suggest that it is entirely something which is to be supported... We were in a much more alarming position in the 1930s, when all these countries were fascist dictatorships.'

At this point, as everyone had to get on with producing the paper, the meeting was adjourned for two days. The news on the radio that day was that Israel had invaded Egypt.

The following day the Soviet troops agreed to pull out of Hungary. As we resumed our meeting on Wednesday October 31, we could read on the front page of our own paper the headline: RUSSIA ADMITS MISTAKES. The story began:

> In a special statement broadcast by Moscow Radio last night the Soviet Government said there had been mistakes and misunderstandings in relations between the Soviet Union and the people's democracies... The Soviet Government had given orders to its commander-in-chief to withdraw Soviet troops from Budapest as soon as the Hungarian Government desires it.

Not yet in the paper, but on the radio, was the news that the Hungarian rebels had released Cardinal Mindszenty from prison. He had been there since his great show trial in February 1949. Some of our comrades regarded his release as proof that the rebels were fascists.

Llew Gardiner opened the resumed meeting by expressing his concern about the splitting of the Party into two parties. 'I abhor the language used by Malcolm about Gollan's speech. I abhor the crack about "reasoners" in Walter Holmes's piece.' In his Worker's Notebook, that morning, Walter Holmes had written, à propos of nothing in particular: 'Of course I know we say something wrong every day, and even when we are right there is no lack of reasoners to prove we are wrong.'

Leon Griffiths declared: 'The split is beginning to appear in this paper.' He pointed out that at the YCL Congress Gollan had denounced the resolution deploring the use of Soviet troops in Hungary. 'Now Moscow is coming out with the same line.'

Leon argued that the demands now being made by Hungary and Poland showed that their economy had been enslaved to the Soviet Union. 'The trouble was that there never was a revolution in Hungary. Socialism was imposed on these countries from the outside.'

Our circulation manager, Phil Piratin, had come to join the editorial meeting. I first met Phil when he was the Party's parliamentary candidate for Mile End in 1945. Addressing a meeting of the Tailor and Garment Workers' Union, he said of his Labour opponent: 'Dan Frankel? Why, Dan Frankel isn't worthy to lick my boots.' Nobody laughed. It was obviously true. Apart from the notorious weaknesses of Dan Frankel, what favoured Phil was the smallness of the constituency. The bombing had killed hundreds of Mile End people, and thousands more moved out when their houses were destroyed. Phil needed only a little over 5,000 votes to win. He became an MP, and a remarkably good one, much loved by people who had no use for his politics, because he dealt so patiently and thoroughly with the problems of constituents who came to see him. He talked to me about this once, on the terrace of the House of Commons. 'If they're Jewish,' he murmured, 'I bully them a little.'

Phil, who did not die until 1995, did not look so much Jewish as Tartar; his clever, lively, oriental face was evidence in favour of Arthur Koestler's theory about the survival of the Khazars.

What I admired most about him, in 1956, was that he had taken the loss of his seat in Parliament so calmly. Redrawn boundaries, a better Labour candidate and the things that Stalin had done to make us unpopular combined to defeat him in 1950. From being a public man he became, almost overnight, a quiet and hardworking backroom boy.

Now he told us frankly: 'I have given numerous lectures on democracy. I would not care to give a lecture on democracy anywhere these days.'

But he pleaded with Malcolm and Gabriel to 'be statesmen'. He assured them that he understood their point of view: 'The very day that Khrushchov and the others flew to Poland, I said that they were wrong. I said they were being ham-handed... I have taken things up in Hungary and Poland, and been rebuked by the Party leadership here for daring to raise it.'

But he wanted the Party to remain united, and give a lead about Suez. 'We are not prepared for knocking the government out. That is our crime.'

Bob Leeson, a reporter, who had spent some time in Hungary in the early days of Rakosi's rule, said: 'To be wise after the event is better than never thinking about it at all... One thing hit Hungary for six. In 1947 Tito was hailed as a hero through the streets of Budapest. In 1949 not only was Rajk shot for Titoism – Rajk's brother-in-law told me that for 18 months nobody spoke to him. Mindszenty might be a criminal. But how can you convince people after dropping a clanger like that? Who can believe you?'

He described how Hungary's football team (which beat England's at Wembley in 1953) was politically exploited.

In the six months leading up to the World Cup, production in the factories was tied to a victory for the Hungarian team. When it lost, there were demonstrations in the streets...

After the Warsaw Pact, more Soviet troops were moved into Hungary. Who is it feels the weight of occupation troops most? The members of the national army...

Practically every young person in Hungary was a member of a youth organisation. Yet they were the backbone of the revolt. The fact that the people had arms showed that the majority of the young people were in the armed forces...

'I could bite my tongue off for the things that I have said up till Monday,' declared Sid Kaufman, a sub-editor. 'The thoughts I express now are the thoughts given to me by comrades in our local branch... I don't believe our Party leadership has begun to learn the lessons of the Twentieth Congress... We have got to look at *The Reasoner* again... At the Saturday meeting Campbell said the discussion was going on apace, and there was no need for *The Reasoner*... At my branch I was accused of stifling discussion, of 'talking like a full-timer'... Phil Piratin says that our Party is not going into action over Suez. The reason is that we have not got a Party to go into action...'

Our correspondent in Glasgow, Phil Stein, had come to London specially for this meeting. He said: 'We, who should have been better informed about the situation in Eastern Europe, were worse informed... When I visited Hungary a few years ago, everyone shouted: "Stalin! Rakosi!" He imitated that rhythmic chanting. 'It made my blood run cold.'

He added that a Scottish comrade, Dr. Robbie Black, had resigned from the Party because the *Daily Worker* refused to print his letter about Hungary. 'He saw the Party members on a special beach on Lake Balaton, protected by barbed wire.'

Phil Stein pointed out that the Warsaw Pact made no provision for the calling in of Soviet troops to put down a revolt. 'Some of our loyalties have been strained to breaking point... I am shocked at the cynicism I have found in this office... I decided not to write to Johnnie Campbell, because he never answered.'

A young reporter, Jim Corbett, read aloud the leading article from the *Daily Worker* the previous Friday, October 26.

'What has happened in Hungary during these past days has not been a popular uprising against a dictatorial government. It has been an organised and planned effort to overthrow by undemocratic and violent means a government which was in process of carrying through important constructive measures to put right past mistakes and wrongs...'

Jim Corbett contrasted this with our own news stories, for example the Monday splash, which was a statement by Imre Nagy, the new Hungarian Prime Minister.

'If the people are not able to defend their own Socialism,' Jim Corbett said, 'then that Socialism is not worth twopence.'

He asked why the paper had not mentioned the YCL resolution condemning the use of Soviet troops, and argued: 'This is not attacking the Soviet Union.'

At this there were giggles from Allen Hutt and Eric Scott. Jim Corbett turned on them and asked: 'Are we going to remain Marxist Bourbons? What is it going to be like here after ten years of Socialism? No free press? No free speech?'

George Sinfield, our industrial correspondent, respected by Fleet Street men as a great expert on trade unions, and by us as a great fellow-worker, was distressed to find us taking the same line as the Labour Party people he had just been meeting. If only we were not in this state of mind, he argued, look what we could do about the impending Suez War! 'If we were organised we could put pressure on the TUC to carry out its own decision, and carry out a general strike against the war.'

The demands of the young reporters, that the Soviet Union should be criticised, shocked him profoundly. 'If the comrades want a slanging match with *Pravda*, I don't think I could work on a paper which did that.'

Sinfield went on: 'It is not much use comrades getting hot under the collar because someone describes what is happening in Hungary as a counter-revolution...

'What we have to be careful about is that similar situations may arise in Bulgaria and Czechoslovakia.'

Sinfield pointed to features of the Hungarian rising which he found sinister. 'How did Sefton Delmer come to be on the spot at the time?' (The *Daily Express* reporter who specialised in spy stories. He was always on the spot when a good story broke.) 'Why was the strongest section of the rebels near the Austrian border?' (It wasn't. The western reporters came in from Austria, because no planes could fly to Budapest, and they described what they saw where they happened to be.) Then the clinching argument: 'Who called the Socialist International together? Their leader, a US intelligence man.'

I was to hear such questions as these for years. In 1990, at a Communist historians' conference on the events of 1956, an 84-year-old comrade rose to her feet to say that one of the Esterhazy family had been somewhere about at the time. With such toys as these do the faithful distract themselves from observing that, wherever 'we' have been in power, the vast majority of the people hate our guts.

All this time George Matthews had been patiently listening to our debate. He was second-in-command to John Gollan, not part of the *Daily Worker* team, but he had come over from Party headquarters to keep an eye on us while Campbell was away. Now he spoke with studied moderation.

'Frank Patterson said some things that a great many comrades are feeling. We all joined the Party because we hated injustice... I would be the last to deny that we have made mistakes...

'The *Daily Worker* treatment of the events in Hungary was correct at the time of writing. We did not follow what the Soviet Union said, because the Soviet Union said nothing.'

Matthews argued that, as a general principle, 'the Soviet Union should be presumed innocent until proved guilty'. So far we could follow him. But then he added: 'We have never adopted the attitude that a Socialist government must never call in the troops of another country... When the Hungarian Government called in the Soviet troops on Wednesday, it said they would withdraw as soon as order was restored.'

And why had the paper not reported the resolution moved at the YCL Congress? Here Matthews became heated. 'I wish you could have seen the bunch of Trotskyists in the public gallery, organising these young people.' (The bunch of Trotskyists was led by Gerry Healy, who sat visibly giving orders to some delegates.)

George Matthews was too honest to give us the usual type of leadership. 'Was the calling in of the troops right or wrong?' he asked. 'My frank opinion is that I don't know.'

Matthews gave a pat on the back to Poland for being 'more or less on the right lines now', and to Gomulka for 'trying to fight the right-wing danger'.

But, as for Hungary: 'We are told this is not a counter-revolution. How do you judge a counter-revolution? Not by the number of people taking part in it. Not by their motives. If Socialism is replaced by capitalism, that is a counter-revolution...

'If we were over-simplifying, Malcolm and the other comrades are over-simplifying in the other direction... I don't think we can accept Malcolm's proposition that the editor should put one view on page one, and Malcolm another view on page two. Some comrades hold up the American *Daily Worker* to us as an example. I hope we shall never do what they are doing.'

What filled Matthews with horror was that the editor of the New York *Daily Worker*, John Gates, was criticising the Soviet Union in his editorials, while on another page the old Stalinist leader, William Z. Foster, put his own views.

Later that day, October 31, two things happened. One I knew about at once, from the radio. The British and French began to bombard Suez. The other thing I did not know about, though its repercussions were to transform my life. Peter Fryer found a phone that worked, and got through from Budapest with his story.

On the morning of November 1 Jack was up first. He came to wake me, saying:

'Good news! When I went into the sitting room the fire was burning. David and his friend have been there all night. They've been arrested for chalking the walls, about Suez.'

I put on a dressing gown and ran downstairs to greet my stepson and his friend (whose name was also David). 'You darlings!' I cried. 'I must make you a really good breakfast.' My stepson had expected this parental approval, but the other David found it slightly bewildering. Both were undergraduates at Oxford, and both had done their National Service first, so that they were now 22. They did not belong to anything; they had heard the news from Suez on the radio, and thought they ought to do something about it. So they got some whitewash and took the train to London, and began to paint the first wall that came handy with the slogan: 'Stop the War.' As they had not the expertise of Party members in dodging the police, they were immediately arrested. The police, they said, seemed puzzled, scarcely believing that British forces were bombing Egypt. One of the policemen said to them: 'If that's true, I ought to be out there with you.'

We had a happy breakfast. The girls were delighted at the sudden appearance of their adored big brother. I could not claim any credit for my stepson; his aunt, with whom he lived, was the one who should be proud of his healthy looks and gentlemanly manners. But Jack and I felt we had educated him politically.

When I had seen Cathy off to school, I put on my press conference clothes to impress the magistrate. The two Davids and I took Stella to her nursery, and went on to Clerkenwell

139

Magistrates Court, where they pleaded guilty. I paid their fines. And how many, many times have I been repaid since then, by the kindness of both men to me!

This was the last time Jack and I felt sure that we were doing the right thing. In the excitement, we scarcely had time to glance at the front page of the *Daily Worker*. It carried a report 'From the Foreign Editor'. (Did Phil Bolsover write this? In 1990 he seemed not to remember.) It began: 'Soviet troops and tanks yesterday completed their withdrawal from Budapest – then gangs of reactionaries began beating Communists to death in the streets. Some reports claimed that only identified representatives of the former security police were being killed, but in fact the gangs seemed to be attacking any Communist they could. According to reports from Prague, whole families were dragged from their beds and shot, including children...'

Reports from Prague? I did vaguely wonder what had happened to Peter Fryer.

That day the radio carried the news that a woman in her sixties, claiming British nationality, had turned up at the British Legation in Budapest. Edith Bone was free. The following day the *Daily Express* reported that she had staggered in and fainted. But she afterwards wrote that she had not staggered, only limped. The rebels who set her free had found her barefoot, and the shoes they got out of the prison stores for her were uncomfortably small. Nor, she insisted, did she faint. She sat down and drank a nice cup of tea.

That same day, there was a broadcast from a member of Imre Nagy's government. 'Our people have proved with their blood their intention to support unflinchingly the government's efforts for the complete withdrawal of Soviet forces.' The speaker was Janos Kadar.

He was, even then, an ambiguous figure. He had been Minister of the Interior after Rajk. In 1956 there were persistent rumours that he had persuaded Rajk to confess, after the Russian General Bielkin had failed to do so. There was even alleged to be a tape recording of his conversation with Rajk on this occasion, which was played to the Central Committee of the Party in the summer of 1956.

In 1951 Kadar was elected to the Central Committee of the Party by its Second Congress. He was arrested so soon afterwards that his name was still in the printed report of the Congress. Dora Scarlett kept a copy of this report, from which Kadar's name had been hastily blacked out. It was still legible through the ink. Kadar was tortured in prison, which gave him a certain respectability in the eyes of the rebels.

On Saturday, November 3, the *Daily Worker* published a statement expressing its horror at the treatment of Edith Bone, and saying that it had made repeated enquiries about her, most recently on September 24. The paper had the promised six pages, but the celebrations of the October Revolution were rather subdued.

That day, too, the paper carried a despatch from Peter Fryer. It consisted of an interview with Charles Coutts, who had been present at the beginning of the rising. I did not know that 455 words had been cut out of this interview by George Matthews. Events were now moving so fast that, in the three days since the Wednesday morning meeting, I had lost touch with what was happening in the *Daily Worker* office. On Sunday, November 4, I had to wake up.

IX

On Sundays we took the Co-op paper, *Reynolds News*, then struggling to survive. Sometimes it would run a bodice-ripping serial, with mildly sexy illustrations, and the circulation would go up. Then the Co-op Women's Guilds would protest that such things had no place in a progressive newspaper. So the paper would become serious and proper, and the circulation would go down again.

That Sunday, *Reynolds* carried the news that Cardinal Mindszenty had made a broadcast. I scarcely took this in at the time, but I quote it now, as one clue to a mystery not yet cleared up. This is the *Reynolds News* version, in full:

> Cardinal Mindszenty last night bitterly attacked the Imre Nagy Government in a broadcast on the Hungarian Radio, describing it as the 'heir of a broken system.'
>
> The Roman Catholic primate, who was released from prison only last week, demanded Hungary should abandon Communism and return to a system of private property.
>
> The broadcast was almost entirely political in tone.
>
> 'What has happened was not a revolution but a battle for freedom,' he declared.
>
> 'The system was swept away by a whole people. The heirs of this broken system should not demand any further proof of this.'

Cardinal Mindszenty demanded restoration of the old rights and property of the Catholic Church in Hungary, and guarantees for Church life and Catholic schools and newspapers.

'We shall now watch closely whether the Government's promises are matched by facts,' he said.

He called for free general elections under international supervision, with every party completely free to name its own candidates.

The mystery is where this report came from. It was almost entirely wrong. The Cardinal made no attack on Imre Nagy or his government. He asked, not for the restoration of Church property, but for freedom of religious teaching.

He did say: 'The fighting which took place was not a revolution but a fight for freedom.' Then he added: 'After a, for us, purposeless war in 1945, the system here was developed by force. Its heirs now brand every bit of it with repudiation, contempt, disgust and whole-hearted condemnation.'

If by 'its heirs' the Cardinal meant the Nagy Government, he was saying that he agreed with them. He did call for free elections under international supervision, but added: 'I, in accordance with my position, am outside parties and will stand above parties.'

What he said about the return of private property was this:

We want a classless society and a state where law prevails, a country developing democratic achievements, based on private ownership correctly restricted by the interests of society and of justice.

Reynolds News (long dead) cannot be blamed for failing to obtain, a few hours after the speech was made, a correctly monitored version. But the version it did use must have had something about it which put all the other Sunday papers off, since none of them used it. Did it come from Tass?

My main concern, that Sunday, was whether I could go to the Suez protest meeting in Trafalgar Square. I could manage it if the article I had sent Malcolm would do as it was, without the additions which I so often had to write on a Sunday. I rang Malcolm. He cut through what I was saying.

'I suppose you know,' said Malcolm, 'the Russians have marched into Budapest.'

I said feebly: 'Oh dear.'

'Quite,' said Malcolm. 'Oh dear.'

I turned on the radio, and heard the recorded last broadcast of Imre Nagy. 'At dawn today the Soviet forces made an unprovoked attack on the capital, with the obvious intention of overthrowing the lawful, democratic Hungarian Government. Our troops are resisting; the Government is in its place. This is my message to Hungary and to the world.'

Between the radio bulletins, Jack and I tried to think of reasons why the Soviet Union could possibly be justified. After lunch we put the girls on the bus to Granny, and went to Trafalgar Square.

On the plinth, Aneurin Bevan was declaring: 'The Tories have besmirched the name of Britain.' I know he said that because it was printed next day. But at the time I did not listen to a word. The banners were all about Suez; the arguments among the banner-bearers were all about Hungary. On the outskirts of the crowd we met an old army comrade of Jack's, Sam Bardell. He told us that this was the only thing the Russians could have done. Jack and I had been trying to think so; now, on hearing it from Sam, we discovered it was nonsense. In the course of the shouting match, Sam asked: 'And what's this about Peter Fryer?'

In this casual way, from a comrade unconnected with the *Daily Worker*, I learned that Peter's first despatch from Hungary had not been published. 'Because they thought it was a pack of lies,' explained Sam.

One thing was clear to me. Peter had not sent a pack of lies. (Nor, indeed, was this ever said by our leaders, to anybody who knew Peter personally.)

Peter was to me a colleague, rather than a close friend. I was seven years older. My particular friends were Sheila Lynd (who, like myself, had two children) and the gentle, reserved, supremely competent Florence Keyworth. But I had the affection for Peter that any sub-editor feels for a reporter whose copy needs no rewriting. That he had naively reported the Rajk trial in 1949 I knew; but I also knew that he had never written a word he did not believe.

Sam added that Peter had threatened to send the story to the *News Chronicle*, but that the *Daily Worker* 'couldn't yield to blackmail'. This didn't sound like Peter either.

That night I said to Jack: 'What's Campbell going to do?' (I had forgotten he was still in Moscow.) 'If he comes out tomorrow for the Russians, he's lost Malcolm and Gabriel. If he comes out against them, he's lost George Sinfield.'

'And you?' said Jack. 'What's he got to do to lose you?'

Until that moment it had never occurred to me that I could possibly, of my own free will, leave the *Daily Worker*.

Jack shook his head over the front page of the *Daily Worker* on Monday, November 5. Yet he said: 'I can see there's a case for it.' The splash headline said: NEW HUNGARIAN ANTI-FASCIST GOVERNMENT IN ACTION. The second deck was: Soviet troops called in to stop White Terror. There was a resolution approving the Russian action by the Executive Committee of the Party.

Also on the front page was the Mindszenty broadcast. This differed slightly from the *Reynold's News* version, and was in reported speech ('The Cardinal said that...') without one direct quote. Both versions of the speech seem to have had a common origin.

An editorial staff meeting had been fixed for that morning. On the trolley bus going to it I found David Ainley, the *Daily Worker* business manager. I had a soft spot for him, because his job was to say: 'No' to people who wanted more money, and this made him unpopular. I thought that unfair; he was just as hard up as the rest of us. His wife, like all the other Party wives, had to work. The perks from Eastern Europe did not affect our lives in Britain. Whether Ainley really saved much money, by telling us to hoard used paper clips, is debatable. But the visible thrift in the office did impress the parties of sympathisers, whom I had so often conducted round the building. They could see that the money we collected from them was being looked after. (Ainley also collected the Soviet subsidy, but I did not know that then.)

I had another reason for liking Ainley. In the Muswell Hill branch, he had put up a fight against our locally culted individual – G. J. Jones (Jonah). Still unable to open his mouth without saying: 'I got 10,000 votes in 1945', and still surrounded with adoring followers, Jonah had been dealt with by that Party discipline, which did indeed distinguish us from other left-wing groups. After his disastrous result in 1950, he had not been allowed to stand for Parliament again. Because of this our comrades in the Crouch End ward of Hornsey found themselves without a place to meet. Jonah's leading mistress, taking umbrage when he was outvoted, refused to have Party meetings in her flat. However, Ainley's faction won. Jonah was told to support Labour at elections.

So I regarded Ainley as the voice of common sense, and was taken aback to find that he did not even question the rightness of the Soviet intervention in Hungary. About Peter Fryer, he said that the banned despatch had been 'hysterical' and that, yes, Fryer had threatened to give it to the *News Chronicle*. (This, I discovered later, was not true.)

Ainley sneered at Fryer, for taking refuge in the British

Embassy. I said: 'So should I.' 'What!' exclaimed Ainley, deeply shocked. I said I wouldn't want to be shot dead in the street.

Our meeting was addressed by John Gollan, with us for the first time since becoming General Secretary of the Party, the previous May.

Palme Dutt said (many years later) that Gollan had argued, within the Political Bureau, against supporting the Soviet intervention in Hungary. This, if true, would not have been known at the time. What happened within the Politburo was kept secret. Once a vote was taken, the minority was bound, not only to accept the view of the majority, but to speak, write and argue for it. The Executive Committee, a much larger body, was not allowed to know even that there had been a difference within the Politburo, much less who had said what.

Whenever the Party line changed, any Party leader who was known by the other leaders to be shaky on the subject would be put up to defend the new line in public. This technique is not peculiar to the Communist Party; Churchill used it in 1940, when he made Halifax denounce Hitler's proposals for a negotiated peace.

In 1991 Mick Bennett denied that Gollan ever argued against the Soviet intervention. In 1976 Gollan himself made a half-apology in *Marxism Today*. He took 20,000 words over it, and not one of those words explains what he thought at the time.

What he said at the time I know. He began: 'We have got to look at the background. Hungary was the original fascist country in Europe.' Then he quoted an article from *The Times* of 4 August 1950: 'The Catholic Church enjoyed unique political rights in Hungary which would undoubtedly have been challenged in the mid-Twentieth Century no matter what regime was in power... Throughout the centuries the Cardinal has held political powers scarcely inferior to the King.'

Gollan told us: 'Industrialisation in a peasant country is always a difficult process. I think everyone here is mature enough to realise that all this would have caused enough difficulties if there had been no abuses...'

Reaction, Gollan said, had been financed and prepared for years. And the Party had rectified its mistakes too slowly. Again he quoted *The Times*: 'The 300,000 Hungarians who turned up at Rajk's reburial came... to proclaim their protest against the regime as a whole.'

Gollan read us this at the cost of admitting that our own estimate of that crowd – 200,000 – had been too small.

He saw two separate, basic trends: 'The just demands of the people, and counter-revolution.'

By this time most of us knew that the people killed by the rebels had been security policemen. But, in Gollan's version: 'The first thing they did in Budapest was to assassinate every Communist they could lay hands on.'

He argued: 'Whatever the excesses and abuses, Hungary was a workers' state. Therefore when the Soviet troops were called in we say this was absolutely correct.'

He said that the Russians had at first been prepared to leave the solution to Nagy. 'But stage by stage Nagy capitulated to counter-revolution.' That is, he formed a coalition including Socialists and peasant leaders. Moreover he announced that Hungary was leaving the Warsaw Pact.

After more quotations from the capitalist papers, Gollan got down to the part of his argument which we were to hear again and again.

'Mindszenty was trying to utilise the religious elements. He made four demands:

'One: Away with Nagy;

'Two: Restoration of capitalism;

'Three: Restoration of the political power of the Church;

148

'Four: Western intervention.'

Mindszenty had made none of these demands. We did not know this at the time, and we were not sufficiently wide awake to ask what effect a broadcast, made at eight on Saturday evening, could have had on Soviet troop movements ordered many hours before. Janos Kadar and another member of the Nagy Government, Ferenc Munnich, slipped away to set up their puppet government in Szolnok on the morning of that Saturday.

'I am glad that the Hungarian Communists rallied,' was Gollan's comment on that act of treachery. 'The question of a bastion of fascism in Hungary is not only an internal class issue. It was a menace to Yugoslavia, Czechoslovakia and the Soviet Union...'

Gollan admitted that there had been a difference of opinion within the Executive Committee. 'It was our industrial comrades who solidly and to a man said that this EC must stand with the Hungarian comrades.'

He admitted: 'It could be argued – better run the risk of fascism than the risk of war. The risk of fascism was not a risk but a certainty... Under Mindszenty there would have been a fascist puppet state under the control of the US... Some comrades are saying: 'Can we have Socialism imposed by force?' This wasn't the case. Socialism was already established and was being torn apart.'

Gollan concluded: 'I know our stand will cause great difficulties for us.'

George MacDougall asked: 'Was the EC decision unanimous?'

Gollan replied: 'No. There were two against.' We later learned that the two were Max Morris (of the National Union of Teachers) and Arnold Kettle (a university lecturer). Both afterwards knuckled under.

Malcolm MacEwen said: 'I think that in the last ten days

everyone has made mistakes. I certainly have... Nevertheless I think the action of the Soviet Government was wrong... It is absolutely impermissible to indulge in brinkmanship. My first reaction was immediately to say: 'Here is the risk of world war.' In the fight for peace at the present time, the Charter of the United Nations is not a scrap of paper. The USSR has forfeited the right to stand up for that charter.'

It shows how confused we all were that, in the middle of this speech, Malcolm declared: 'If you say: "Do I support Comrade Kadar?" I say: "Yes, I do." '

Then he reverted to sense. 'The Poles say that all their difficulties are the fault of the Soviet Union... When Gollan was in Moscow to discuss the Stalin revelations [the previous July] Khrushchov said: "This thing will die down in three months." Gollan said: "I disagree." Khrushchov said: "I am glad you raised that point. What I mean is that the present sensation will die down, but the thing will go on for years." '

Gollan confirmed that this conversation had taken place. Malcolm then announced: 'It would be better for the paper if I were to leave.'

'I think that Malcolm's statement reflects what we have been thinking,' said Llew Gardner. 'It is wrong for the troops of any nation to be used against the people, or any section of the people, of another country...'

On the other hand, Llew Gardner argued, fascism was a certainty. 'I believe, therefore, that the greater evil had to be defeated... I am not satisfied with the way this is put in our paper... But I stand by the EC.'

'I can't accept the EC resolution,' said Gabriel. 'I think the Soviet Union had no right to make this criminal gamble with the people of the world.'

Then he announced: 'I drew a cartoon on Hungary. It was rejected. All right, I accept that. But that is my last cartoon for the *Daily Worker*.'

Frank Gullett, the news editor, said he knew how Malcolm and Gabriel felt. But he asked them: 'Would the danger of world war be less if things had been left to go on as they were?'

Robin Jardine of the library said: 'When I read the EC statement at first I was inclined to the view expressed by Malcolm and Gabriel... Jesuitry is Jesuitry.' Yet, he argued: 'I still believe in the Communist Party and in the need for it.'

The stenographer Doris Tuckfield said: 'I am old enough to remember 1919, and the White Terror in Hungary... Class struggle is war.'

To which Frank Patterson rejoined: 'I joined the Party 23 years ago, out of the class struggle. We *lived* it. But if Hungary is what I joined the Party for...'

Peter Zinkin spoke in whole-hearted support of Gollan. 'When I leave this room I will have to go to the House of Commons and mix with MPs. No-one on this paper will have to face a more difficult job.'

How much mixing Zinkin did was a moot point. He had once told an editorial conference: 'We're really making headway with the Labour Party. I saw Nye Bevan in the corridor yesterday, and he almost spoke to me.'

Now he declared: 'I am not worried about facing Labour MPs... Hungary is a big dagger with its point near the heart of the Soviet Union.'

Leon Griffiths protested: 'Gollan said that the forces of reaction turned up at the Rajk reburial – 300,000 people! But that was the entire working-class population of Budapest. More than come out for May Day!'

Leon was the first to mention Fryer's banned despatch. 'He said it would take generations for the Party to regain the respect of the people... There is not the slightest bit of evidence that the Hungarian workers are supporting Kadar... We can ill afford to lose people like Malcolm and Gabriel... I have heard that Hutt made a speech at the EC imputing all sorts of odd motives to the people who signed this petition.'

The petition was another thing I had missed in my few days outside the office. It protested at the treatment of the news from Hungary. Out of the full-time staff of 31, 19 had signed it.

George Sinfield had not. 'The more I listen to Malcolm and Gabriel,' he said, 'the more I admire them. But I profoundly disagree... Isn't what we see going on in Hungary precisely what the reactionaries have been working for all these years? Isn't that their whole purpose? At the Labour Party conference Zilliacus said that social democrats were working for counter-revolution.'(Zilliacus had unbecome an unperson, now that we were friends with Tito.)

I was by now so much occupied with what I ought to say that I did not make notes of what Bob Leeson said. In 1990 he remembered urging Gabriel to 'stay in and fight for change'.

What I said was that I could not make up my mind. 'From a military point of view,' I said, 'I can see the Soviet case. They thought their frontier was in danger. But does the class war justify everything? When I first joined the Labour League of Youth in 1935 I said: "We must always act legally, to put ourselves in the right." Someone told me: "You're taking it for granted that there's somebody above both classes, who will judge us." And I realised that that's what was at the back of my mind, and that it wasn't true – there was only the working class and the capitalist class. But nowadays there is a great new force – the force of world public opinion, to an extent that never existed before the war. Isn't that of much greater importance for the Soviet Union, even from a narrow military point of view, than what happens on the frontier?'

Hutt then made a reluctant retraction of what he had said at the EC meeting, about the staff members who signed the petition. 'I meant no reflection on George MacDougall and

Phil Bolsover.' A few minutes later Hutt snarled at Bob Leeson, as he left the meeting: 'If you want to fight you ought to clear out.'

The meeting was adjourned for two days, until Wednesday November 7. We barely noticed that, on the Tuesday, President Eisenhower was re-elected with an increased majority. The United States, at that moment, was the only world power with clean hands. It was telling Britain and France to get out of Suez (as they soon did) and the Soviet Union to get out of Hungary (as it did not).

Jack and I clung together. All round us the marriages of Party members were cracking up. Some couples stayed together only by never holding those discussions which to us were the breath of life.

Jack and I talked far into the night, and when we fell asleep we fell into nightmare. I dreamed that the Russians were hanging people along the roads. In the morning Jack woke me with the words: '*The Daily Telegraph* says that the Russians are hanging people from all the Danube bridges. If that's true my Party card goes straight into the fire.' It seemed not to be true, though other nightmares were.

I dreamed that George Fles was rising up, covered with earth, into the middle of our sitting room. Who was he, and why was he on my conscience?

George Fles was a Dutch Communist, who in the 1930s had married an English girl, Pearl Rimmel. They were thrilled when a great opportunity came their way – going to live in the Soviet Union. In 1937 Stalin sent out his ukase: foreigners must leave. Pearl came back to England first, because she was pregnant. George was about to follow her, when he was arrested. He had become disillusioned with Stalin's rule, and was not always careful when he said so. He was not, however, sentenced to death. With other political prisoners, he was sent to work on a military highway from Smolensk to Moscow.

Pearl was, at first, able to write to him. Then her letters began coming back marked: 'Address unknown.'

Why did I feel guilty? Because I had heard about this, even before Stalin's death, *and had chosen not to know more.* Since the Khrushchov speech, Pearl's sisters (still in the Party) had begun to talk more freely.

So I now knew that in 1937 Pearl had been to see Harry Pollitt, and had begged him to intercede for her husband. Pollitt said: 'What can I do? They won't listen to me. They've arrested Rose Cohen. I know she's innocent; I've known her from a child.'

Pollitt had been in love with Rose Cohen in the 1920s, and had asked her to marry him. She turned him down and married the Comintern agent in England. He was known as A. J. Bennet, a name which carried no conviction, as he had a thick East European accent. In Russia he was known as Petrovsky and in Poland as Goldfarb. He had been one of the leaders of the Bund, an organisation of Socialist Jews. Stalin killed millions of people who were not Jews. However, if you were under suspicion already, being Jewish might be one more point against you.

Long after this, Pollitt continued to assure all us humble Party members who did the work that the stories of innocent people being arrested in Russia were lies. I had, by November 1956, no respect for him. But how much respect ought I to have for myself? Looking back, I could see that I had insisted on being lied to.

When we resumed our meeting Gabriel had already gone, and Malcolm had given notice. A dinosaur came raging at us from the past. It shows how fast events were moving that the past was three weeks earlier.

The veteran industrial reporter Ben Francis had been ill for that time. He had thus missed the coming of Gomulka to power and the entire course of the Hungarian rising. Now he came back to find, as he put it, 'the counter-revolution in this building'. As for Malcolm resigning, 'Malcolm should have been put out of his job'. Ben was shocked by the letters on the features page, some of which criticised the Soviet Union.

'Ben has made a very bad speech,' said Ainley. 'It is hard for all of us to break the habit of thought of a very long time... All the comrades are trying to grapple with their consciences... Terrible things have happened in Hungary, and I feel that the Soviet Union, together with the Hungarian Party, have made serious mistakes... But I disagree with those comrades who think that these mistakes should be expiated in the blood of the Hungarian workers.'

Then Ainley presented what was to become the official view. 'It was a mistake to send Fryer. He was hysterical on certain questions. A number of our comrades are outraged because a report which he sent is not printed in our paper. The role of the *Daily Worker* is to express the views of our Party and its leadership.'

Sheila Lynd said: 'The more we hear about the leadership of the Hungarian Party, the more criminal its record becomes... The Party succeeded in uniting the people against it... There are some crimes that we really do have to pay for with our own blood, and not with the blood of other people.'

Sheila had been listening to the hardliners in conversation. 'I have heard so many sneers at democratisation as the cause of the trouble. Sneers at the promise of free elections, and remarks to the effect that if the Soviet Union had had any nonsense about free elections in the twenties there would not have been a Soviet Union today. I believe there was real democracy in the Soviet Union in the twenties.'

Sheila pointed out: 'We all believe in self-determination. So much so that we support the union of Cyprus with fascist Greece... There is a real danger of us following blindly a very short-term part of Soviet policy, as we did in 1939. I am not prepared to do that again.'

'I can see that White Terror had to be defeated in Hungary,' said the sub-editor Ted Armitage. But he added that the EC ought to have said that the trouble arose from 'the cult of the individual – the individual country'. To those comrades who had been arguing that the crimes of Stalin were 'unavoidable' Armitage repeated: 'Unavoidable? If the British working class gets that idea, we are sunk.'

(The British workers had a pretty good idea that Communist policy made slave camps unavoidable. That was why our circulation was so small.)

The stenographer May Hill was horrified at a report that Fryer's banned despatch had been read aloud to a Party branch. She said: 'Malcolm's attitude reminds me of Neville Chamberlain's. Peace in our time! We had to face up to intervention in Spain.'

Malcolm called to her: 'Are you in favour of intervention in Spain *now*?'

'Let me speak,' said May. 'I have heard enough from you. There is no such thing as neutrality on the Continent.' (She was referring to the attempt of Imre Nagy to take Hungary out of the Warsaw Pact.)

As for the Party line being unpopular, she did not mind that. 'My life in the Party has been one of unpopularity.'

George MacDougall said: 'It is not a question of an unpopular line. I oppose the EC statement on three lines:

'One: Working-class principle;

'Two: Right of self-determination;

'Three: Its effect on the British working class.'

'I believe, with Sheila, that the whole situation has arisen because of the policy of the Hungarian Communist Party... You cannot save the country with foreign arms.' As for there being no such thing as neutrality, he pointed out that Finland was a neutral, independent state.

MacDougall went on to show how little basis there had been for Gollan's boast that the industrial comrades were solid. He listed the trade unions which had come out against the Russians: the Fire Brigades Union, the National Union of Railwaymen and the Yorkshire miners. He concluded: 'If the Soviet Government are sincere, then they are too stupid to be the leaders of the first Socialist state.'

I listened eagerly to my dear friend Florence Keyworth. Her modesty always made me feel like a noisy show-off. Now, I felt, she was taking modesty too far. She was prepared to believe that the Party leaders knew best.

'I did not sign the petition,' she said, 'because I thought it would split the staff.' On the other hand she did not agree with Ben. 'That sort of speech is splitting the Party.' She pleaded with Malcolm not to leave. 'The Party needs comrades like him.'

Phil Bolsover said: 'Our attitude to the Polish and Hungarian events has been completely wrong... The Poles sent a protest from their Party paper to us... The Soviet domination of these countries is not only military domination, but in all spheres.' He instanced the imposition of unrealisable five-year plans.

The same pattern of domination was felt, he argued, in the British Communist Party. 'I would like to know what would have happened if the Soviet Union had withdrawn its troops. The EC would have come out with another statement saying that was a good thing.'

He derided the talk of class war. 'I come from a working-class family. My father was a steel worker, unemployed for five years.'

Eric Scott declared: 'I have been in agreement with almost everything *everybody* said... If in these countries they managed to get some elections and it was discovered that the people were going to vote Communist, the election would be suppressed, as in Southern Vietnam...'

Claire Madden pursued her own line. 'I agree with the EC statement, but for one thing. *Mister* Khrushchov, not content with the attempt to discredit *Comrade* Stalin, gave Hungarian reaction its opportunity, by sacrificing Rakosi in order to appease Tito.'

Mick Bennett said he saw the paper's job as helping the Kadar Government to win the confidence of the people. 'The more that Radio Free Europe can quote our paper, the more it will spread demoralisation inside Hungary.'

We listened to Mick without any great interest. We were all waiting for one thing: the return of Campbell from Moscow.

X

I still did not know what was in Peter Fryer's banned despatch. Mick Bennett and George Matthews were not allowing any more people to see it. I could not ask Peter, who was inside the British Embassy in Budapest – safe, but incommunicado.

The third issue of *The Reasoner* came out just after the Soviet tanks went into Hungary. Thompson and Saville wrote in their editorial: 'One thing only might have restrained the Soviet forces from their final criminal action – an outspoken call for restraint from the Communist Parties of the world. In this crisis, when the Hungarian people needed our solidarity, the British Communist Party has failed them.'

In the same issue, Derek Kartun's article, written before the tanks went in, declared: 'We must stop once and for all abusing the meaning of the phrase "international solidarity". It has made puppets and parrots of us in the past. It has been bad for the Russians and disastrous for us.'

Now the obvious difference between intellectuals and workers was that the intellectuals left the Party slowly, arguing to the last, while the workers just left. Trade union leaders who went out as the tanks went in included John Horner, general secretary of the Fire Brigades Union, Les Cannon, an official of the Electrical Trades Union, and Alex Moffat, an official of the Scottish District of the National Union of Mineworkers. Many rank-and-file Communists in these unions followed them out.

The firemen, the electricians and the miners had provided the Communists with some of their most firmly entrenched positions. When Campbell told us: 'We have made some impact on the Labour Movement', he meant that, however small our vote, we had our trade union stronghold.

Whatever else the Soviet tanks in Hungary ultimately failed to crush, they did crush that stronghold. The Party's power base in the unions, which had taken years to build up, vanished in one week. It never was rebuilt. Arthur Scargill, when he led the miners to disaster in 1984/85, was a poor caricature of the tough, wily, practical trade union leaders the Communists used to train.

True, they had some good human material then. Until 1945 it was extremely difficult for the child of a working man to reach a university. It was still far from easy in 1956. So there were always plenty of clever, ambitious young people getting an education in the best way open to them – through the Workers' Educational Association and the trade unions. The Communists could offer them a sort of training more intense, more all-embracing, more seductive than anything available from the Labour Party. At summer schools a boy or girl whose formal education had ended at 14 could meet Professor Haldane and Professor Levy.

One of the bright boys the Party trained was Jack's old friend Ben Smith. He was born in 1906 and brought up in an orphanage in Hackney. In those days all orphanage girls went into domestic service, and all orphanage boys became boot boys at hotels.

Ben did not stay among the boots for long. His gift of the gab made him, while still in his teens, a patent-medicine salesman. That was when Jack first met him. Ben was going through the dictionary every day, in search of words he didn't know. When he found one he would use it until he did know it.

On the top of a bus he asked Jack: 'Will you settle with the numismatist or shall I?'

'Numismatist?' Jack asked.

Ben had looked it up. 'A numismatist is a man who collects coins. Well, the bus conductor does that.'

Ben soon found better ways to learn. He made love to a woman (he once explained to us) only if she could teach him something.

By 1956 he had settled down with his second wife (a lady with a good degree) and was in Glasgow as the Scottish organiser for the National and Local Government Officers. He had long ago left the Party, but he never denied how much it had taught him. 'I'm better than Walter Citrine and Victor Feather or any of them,' he said, 'because they don't know how good the Party line is, and I do.' He meant that the Party had educated him out of the British trade unionist's traditional contempt for foreigners, blacks and women.

Ben had been ringing us up fairly often since the Khrushchov speech, to ask: 'Are you still in the Party?'

He now found us willing to discuss whether we were or not. Jack said: 'I am not prepared to belong to no party. It's this one or the Labour Party. But I still believe that this one can be changed. There's going to be a special conference, next March...'

'You think you can change the Party?' said Ben. 'All right. You try that. But just promise me one thing. From now until this conference, you go to every single meeting that you're entitled to go to, and argue for a change of line.'

Jack said he meant to do that anyway, but thanked Ben for the advice. It turned out to be the best advice that anybody ever gave us.

According to the rules, the only way to alter anything within the Communist Party was through one's own branch. This meant that Jack and I had to become assiduous attenders at the Muswell Hill branch.

What we found there shook us to the core. Inside the *Daily Worker* office even the hardliners were admitting that terrible things had happened, that innocent people had been framed and murdered, that the tragedy now unfolding in Hungary was, at least in part, the result of a great human revulsion against these crimes.

But, for some of the Muswell Hill comrades, none of this had happened. They had not, like Claire Madden, worked out an elaborate logical structure for proving that Stalin was innocent. Nor had they, like Mick Bennett, decided to acquit Stalin of stifling Jewish culture because he had stifled all culture. Their view was summed up in a letter which the *Daily Worker* printed on November 9, from the lifelong Soviet apologist D.N. Pritt.

'There is a wave of anti-Soviet hysteria in this country... We get these waves periodically. I have lived through quite a few of them; they arose, for example, over the Ribbentrop agreement of 1939, the Finnish war of 1939-40, and over Korea... Those who kept their heads and waited soon learnt that there were good reasons for what the Soviet Union had done.'

A few days later a reader rejoined: 'The letter from D.N . Pritt represents an incredible state of mind...'

For the comrades in the Muswell Hill branch – that is, the three-quarters of them who stayed in the Party after November 4 – there was nothing incredible about it. This was their habitual state of mind, in which they felt comfortable. Nor were they alone in this. A member of a neighbouring branch, who urged his comrades to think critically about the Soviet Union, was rebuked in the words: 'Oh, ye of little faith!'

On November 11 the Executive Committee of the Communist Party met again. It dealt with the rebellious editors of *The Reasoner* by suspending them from membership for three months – a prelude to expulsion. (Thompson and Saville did not wait to be expelled, but left of their own accord.)

The EC also decided that the special conference promised for Spring 1957 would be a Congress – that is, a body with the right to change policy and elect a new leadership – and that it should take place at Easter. This was our traditional time. Very few people want to ask their employers for days off to attend a Communist Congress, but the four days of Easter are free for almost everyone.

So on Monday morning, November 12, I went to the *Daily Worker* staff meeting in the belief that it was possible to shift the leadership. We'd got the Congress we wanted.

What I did not know, until just before the meeting began, was that Peter Fryer had reached Vienna, and had sent his third despatch from there the day before. This time it was Campbell himself who banned it. Peter Fryer's wife, who worked in the accounts department of the paper, got through to him and said: 'The editor won't even let the staff see it.'

So scarcely anyone had read it. Nevertheless, the existence of this latest banned report darkened our mood.

Mick Bennett reported on the EC meeting the previous day. He begged us not to be diverted into arguments about Hungary. 'The main danger is the war in Suez.'

But the war in Suez was already over. The United Nations had imposed a ceasefire. UN forces were about to replace those of Britain and France.

Campbell said: 'What has happened in Hungary is a tragedy for the international working-class movement. It is no use pretending otherwise... The Soviet comrades think that the Hungarians failed to end the cult of the individual when it was being ended in other Communist Parties. There was a wide growth of anti-Semitism, directed at Rakosi and Gerö. There was a split within the Party for several years. Nagy brought those splits into the streets.'

163

Campbell spoke as if it had been a crime for Nagy to let the leaders' divisions be known to the people in the streets. His tone was, to me, like the cold wind off a glacier. I had been campaigning, in my column, against the 'Fourteen-day Rule' which forbade any mention on radio or TV of any topic due to be debated in Parliament within 14 days. The radio programme 'Any Questions' was taken off the air for five minutes on Friday, November 2, because a right-wing journalist, Henry Fairlie, defended the British attack on Suez. My report of this event was on the front page of the *Daily Worker*, and I had since been giving the readers a blow-by-blow account of the crumbling of the rule.

Now Campbell was making it clear that he thought the people of Hungary should have been subjected, not to a fourteen-day rule, but to an indefinite rule of silence on matters too high for them.

The first use of Soviet troops, on October 24, was, Campbell admitted, 'unfortunate.' Then he described the killing of security policemen as 'a massacre of comrades, a St. Bartholemew's night'. He added: 'Gerö was murdered.'

Gerö was not murdered, though someone may have told Campbell that in Moscow. Gerö fled to the Soviet Union and died years later, in bed.

The efforts of Nagy to broaden his government were described by Campbell as 'giving up position after position to reaction'. He added: 'Not only were all political criminals liberated, but all ordinary criminals too.'

According to Campbell, the Russians denied that the standard of living had gone down in Hungary. (Peter Fryer, in his August articles, said it had.) 'The main reason for the revolt going as it did was the political mistakes, the imprisonment of innocent people... It was not realised that guilty people had been imprisoned too... Why were there so many people supporting a change? There had been too much weight on industrialisation. There was too much blind copying of the Soviet Union. Too much of the national income had gone to the Soviet Union... Budapest was building an underground railway... How could the masses be so split from the Party? The reburial of Rajk was an unnecessary ceremony, which turned the people against the Party as a whole. Remember this was done under Rakosi!'

It wasn't. Rakosi was in power until July 18, and as long as he was there such people as Miklos Gimes were expelled from the Party for demanding a formal, public rehabilitation of Rajk. The 'unnecessary ceremony' took place while Gerö was in power, on October 6.

It is understandable that, in the rush of events, Campbell should have become confused. But he had, on the other end of the phone, the man who could have put him straight. He had Peter Fryer.

Campbell added: 'A special problem was the writers. Most of them were middle-class, and the Party had driven them into opposition... The fact that a man can write a vivid article is no guarantee that he has twopennyworth of political judgement.'

He admitted: 'All this will create many difficulties for us. There cannot be any question about it; this was a people's movement. The people were for the time being against the Party... This has been a godsend to reaction in Britain.'

Campbell made it clear that one set of people thought themselves perfectly guiltless of these events – the Russian Communists. He insisted that the Hungarians had embarked on their over-ambitious industrial schemes without consulting the Russians.

Phil Bolsover commented: 'Johnnie Campbell tells us that this was a mass movement against the Hungarian Government. I cannot believe that the people would be willing to permit the restoration of a fascist regime... It is now agreed that it was wrong for the Soviet troops to intervene in the first place... If the tendency of the EC always to find excuses for the Soviet Union goes on, it will lead to the dissolution of our Party.'

The hardliner Stan Harrison declared: 'This is a war without quarter. If you want to see what it costs when the working class suffers a historic defeat, read the report of the Spanish Communist Party.'

Leon Griffiths described his own visit to Hungary. 'People talked with nostalgia of 1947/48. Fryer earlier this year said that standards were going down and down.'

Then Leon spoke of Peter's first banned report. 'Fryer saw the corpses of 80 men, women and children who had been shot down, and the bodies of the security policemen responsible.'

This was at Magyarovar, near the Austrian border, where Peter arrived on Saturday October 27. The previous day a peaceful, unarmed demonstration had been fired on without warning by the security police. Peter saw the bodies, including that of a baby 18 months old. He then witnessed the lynching of Lieutenant Jozsef Stefko, believed to have given the order to fire. Peter also established that the people had no arms, until the soldiers at the local barracks gladly handed them over.

On October 31, when Peter was trying to tell Mick Bennett about this, Mick insisted on reading him a long extract from a resolution of the Central Committee of the Polish Workers' Party (i.e. Communist Party).

The part of Peter's despatch which caused particular offence to Mick was: 'This was no counter-revolution, organised by fascists and reactionaries. It was the upsurge of a whole people...'

I put these words here although I had not then read them. Leon had. He said: 'There is absolutely nothing to suggest that there was any great western intervention.'

Llew Gardner, too, had read the first banned despatch. He admitted: 'A week ago I said I supported the EC resolution. However, I think I was wrong... The Communist Government disgraced the name of Communism... We have not been able to produce one worker who is fighting on the side of the Soviet Army.'

I recalled that, a week earlier, I had not been able to make up my mind. 'I have made up my mind,' I said. 'I am now certain that the Soviet action was wrong.' I reminded Campbell of the day when he had said that the Soviet Union might invade Yugoslavia 'in defence of its own legitimate interests' and that he would then support the Soviet Union. 'What a great and glorious thing that would have been, wouldn't it?' Campbell looked uncomfortable, but made no reply. I went on: 'But Stalin, though he may have been mad, was only mad nor' nor' west; he had more sense than to invade anywhere when he knew the west would be united against him. What would Khrushchov have done if the west had been united this time, if the west hadn't been split over Suez?'

I refused to believe that the Hungarians had built their heavy industries and their underground railway without the Russians telling them to. I suggested that the Russians had forced these countries to rearm, lowering their standard of living.

'To continue this discussion would be a diversion from the main action!' Mick Bennett exclaimed. But several people quietly congratulated me, on remembering Campbell's remarks about Yugoslavia.

Campbell did not mention Yugoslavia when he summed up. He said: 'The two greatest mistakes of my career were to go to the Soviet Union on the day the Hungarian rising broke out, and to send Peter Fryer to Hungary... The staff here is infected by Trotskyist lies and slanders... It is a classical mistake when Peter Fryer says it was only a workers' rising against genuine grievances, and not to see the reactionary side... You cannot make a counter-revolution by dollars. But you can enormously strengthen whatever forces are in the counter-revolution... In any case, rightly or wrongly, that is the line I am sticking to in the paper.'

After this tirade Sheila Lynd, Phil Bolsover, Llew Gardner and Leon Griffiths gave notice. (Malcolm had done so earlier, and Gabriel was already out.)

Leon Griffiths told me that his wife was waking in the night, screaming about what the Russian tanks were doing. 'Me too,' I said. Leon could hardly believe it. 'What a nice restful job you've got! You only have to sit and watch the TV and write about it. You're not really involved in all this.'

I said that I, too, liked to sleep quietly at night. But from then on I did.

The previous night Jack had woken me by saying: 'Do you realise the Russians massacred those Poles at Katyn?' I said: 'Yes, of course they did.' After that we both slept well. Whatever violence was raging in the world around us, we were no longer doing violence to our own natures. We had given up making excuses for the Russians.

Sheila Lynd told me that the comrade who wrote the cookery column, whose improbable but real name was Vanda Cook, had quit. Her letter announcing this to Sheila ended: 'Yours in hate.'

Our film critic, Paddy Goldring (who wrote as Thomas Spencer), left the Party as well as the paper. His letter to the *New Statesman* the following Friday said: 'By giving uncritical support to Soviet repression in Hungary the British Communist Party has committed suicide as an effective political force in this country, at a time when it had the chance of making real progress.'

Malcolm and Sheila stayed in the Party. Malcolm said: 'If Gomulka can come out after seven years in prison, and still be a Communist, I can stay in the Party too.'

I went to the library to see the New York *Daily Worker*. I discovered that, on Campbell's instructions, it was no longer available for us to read.

And still I hesitated about leaving. What made me hesitate was that everyone who left the *Daily Worker* was gloated over by the capitalist press. Jack and I were now reading the capitalist press; we took the *Telegraph* every day to find out what was actually going on. But most of the people I met, when I went to press conferences, were from papers of a very different character.

On November 16 the BBC told the press about a new series on pregnancy and childbirth, based on the work of University College Hospital. Derek Kartun's wife Gwen was at the press conference because she was a midwife (and surely the most glamorous one in London). She and I were taken aback to find that all the male journalists present thought childbirth (a) disgusting and (b) uproariously funny. Looking round at these ignorant slobs, I reflected that they would be gloating, if I left the *Daily Worker*.

That was the day the *Daily Worker* printed Peter Fryer's letter of resignation. Campbell had refused to print it, until Peter told him that the letter was already with the *Manchester Guardian*. Then Campbell printed it side by side with his own comments, accusing Peter of hardly seeing anything in Hungary. What Campbell wrote was tedious and absurd, but it was nothing to the whispering campaign conducted against Peter.

It began with the sneering and jeering because he had taken refuge in the British Embassy. 'But what ought he to have done?' I asked Mick Bennett. 'He could have gone to the Yugoslav Embassy,' Mick said. He went on saying that until

November 23, when he had to stop rather suddenly.

'Peter Fryer's been seeing a psychiatrist for months,' I heard in the Muswell Hill branch. Other people in other branches, all over the country, heard it at about the same time. Perhaps we should all have seen psychiatrists, before we joined the Communist Party, but in fact Peter had never met one.

There was also a whispering campaign about Peter's wife. She resigned from the accounts department when he resigned. Within a few days Peter Zinkin was taking aside journalists from the capitalist press and saying: 'You want to know the real reason why Peter Fryer resigned? His wife was caught with her hand in the till.'

As soon as he had resigned, Peter explained his reasons to the *Yorkshire Post*, the *Glasgow Herald*, the *Daily Mail* and – his great crime in the eyes of the Party – the *Daily Express*. It was the *Daily Express* which gave him the most space on Saturday, November 17. Now, for the first time, Jack and I were able to read what Peter had seen in Hungary.

The text of the banned despatches was included in Peter's paperback, *Hungarian Tragedy,* published within a few weeks by Dennis Dobson (and reprinted 30 years later by New Park Publications).

But, even before we had the full text, the moral issue was clear to Jack and me. While we were desperate for information about Hungary, while we could not sleep for want of the facts that would help us to make up our minds, the very facts we needed had been available, and had been deliberately kept from us by Mick Bennett, George Matthews and Johnnie Campbell.

In 1990, in the course of a TV programme on the *Daily Worker*, George Matthews said of Peter Fryer's despatches:

I don't think the first one was printed at all. Parts of the second one were printed, er, and he says in his book that I, er, blue-pencilled it to ribbons, if I remember rightly. Actually I don't really remember – I'm not quite, er, quite sure – because I, although I was only assistant editor, the assistant general secretary of the Party [George Matthews was in 1956 not the assistant editor, though he was assistant general secretary of the Party] Johnnie Campbell, the editor of the paper, was in Moscow and so I was sent to help Mick Bennett, the assistant editor of the paper at that time, and, er, I may well have subbed the story. I think the first stuff wasn't published. Now again, it, it was understandable at the time why there was a feeling they shouldn't be published, because it was totally contrary to the estimate that was being made by the Party and the paper of the situation in Hungary, totally contrary. I mean, Peter just saw the popular side of it and more or less discounted the anti, anti-socialist side of it, so his despatches were very pro the revolt and so, you know, there was an obvious feeling among people that – but, looking back, I think they should have been published.

Peter Fryer himself took this down, in his excellent shorthand, and played the video back several times to make sure of every last 'er'. He was happy to hear it. Not all the people who were called traitors and renegades then have lived to get an apology, or mumbled half-apology, from those who denounced them.

That weekend, November 17 and 18, I felt more than ever like leaving the *Daily Worker*. I was not short of advice. Jack had tracked down the man who, when he and Ben Smith were teenagers, was their most admired mentor – J. T. Murphy.

Jack Murphy had his niche in history. He had been the British representative on the Communist International, and in 1927 he was the man who moved the expulsion of Trotsky. He regretted that, he told us, not because he thought Trotsky was right, but because, once he was expelled, the whole thing ceased to be a dispute among comrades, and became a matter for the police.

Isaac Deutscher wrote in *The Prophet Unarmed*: 'JT Murphy, an insignificant envoy of one of the most insignificant Communist Parties, the British, was chosen to table the motion of expulsion. The disdain which Trotsky hurled at this conventicle was proportionate to the insult...'

Murphy himself was threatened with expulsion from the Communist Party in 1932. Rather than be thrown out, he left. As the Party organiser in Sheffield, he had been moved by the sufferings of the unemployed, and had suggested that they might be alleviated by trade with the Soviet Union, which would also reduce the danger of war. The Political Bureau said: 'J. T. Murphy's childish argument that international trading relations reduce the danger of war is nothing but vulgar capitalist propaganda.'

This looks like a bizarre excuse for expelling anyone, even by Communist standards. Murphy never knew that Trotsky had written an article on trade at the same time, and that the Russians took this as evidence of collusion. Even without such encouragement, the British Communists of the early 1930s had a passion for expelling each other. Ben Smith once moved Jack's expulsion from the Party, on the grounds that he had given £5 to the funds. How's that again? It was logical; Jack was using his position, as a relatively well-to-do shopkeeper, to buy himself into good standing with the Party. He should have been out collecting the money, penny by penny, on the doorsteps of the working class.

Murphy was a delightful man to meet. He had never regretted leaving the Party; the Labour Party was to him the mainstream of British politics, and he was proud of his years as an assistant to Stafford Cripps.

However, he still worshipped the memory of Lenin.

That he had met Lenin more than once is certain; that Lenin (who spoke English) could communicate with him easily is also true. But whether the friendship between them was quite so close as it retrospectively became, on evenings when Murphy had drunk a whisky or two, may be doubted. Once Murphy gave us a graphic account of Lenin expounding the military tactics with which he was planning to defeat the White armies. 'Lenin told you all this?' asked one of his hearers. Murphy held up two entwined fingers. 'Lenin and I were like *that*.'

What we could not get from Murphy or his lively wife Molly (a veteran suffragette) was any picture of what the Russian people were living through in Lenin's time. The Murphys lived as other foreign comrades did, in the Lux Hotel, getting meals which were poor and monotonous, but regular. Neither ever quite mastered Russian. In 1957, when I began to learn Russian, Murphy gave me his old Linguaphone records. They were worn and scratched up to Lesson 10. The remaining 20 records were virgin. So how had he known what was going on, in those famous Comintern meetings? He said that, until Stalin came out on top, the Comintern conducted its business largely in German.

Because they had seen so little of the life around them, the Murphys always insisted that Lenin was kind to the peasants and unopposed by any great section of the people. Murphy had been in prison for a time ('a mistake') but the episode had done nothing to shake his faith.

As for Stalin, whom he had backed because of what seemed to be his practical, commonsense views, Murphy was simply unable to believe the scale of the crimes which in 1956 were coming to light. When I said that, as near as anyone could reckon, 20 million people had been arrested in the purges, Jack and Molly Murphy both exclaimed that this was obviously ridiculous. (It was; in 1990 the Russians were estimating it at 40 million.)

And yet both knew a great deal about British politics. However they romanticised their past, they had no doubt that their present allegiance was to the Labour Party. Just as Molly Murphy, when she found herself pregnant, had turned her back on Soviet Russia and come straight home to Britain, they had both turned their backs on the Communist Party and settled where they belonged.

Jack and I were still not sure where we belonged. We spent the ensuing five months finding out.

XI

On November 19, when the staff next met, the paper was full of denunciations of Peter Fryer, most of them by Campbell. Our editor was appealing to the Party faithful. For them, what Peter had said no longer mattered; it was crime enough that he had said it to the *Express*.

With us, however, Campbell was trying to be conciliatory. He said: 'In the past, through all twists and turns of Party policy, the Party and the paper stood as one. There were doubts, but they were kept within the organisation... We had in those days one authority – the Soviet Union...

'Now of course we know that the Khrushchov report marked a break. We could never go back to where we were. It did a lot of good because the old authoritarian way had outlived its usefulness.'

That wasn't what he'd said the week before. Now he was pleading with us. 'I find nothing abnormal in differences of opinion. But what I do find abnormal is differences as a basis for leaving the paper... I can't understand comrades who say: "I am leaving the paper but staying in the Party" ...There are comrades who are leaving at a time when the capitalist press is gloating over every comrade who leaves the paper... I am dragged out of bed by people asking: "Who is leaving next?" We have, right in view of the public, two offices, with two different views.'

Campbell went on: 'In my own disagreements with the Party, the Party sometimes turned out to be right.' He did not really think so; he had often remarked, in conversation, what a disaster it was that the Party had not followed his line at the beginning of the Second World War.

He conceded that 'comrades in a key position' had to leave, rather than write leading articles with which they disagreed. 'But there are comrades who are not called on to write anything with which they disagree.'

That was my situation. I never had to write a line which went against my conscience. But people who saw my name still appearing in the paper would think that I agreed with the Party line, and this was tormenting me.

'I am one of those who detest any possibility of a return to Stalinism,' Campbell said. 'I have a very simple request to make to any comrades planning to leave the paper. Think it over for 24 hours! Do not do it in a way which will inflict the maximum injury on our paper... If a leading member of the staff leaves the paper at this moment it is not an ordinary act but a deadly blow.'

George MacDougall said: 'Although I am opposed to the EC, I feel we should stay on the paper. I feel that Gabriel had to resign because he was the cartoonist. Peter Fryer also had to resign because his despatches weren't printed. But I feel that every other comrade should stay on the paper.'

He spoke of Malcolm MacEwen. 'Malcolm was last Wednesday subjected to something I can only describe as a witch-hunt. When he walked out I felt like walking out with him.'

George was talking about an editorial executive meeting. In 1990, Malcolm described this occasion at a conference of Communist historians. He began: 'I don't think I've ever loved anybody more than I loved Johnnie Campbell – ' and broke down. When he could go on he said that he had found his best friend suddenly transformed into his worst enemy, denouncing him so venomously that he knew what Rajk and Slansky must have felt.

Malcolm's crime had been to draft the petition signed by 19 members of the staff, and read it aloud to the Party's Executive Committee on November 3:

> The imprisonment of Edith Bone in solitary confinement without trial for seven years, without any public inquiry or protest from our Party even after the exposure of the Rajk trial had shown that such injustices were taking place, not only exposes the character of the regime but involves us in its crimes. It is now clear that what took place was a national uprising against an infamous police dictatorship...

Malcolm was also guilty of talking to Gordon Cruickshank, our correspondent in Poland, and of telling people what the Poles were saying.

On 19 November 1956 I knew nothing about the treatment of Malcolm – only that he had gone. Bob Leeson explained his own reasons for not going. 'The more I study the Hungarian situation, the less I feel inclined to agree with the EC... The movement as a whole has a conscience. And I don't want to leave that conscience in the keeping of people with whom I disagree... Stay in! The battle is beginning to be won!'

'I am a little bit concerned,' said Allen Hutt, with studied under-emphasis, 'at the way George and Bob put their points... Putting their views in the Party is one thing; making the staff of this paper a battleground is another... You can't have freedom of action when navigating a ship.'

Hutt said some comrades had been complaining of 'an atmosphere'. He asked: 'Who created it? Not those of us who support the Party line.'

Hutt then shot himself in the foot, by mentioning the Finnish War. 'Seventeen years ago William Forrest [a *News*

Chronicle reporter] was approached to become the editor of this paper. The same year he was standing with the Finnish "freedom fighters" against the Russian tanks.'

Hutt saw this as a parallel with Peter Fryer. So did we, but we no longer thought that the Finns were obviously in the wrong.

'I know I have my own faults,' Hutt went on. 'I do tend to argue when I am argued with.'

Leon Griffiths, who was about to leave the paper, said: 'We are not elected. It would be dishonest and undemocratic in the extreme if we are to stay on in order to fight the EC. I think Malcolm and Fryer had no alternative but to resign.'

Fred Pateman went one better than the other hardliners. 'Personally, 24 hours before the Soviet intervention in Hungary, I was in favour of intervention.'

He asked us what other sort of paper we wanted to work on. 'A paper which is supporting the British in Cyprus, Kenya, Malaya?'

I contended that it was obvious, from what Hutt had said, why people were leaving the paper but staying in the Party. 'You can't make the office a battleground while the paper is being produced, as he says. But you can go into your branch and fight for a better leadership.'

I said only one thing was keeping me on the paper. 'I can't bear to think of seeing my name in the capitalist press. And that's all! Until a week ago I would have said that what kept me on the paper was my great respect, lasting over many years, for the editor. But then he came back from Moscow and told us that we were "infected with Trotskyist lies". That's not the language of Party controversy.'(I was thinking of Murphy, moving the expulsion of Trotsky.) 'That's the language used when one side in the controversy is going to hand the other side over to the secret police to be tortured in a dungeon, and if you haven't got any dungeons or secret police, you'd better not use it.'

At this everybody laughed, including Campbell. That didn't stop me. I said: 'Our leaders shouldn't have the face to talk about lies. George Matthews came here after the Twentieth Congress and told us he had no inside information. The following week Mick Bennett told us that Stalin had been mad in his last months and had thought Voroshilov was a British spy. That bit of inside information could only have come from George Matthews.'

(Nobody contradicted this then. But in 1990 I was assured by Matthews that he really did have no inside information. Mick, in 1991, could not remember who had told him about Voroshilov.)

I reminded the meeting that Gollan had told us the industrial comrades were solid. I said: 'He already had John Horner's resignation in his pocket.' John Gollan's wife Elsie, who worked in the building, called out from the back of the meeting that Gollan had meant the comrades on the EC. Horner wasn't on the EC.

I hadn't finished. 'Why aren't we allowed to see what the American *Daily Worker* says? What is really going on inside Russia? Those who do know won't tell us, so we have to speculate. One of the things Stalin did was to open military academies for officers' sons – not soldiers' sons – thereby creating a military caste. This military caste must have had a lot to do with the decision to march into Hungary.'

I pointed out a letter which had appeared on the feature page that morning, demanding Fryer's expulsion from the Party. His interview with the *Express*, which the letter described as 'vile' did not appear until Saturday, and the Monday feature page was normally made up on Friday. Things could be put in at the last minute, but only if they were written in the office.

Robin Jardine explained that he had brought the letter in

by hand on Sunday morning. It had been given to him by Frieda Devine, wife of Pat Devine, who really did write it. 'All right,' I said. 'I'm sorry if I was too suspicious, but we've been told so many lies we can't help it.'

After I had said that, Allen Hutt did not speak to me for months.

Our lawyer, Maurice Tarlo, complained: 'The way in which we are all torn with dissension here is making work impossible. How the hell the paper is brought out every day I don't know.'

Frank Gullett, the news editor, said he had been extremely sorry to see Fryer's interview with the *Express*. Gullett's memory is dear to me; he was a former merchant seaman, and we all called him 'the bo'sun'. He used to call the reporters to order by crying: 'Muster on the poop deck!' Among the sayings which he had learnt in the Merchant Navy, my favourite was: 'What are the three most useless things in the world? A man's nipples, the Pope's balls and a vote of thanks to the staff.'

The bo'sun's outlook was aggressively masculine, and a bit brutal, but he was not given to talking nonsense. So I was disappointed when he said: 'After the Twentieth Congress Peter had a greater shock than anyone else in this office. Peter came back from Hungary in the summer very distressed at what he had seen, and at what he had learned about the Rajk trial. I opposed sending Peter to Budapest.'

This was to be said again and again. It implied that there was some kind of a rock-like reporter who should have been sent instead, a reporter who would have looked at the bodies in Magyarovar and felt nothing, because 'we' had shot them. This imaginary reporter would have known about the sufferings of Julia Rajk, because he could hardly have been in Hungary without knowing, but he wouldn't have cared. Though some of the reporters were less sensitive than Peter, I can't think of one who would have been such a brute and fool.

Frank Patterson said there had been 'not enough dictatorship by the proletariat, too much dictatorship to the proletariat'. He added: 'We will not win the support of the working class by twisting things. The critics must not be labelled as purveyors of Trotskyist slogans.'

Campbell, still conciliatory, said: 'It is a pity when comrades like Al Hutt urge people to stay, and then make speeches calculated to drive them away... This was the best staff we'd had for a long time. If we hadn't had a high-powered staff of capable people, it wouldn't be such a tragedy as it is... I used the word "Trotskyists". The fact that people have been labelled wrongly doesn't mean that there are no Trotskyists.'

He appealed to all those who were staying on the paper to do something extra, such as making fund-raising speeches. This I was not prepared to do, so long as the paper was full of rubbish about Hungary. The day after this meeting, Campbell refused to print a letter on Hungary because it was signed by Party members from different branches. By getting together, they were 'forming a faction'.

On Wednesday November 21 Charles Coutts, who had talked to Fryer in Budapest during the rising, explained on the front page why he had changed his views. There was a fascist danger in Hungary. The proof of it was that somebody had wanted to shoot Charles Coutts. Why they wanted to, and why they decided not to, he had not fully understood. During his three years in Budapest, he had learned little Hungarian. He gathered that the armed patrol which grabbed him thought a foreigner could not be living in Hungary, unless he was a Communist. (Which was true.) Nothing Coutts wrote, then or in his ensuing articles, contradicted anything Fryer had written. He did not, any more than Fryer, meet one American agent or see one American gun. But he stressed the lawless nature of some armed gangs. If his articles and Fryer's had both been printed in full, the readers would have been able to make up their own minds.

They did get some vital facts, if they looked carefully for them on the back page. Sam Russell was sent from Moscow to Budapest, to talk to the victorious Russians.

Sam reported the Soviet commander in Hungary, Major-General Grebennik, as denying that there had been any deportations.

Dora Scarlett had now left Hungary. Later she heard about one of these deportations from a refugee:

> One evening, while he was walking down a street, Soviet troops sealed off the outlets and forced everyone who happened to be there at the time to get into lorries. They were taken to the railway, put into cattle trucks, and sent over the north-east border of Hungary into the Carpathian Ukraine. They were put into an ordinary prison, men and women together, about forty to a room. They were there for five weeks. They did not have to work; they had nothing to do; their heads were shaved, but they had no washing facilities and did not wash once during the whole five weeks. After that time they were put on the trucks again and sent back to Budapest where they were released... the deportations were indiscriminate; it was sheer terror tactics aimed at breaking resistance, not punishment inflicted on known individuals.

While Sam reported that this wasn't happening, Imre Nagy and other leaders of the uprising were in the Yugoslav Embassy. (Where, according to Mick Bennett, Peter Fryer should have gone.) On November 23 they left in a bus, under a safe conduct from Kadar, intending to go to Yugoslavia. Russian troops boarded the bus, forced off the Yugoslav officials at gun point, and drove Nagy and his friends to an unknown destination.

Even the Russians could not have expected this to remain

a secret; the Yugoslav officials protested to the press of the world, and the story was on every front page, even ours, on Saturday November 24. That day Communist journalists, including those working for capitalist papers, met at the *Daily Worker* office.

Malcolm MacEwen attended, as was his right, since he was still in the Party. He launched an all-out attack on the way the paper was run. He said it was full of 'old boys' who could not be removed. I supposed that he was talking about Peter Zinkin.

Malcolm attacked the cowardly treatment of the Khrushchov speech. Campbell insisted that 'a fair summary' had been published. Here I think he had become genuinely confused. He had forgotten the difference between Sam's two despatches on March 18 – the anodyne report which was published, and the six-page summary of the speech, which was not.

But the main attack on Campbell at this meeting, from Malcolm and from the Fleet Street people, concerned Peter Fryer. Like Haldane recognising nonsense if it was about genetics, the comrades from Fleet Street recognised nonsense about an editor's treatment of a report from a man on the spot.

Campbell defended himself by saying that Peter's third report, the one he personally had suppressed, had not consisted of eye-witness reporting, but of analysis, and that it was the analysis he rejected. At last he offered to let any comrade present read Peter's third despatch. This was a tremendous concession.

Peter's fellow-journalists could now judge for themselves whether there was any lack of eye-witness reporting in this.

Vienna, November 11

I have just come out of Budapest, where for six days I have

watched Hungary's new-born freedom tragically destroyed by Soviet troops.

Vast areas of the city – the working-class areas above all – are virtually in ruins. For four days and nights Budapest was under continuous bombardment. I saw a once lovely city battered, bludgeoned, smashed and bled into submission. To anyone who loves equally the Socialist Soviet Union and the Hungarian people it was heart-breaking.

The people of Budapest are hungry today. Many are almost starving. By eight each morning hundreds of thousands are standing in long silent queues all over the city waiting for bread. Shops and restaurants are still closed, and the workers refuse to end their general strike, despite frantic appeals by the new 'Workers' and Peasants' Government'.

Corpses still lie in the streets – streets that are ploughed up by tanks and strewn with the detritus of a bloody war: rubble, glass and bricks, spent cartridges and shell-cases. Despite their formidable losses in the first phase of the Hungarian revolution, Budapest's citizens put up a desperate, gallant, but doomed resistance to the Soviet onslaught. Budapest's workers, soldiers, students, and even schoolboys, swore to resist to the very end. And every foreign journalist in Budapest was amazed that the resistance lasted so long.

In public buildings and private homes, in hotels and ruined shops, the people fought the invaders street by street, step by step, inch by inch. The blazing energy of those eleven days of liberty burned itself out in one last glorious flame. Hungry, sleepless, hopeless, the Freedom Fighters battled with pitifully feeble equipment against a crushingly superior weight of Soviet arms. From windows and from the open streets, they fought with rifles, home-made grenades and Molotov cocktails against T54 tanks. The people ripped up the streets to build barricades, and at night they fought by the light of fires that swept unchecked through block after block.

On the Sunday and the Monday, while the din of the artillery bombardment and the ceaseless tank-fire mingled with the groans of the wounded, the battle spared neither civilians nor those bringing aid to the wounded. Bread queues were fired on by Soviet tanks, and as late as Thursday I myself saw a man of about seventy lying dead outside a bread shop, the loaf he had just bought still in his hand. Someone had half-covered the body with the red, white and green flag. Soviet troops looted the Astoria Hotel as far as the first storey, even taking the clothes from the porters' rest room; they ransacked the Egyptian Embassy; they even shot dead a Yugoslav diplomat looking out of the windows of his Embassy. On the other hand, five Hungarian bullets broke five windows at the British Legation. These are things that happen in the heat of battle,* and it should be said that the Soviet troops are now making efforts to fraternise with the people. Some of the rank-and-file Soviet troops have been telling people in the last two days that they had no idea they had come to Hungary. They thought at first they were in Berlin, fighting German fascists.

Campbell had another line of defence, though he did not use it at this meeting, where everybody knew Peter. He would tell the less-informed comrades that Peter could not have seen all this, because he was inside the British Legation. Peter slept there, certainly. But in the daytime, like the other British reporters, he took great risks in order to roam the city.

As the journalists' meeting broke up, somebody told me that Hyman Levy, since his return from Moscow with Campbell, had been addressing two meetings a day. Another comrade said that the most important thing we could do was to rewrite the section on the press, in the *British Road to Socialism*.

That struck me as a diversion of effort from our first job

---

* According to Sandor Kopacsi, the Yugoslav was not shot in the heat of battle. He happened to look like Imre Nagy, for whom a Soviet sniper was lying in wait.

– to change the leadership. But we were so far from being an organised opposition that it was easy to divert us. Malcolm spent many hours as a member of the Commission on Inner-Party Democracy. His findings could have been summed up in one sentence: there wasn't any inner-party democracy. A small clique of full-time officials bent the rules to suit themselves. When there wasn't a rule that could be bent, they invented one.

There was no rule that instructed a Party member not to see an old man shot dead in a bread queue. Nor was there any rule forbidding him to mention the matter to other journalists, who had seen for themselves the bodies of non-combatants in the streets. Nevertheless the London District Committee suspended Peter Fryer from membership on November 26.

The same day, the *Daily Worker* printed Sam Russell's interview with Lieutenant-General Lashenko, who denied that the Russians had kidnapped Imre Nagy.

The following day, November 27, the *Daily Worker* ventured to protest against this blatant lie. Its front page carried the headline: THE MYSTERY OF NAGY. The second deck read: An explanation is wanted. The vital part of the text, very timidly asking the Russians to come up with a believable story, was written by Mick Bennett.

Mick presided over a staff meeting that morning. He said that the movement against the Suez War had evaporated. Stan Harrison pointed out that it was bound to do that, since the Suez War was over.

Bob Leeson said: 'Reaction has sought to cast us in the role of friends of the Soviet troops first and friends of the Hungarian people a long way after.' He suggested that we should prove we were friends of the Hungarian workers by helping the Red Cross.

'Friends of the Hungarian workers?' said Phil Bolsover. 'With our present attitude that's impossible. It's a good thing to help the Red Cross. But we can't get away with that. There is no doubt that the Hungarian workers are on strike, and have been for three weeks. We can't pose as friends of the Hungarian workers when we get the sort of material we are getting from Sam Russell... The next despatch we get from Sam is that the Kadar Government has secured a great victory, by giving the workers their demands.'

Phil Bolsover pointed out to Mick, who had called for campaigns on domestic issues, that what we were printing about Hungary must affect all our other campaigns.

'I am no friend of Sam Russell,' said Frank Gullett. 'But it is his job to go to the men at the top.'

'How does Sam appear to a Hungarian worker?' asked Robin Jardine. 'Are they going to talk to him with any sense of freedom? I don't think they are... We must come out with our own line... We have been following the Soviet line quite slavishly.'

Eric Scott was worried about the idea of being on the side of the Hungarian working class. 'Sometimes the majority of one national working class may be wrong.'

'What is our interest?' asked Stan Harrison. 'To get a little working-class law and order in Hungary.' He scoffed at comrades who had been pointing out that the Soviet Army had been on the verge of invading Poland, until all the Polish leaders backed Gomulka. 'Are we to criticise the Soviet leaders for something they nearly did in Poland? I am not interested. I do not believe that all Hungarian workers are against the Soviet troops.'

Peter Zinkin said: 'I have been in more strikes than most people in this Party. When I was in the shop stewards' movement we did support strikes which were wrong... We are never going to get the solution in Hungary until we get the restoration of normal order.'

George Sinfield wanted a world conference of

Communist Parties. 'Gordon Cruickshank told me that the Poles were being careful because there were 40 divisions of Soviet troops on their border.'

I asked why comrades needed Gordon Cruickshank to tell them that. It was common knowledge, I said, that the Soviet leaders had been prepared to start a war in Poland. 'Why doesn't our paper publish what the American Party says? There's been a row between the French and Polish Parties, because *L'Humanité* didn't publish a word of the Gomulka speech until several days late, and then only five paragraphs. The French said they couldn't, because the speech 'contradicted the decisions democratically arrived at, at the French Party Congress'. In other words the French party had said the Poznan riots were the work of fascist agents, and Gomulka said they weren't. I wouldn't know about that if I hadn't read it in the American *Daily Worker*.'

'It's not our job to publish the row between the Polish and French Parties,' replied Mick Bennett. 'The only reason why we have elected two delegates to the Italian Communist Party Congress is that we want to agitate for a world conference of Communist Parties. It's not so simple to organise. Who convenes it?'

Mick meant that the feeling among some foreign Communist Parties was such that they would not come to any conference the Russians convened.

The same evening, I went to a meeting of the Muswell Hill branch. Some of those who had supported the Party line were now having second thoughts. One woman said: 'When Labour Party people speak to me these days, I can't answer back. I just cry and cry.'

David Ainley was there, as convinced as ever that he knew best. But suddenly his quiet little wife Edna had something to say. 'When I listen to the radio, and hear about the Russian troops shooting people down on the frontier,

David tells me not to listen to capitalist propaganda. I should take my news from the *Daily Worker*. But what it says on page one of the *Daily Worker* this morning is different from what it says on page four.' She was talking about the kidnapping of Imre Nagy.

One of our local comrades, Roy Zemla, was so orthodox that he refused ever to buy an evening paper. He couldn't bear the capitalist propaganda, he said. Now he confessed: 'At first the news from Hungary put me into a completely negative frame of mind. It even seemed to me that Communism had nothing to offer humanity.'

He was proud of having got over this weakness. To show he had got over it, he attacked me with a venom which (I am ashamed to say) I was never able to forgive. I was arguing against the London District decision to suspend Peter Fryer. Palme Dutt, also a member of our branch, and now attending it regularly for the first time in his life, explained that what Peter Fryer had done was exactly like what Zinoviev and Kamenev had done in 1917.

They wrote an article which was published just before the Bolshevik Revolution, in *Novaya Zhizn*, a paper edited by Maxim Gorky. They said that the Bolsheviks were planning an uprising, and that they considered it adventurist.

Dutt's account of this was not right. True, Lenin was furious at the time. However, Zinoviev and Kamenev were not expelled from the Party, but given responsible posts. The 1917 episode was raked up by Trotsky, in 1924. Zinoviev and Kamenev were then two-thirds of the 'troika' ruling Russia, the other third being Stalin. In his *Lessons of October*, Trotsky, discussing the recent failure of the German revolution, said that Zinoviev and Kamenev had shown the same vacillation as in 1917.

Dutt was not thinking of this, but of Stalin's excuses for shooting Zinoviev and Kamenev in 1936.

Somebody at the branch meeting asked, in the tone of one rooting out saboteurs: 'Who was responsible for sending Peter Fryer to Hungary?'

I said: 'Johnnie Campbell was. And why not? Peter Fryer had been in Hungary in the summer; he knew what was going on there. I can't see why it should be a disqualification for his going to the country, that he knew something about it.'

Roy Zemla said: 'I'm not going to believe that Campbell was responsible, just because somebody vaguely connected with the *Daily Worker* tells me so.'

I had been at the *Daily Worker*, with intervals for babies, for 12 years. To be told that I was 'vaguely connected' with it made me so angry that I was perhaps distracted from putting the case for Peter Fryer.

Not that anybody was in a state to listen. People had wild swings of mood. Peggy Aprahamian (who, as Peggy Lucas, later took my place as TV critic) exclaimed: 'One paper says the security police are back, in their jackboots, knocking on the doors and arresting people. That's terrible.' A few days later the same woman said of my husband: 'This hysterical comrade, who actually says he prefers the *Observer* to the *Daily Worker*...'

I asked her: 'And what paper did you read the Khrushchov speech in?'

Sticking out a firm, Bolshevik jawline, Peggy said: 'I can't remember.'

On Friday November 30 *Tribune* did us all a service. It printed a splendid article by Mervyn Jones, comparing the *Daily Worker* version of the Mindszenty broadcast with a monitored transcript. Anyone who said, from that time on, that the Cardinal had called for the restoration of capitalism, was deliberately lying.

One of the 'solid' industrial comrades on the EC, Brian Behan, a building worker, had supported the Party line because he thought the Cardinal's speech indicated a Catholic plot to restore capitalism. He now became one of the foremost critics of the leadership.

That he and I and all the other critics were bashing our heads against a brick wall must by now be obvious. We suspected it at the time. But, if I had walked out in November 1956, I should have missed the strangest part of the story. I should never have known the truth about Campbell's divided nature.

XII

Unity Theatre was not what it had been in 1938, when the wicked uncle in Babes in the Wood was played, amid roars of delighted laughter, by an actor got up to look like Neville Chamberlain. Jack and I had sat through some terrible plays there since. Once Jack failed to sit through a play about oppression in fascist Spain. Fleeing at the interval, he ran straight into the author. Some days later, Gabriel thought of the right remark for the occasion: 'I had to see your first act again.'

Now, inspired by Suez and Hungary, Unity regained its old form. Roger Woddis wrote *World on Edge*, a living newspaper, which went into rehearsal as the sheets came off his typewriter. The first night was November 23.

The Communist leaders were horrified. Not only did Unity show on the stage a Party member tearing up his card; it showed a Russian soldier's face being slapped by a disillusioned woman Communist. 'I'm sick ashamed of you!' she cried.

Whether all this was acted and produced to fully professional standards nobody noticed. The audience was with it, from the first moment to the last. Every night, after the show, there was a general discussion, led by a politician. The night I was there, the politician was the left-wing Labour MP, Konni Zilliacus.

He said that people who went in for *Realpolitik* were asking to be judged by the results. Since Britain and France had gone to war to keep the Suez Canal open, and the result was to close it, that was not successful *Realpolitik*. And the same thing went for invading Hungary to save Socialism, if the result turned out to be that Socialism became forever impossible there. (I often thought of this prophecy afterwards, when Kadar succeeded in governing Hungary only by bringing back the free market.)

One of the audience rose and said that Stalin had made mistakes, but that these mistakes were inevitable. I said that if a thing was inevitable it wasn't a mistake. It hadn't, I said, been inevitable to stage the Slansky trial, and to denounce Zilliacus as a western spy. Zilliacus laughed. As far as I know, this was the only public apology any Communist ever made to him.

In the audience was Alfie Bass, then a rising star of TV. I had known him in 1938, when he was a working-class boy, desperate to become a professional actor, and finding his way through Unity Theatre. In those days Jack used to teach him Marxist economics. While Jack was explaining, on what we then considered scientific principles, the mechanism by which the capitalists intensify their exploitation of the workers, Alfie suddenly got the point. He showed it by crying: 'The bastards!'

Now he gave me a lift home, keen to see Jack again. We made tea and settled down to a night of discussion. Little Stella woke up. Jack brought her downstairs and said: 'Look! Alfie Bass has come out of the television to see you.' She fell blissfully asleep while we talked.

What we talked about (besides Alfie's arguments with script writers) was the fact, which I had learned only that evening, that the Party leaders were boycotting Unity Theatre. Zilliacus might lead a discussion there; Pollitt or Gollan would not. Informally, the word had gone out to the Party branches that they were not to make block bookings. (Some of them did, though.)

I spoke to Campbell about this, a few days later. Did the supporters of the Party line, I asked him, not dare to defend it in public? Campbell's only reply was to sneer at Unity Theatre. 'Who do they think they are? The Petöfi Circle?'

That was the hard-line Campbell. The other Campbell emerged on December 4, when he gave the *Daily Worker* staff his report on the Soviet Union.

He said that in the course of 'a long scuffle' with the staff of the theoretical journal *Kommunist*, the British delegation had told them it was no use to say that the Stalinist practices had nothing to do with Socialism. The British had also asked why the legal system had not protected the rights of the individual during the purges.

'Most of the cases avoided the civil courts altogether. They were taken to the military courts and to a "Special Conference" which had been set up to deal with counter-revolutionaries. Now the "Special Conference" has been abolished.'

It had been abolished over three years earlier. That was the subject of Ralph Parker's article, which Brian Pearce brought back from Moscow, only to have it declared unpublishable by Sam Russell. Campbell must have seen it then.

'All cases of those imprisoned on political charges have been reviewed,' Campbell assured us.

As for the death penalty: 'They insist on it for: one, high treason; two, murder with robbery; three, rape followed by murder. They say it would be possible to abolish death for treason if the west would stop sending agents in... It is one thing for an individual to strangle his loved one in a fit of exasperation, and another thing for a gang to plot cold-blooded murder for gain.'

Campbell told us how democratic the trade unions were becoming, and then got down to the delegation's real purpose.

'Is there anti-Semitism in the Soviet Union? If that means that a Jew has less rights as a citizen, I would say no. With one qualification. There was an attack on Jewish culture as expressed in Yiddish publications. There were also attacks on other culture, but that doesn't excuse them.'

Campbell admitted: 'Up to 1948 there were publications in the Yiddish language. After that – nothing. Members of the Jewish Anti-Fascist Committee were framed and shot; people with connections in the west broke off connections... An old comrade, Levine, was able to give me a list of her nephews who were doctors, etc. But there was an attack on Yiddish culture... I should say their attitude is still inconsistent. First, they argue that Jews are not a nationality. But on all applications and passports there is a space for 'nationality', which the Jews are meant to fill in as Jewish... Soviet comrades argue that the way is open to their full assimilation. They argue that the deliberate spreading of Yiddish culture among people who speak Russian is an attempt to put them in a cultural ghetto. They claim that the Jewish theatre was losing money. My own stepson says that the Jewish theatre was doing badly.'

We knew that Campbell's stepson in the Soviet Union was a variety artist, who had toured the front line in the war to entertain Red Army men.

'We were told,' Campbell went on, 'that the great Yiddish writers are going to have their works printed in the Yiddish language for anyone who wants to buy them. The reopening of the theatre is under consideration – if it can pay for itself... I told them that if anyone wants a Yiddish paper it should be published.'

Finally he exhorted us: 'We have got to steer between adoration of the Soviet Union and insensate criticism.' But the whole paper was filled with 'adoration', and had been since the tanks went into Hungary.

Our questions to him centred round the passports. Sid Kaufman asked: 'Are you just supposed to fill in 'Jew' on your passport if you feel Jewish, if you don't want to be known as Russian?'

Campbell said that Gabriel Cohen (the brother of a prominent British Communist) had no desire to put 'Jew' on his passport. 'But he has to, and so has his daughter, born in Russia.'

I pointed out that these passports were identity cards, not passports for travel. Soviet citizens must have them to live in the country at all. Campbell agreed that this was so.

Sheila Lynd asked Campbell what he had said to the staff of *Pravda*.

'On Jews, the *Pravda* comrades are completely split,' Campbell said. 'The Jews on *Pravda* did not want the Jewish theatre; the Russians did.'

A hint of national pride crept into his voice, I thought, when he said that Soviet citizens, fed up with the lateness of the news in *Pravda*, got their information from the World Service of the BBC.

Claire Madden hadn't given up. 'Capital punishment was abolished under Stalin. Under Khrushchov there are 21 reports of executions of leading Party members.'

Campbell said that the death penalty was intended to deal with gang robberies. 'One of the main troubles of the Soviet Union is the absence of fathers.' The fathers had been killed in the war; that was why they had so many juvenile delinquents.

And the secret trial of Beria? 'Representatives from the factories were at the Beria trial, but it was not in public because it was concerned with state secrets... Other trials were reported in the local papers.' (He meant papers printed in languages other than Russian. Very few western correspondents ever saw these, or could understand them if they did. That was why news of executions filtered through so slowly.)

As the meeting broke up, George MacDougall said to me: 'Well, Alison, are you glad you live in Britain?' I said I was, and added that I wasn't so much afraid of Palme Dutt coming to power and tearing my fingernails off as I was afraid that the British people, rather than risk the state of affairs which Campbell had described, would put up with anything the Tories liked to impose on them.

In the canteen, Sheila Lynd seethed at the suggestion that juvenile delinquents, because they had no fathers, needed to be shot. But it no longer surprised us that this was the way the Russians thought. What did surprise us was Campbell's genuine indignation about the treatment of the Jews.

'Khrushchov never mentioned anti-Semitism in the secret speech,' Sheila pointed out. 'But then, he wouldn't; he's anti-Semitic himself.'

The following day the paper carried a letter from me, which Campbell had unexpectedly agreed to publish. It began: 'I appeal to every Communist who feels, as I do, that our Party's present policy on Hungary is wrong. Don't fail to pay up your 1956 dues. Don't fail to re-register.' I wanted all the critics of the leadership to stay in, and elect a new leadership at Easter. 'As a very noisy critic,' I wrote, 'I'm not quitting.' I meant it, then.

Because this letter appeared, I learned that two old friends, Jane and Dennis Swinnerton, were holding a meeting of rebellious Party members in a pub, the Pindar of Wakefield, on December 7. As our children were so young, Jack and I could seldom go out together. We were following Ben Smith's advice, and going to every possible meeting, but in turn. For the Swinnertons' meeting, it was Jack's turn.

He found some Trotskyist pamphlets on sale there. One

of the Party members at the meeting objected to this. Jack exclaimed: 'Now, this is the sort of thing we've got to stop! We may not agree with these people, but we ought to read what they say. Some of them were more right than we were about Stalin.'

The 17 comrades present came from 12 different branches, which meant that they were 'forming a faction' and thereby defying Party discipline. Unless we did that, we could now see, it would be impossible ever to shift the leadership. They had their own permanent faction. They knew what was happening in each branch, but they made sure that nobody else could know, by insisting that the branches must not write to each other.

The statement issued after the Swinnertons' meeting denounced the Party leaders for their fear of discussion, shown by the ban on *The Reasoner*. 'The weaknesses in the Party were brought into the open by the revelations of the Twentieth Congress and the events in Hungary. These things showed a basic weakness in the CPSU. [Communist Party of the Soviet Union.] Such a weakness could only be reflected in our own Party because it has always been modelled on the Soviet pattern.'

Those present agreed to put forward a proposed new rule:

'Every Party member has the right and the duty to publish ideas which he considers to be beneficial to the Party and the working class.'

For months after this, the Party leaders conducted a whispering campaign against the Swinnertons, quite as vicious as the one against Peter Fryer. Incidents long since officially forgiven by the Party were now raked up, with fictional embellishments. An emissary from Party headquarters visited branches, to tell them that Dennis Swinnerton was a liar; he had never, as he claimed, been a full-time Party official. (I had first met him when he was a full-time organiser in Bristol.)

Nobody ever quite got around to denying that he had been in the International Brigade.

Jane's crime was to be extremely beautiful. A few years earlier she had worked as an artist's model. She wrote an entertaining article about that for the *Daily Worker*. Sheila Lynd was horrified by the spitefulness of the letters which then came in, from female comrades who knew Jane and hated her. Apparently they were not themselves well qualified to work as artists' models.

I have always felt that people of either sex who go about looking beautiful are doing me a favour, as much as if they were painting a picture for me, or planting a flowering tree. Jane told me, however, that my attitude was unusual. She was more accustomed, she said, to arousing resentment. (Not that it discouraged her; she continued to look lovely when she had several grandchildren.)

In our house, late at night, Jack and I and the Swinnertons talked about the episodes for which we felt most remorse. How could we have swallowed the change of line at the beginning of the war? How could we have justified Uncle Joe's attack on Finland?

Dennis contrasted our indifference to Stalin's victims with the demonstration about the Rosenbergs, in June 1953. 'When I think of it,' he said, 'when I think of the whole Party aktiv turning out and shouting all night because two people, after every process of law and every chance to appeal, had been condemned for something which, obviously, they did...'

Jane said: 'All the same, I can't think the Party's useless, because, if I think that, I've wasted my life.'

'You mustn't let that stop you thinking,' Jack said. 'If you've wasted your life up to now, the important thing is not to waste any more of it.'

And yet we were still in the Party. The Muswell Hill branch gave me some leaflets to distribute, for the *Daily*

Worker bazaar. Since I was working for the paper, and taking its money, how could I refuse to take part in its fund-raising activities? On the other hand, how could I let the neighbours see me pushing *Daily Worker* leaflets into their letterboxes?

I compromised. I gave out the leaflets after dark.

On December 9 martial law was declared in Hungary, with summary courts to try all those who still resisted the Kadar Government.

The next day Campbell continued his report on the Soviet Union. He was asked what explanation the Soviet comrades gave for the Jewish repression.

'They gave none,' said Campbell, 'except that Beria had fun playing one nationality off against another... All our conversations with them assumed that these persecutions had taken place.'

Was it correct to speak of 'the Jewish problem in the Soviet Union'?

'Anti-Semitism,' said Campbell, 'means that people of Jewish origin must be given the status of inferior citizens. There was no such thing in the Soviet Union. Still, if you are savagely persecuted, and some of you are shot, it certainly isn't Socialism. After the closing of the Jewish theatre and so on came the sacking of Jews from certain ministries.'

Campbell said it was the British comrades who had used the words: 'Jewish problem'. The Russians had said there wasn't one. 'Before the revolution the Yiddish language and the separation of the Jews had been kept in existence by the Tsar's regulations. Since then the Jews had come into the full stream of Soviet life... We were not disputing the possibility of assimilation. But when you consider how touchy – rightly touchy – world opinion is, the stopping of Yiddish papers was, to say the least, unfortunate.'

Somebody asked: 'Is there Socialism in the USSR?'

Campbell did not give a direct answer. 'Levy asked them

– did they think the practices of the Stalin era had nothing to do with Socialism? They said they were just a foreign body on a tree. Levy said that the foreign body draws nourishment from the tree.'

Campbell told us where *L'Humanité* had got its five paragraphs about the coming to power of Gomulka. They were, word for word, the same five paragraphs that had appeared in *Pravda*.

'What about the heavy sentences on the Zionists?' asked Sid Kaufman.

'They denied it,' Campbell said, 'and we could get no proof.'

George Sinfield asked: 'Was there anything said about how the Communist Parties could clear up the mess resulting from the Khrushchov speech?'

By 'the mess' he did not mean the mess left by Stalin's crimes. He meant the mess the Communist leaders were in, since the crimes had been disclosed. Campbell did not answer him – at least, not then.

I asked for news of British comrades who had been imprisoned.

'Len Wincott is back in Moscow,' Campbell said. 'He proposes to do something on his experiences. He is not at all hostile.'

Len Wincott was one of the leaders of the Invergordon Mutiny in 1931. He fled to the Soviet Union and had been there ever since. One of the things we had refused to believe, because it was said by Trotskyists, was that Len Wincott had been sent to Siberia. He had, though.

And Edith Bone? Campbell said: 'Edith Bone went to Hungary on her own account, in her own pursuit of glory and lucre.'

This was an odd way to describe her visit to Budapest to translate an English scientific book into Hungarian. (She had to do it on the spot because the publisher could pay her only in Hungarian money.) Translators get little lucre and less glory.

'She came in here and offered to do an occasional job for the *Daily Worker*,' Campbell went on. 'I never protested against her being imprisoned, because I did not know. But we asked where she was... After the death of Stalin we raised it more sharply... If a *Daily Worker* correspondent disappeared I would have protested.'

Why should Campbell speak so coldly of an elderly woman who had been kept for seven years in atrocious conditions? Because she, like Fryer, had talked to the *Daily Express*. It had serialised her story under the title: I SUFFERED AND I ACCUSE.

Did the Party leaders, then, expect a loyal silence from comrades who had been treated like this? That was indeed what they expected. Sometimes they got it. Campbell, when he said that Len Wincott was 'not hostile', said it with approval. In any other context, an innocent man who had endured years of suffering, without becoming hostile to the power which inflicted it, would have been regarded by Campbell as soft in the head.

The Fields, ever since their release, had been silent about their experiences, even in the company of close friends. And Stan Harrison, a conspicuous hardliner at these meetings, did not tell me until 1990 that, while he was living in Czechoslovakia, he had been six months in disgrace. He and his wife had been 'on brigade' – that is, sent to do manual work on a farm. The weather was pleasant and the work light, consisting mainly of pulling insects off trees. When they were allowed to come back to Prague, in the autumn of 1949, they found themselves back in the Party's good books. Their friend Otto Katz (André Simone) was not so lucky; he had disappeared, not to be seen again until three years later, when he made his deliberately preposterous confession at the Slansky trial.

Brutal as Campbell's manner was, when he spoke of Edith Bone, it may have been concealing something even worse. In her book, *Seven Years Solitary*, she accused Campbell of repudiating her when Rakosi first made enquiries, thus facilitating her arrest. By the time this book was published I was no longer close enough to Campbell to ask him if it was true. But I am not aware that he ever denied it.

The day of that meeting, December 10, was also the day of the first meeting of the Party's History Commission. The Executive Committee had decided, the previous July, that this commission should be set up to write the history of the British Communist Party. Brian Pearce was a member of it.

Now that it met for the first time, Harry Pollitt appeared and threw a spanner in the works. 'I wasn't present when the EC made this decision,' he said. (He had been recovering from his illness.) 'I'd have voted against it. You can't write a history of the Party! You can't write about what happened when Albert Inkpin was taken off the leadership, and I was put in.'

Pollitt's use of the passive was (as we used to say) no accident. He meant that in August 1929 he was put in by the Russians, because they were changing the line. That was when the Party began to call the Labour leaders 'social fascists'.

Afterwards, talking to Brian Pearce, Pollitt said: 'You can't write the history of the Party until we're in power. And even then there are difficulties.' Rakosi, he said, had shown him an advance copy of a history of the Hungarian Communist Party, expensively produced. In this, all the errors of the Party in its earlier days were attributed to that enemy of the people, Bela Kun. 'And just then,' said Pollitt, 'the Russians went and rehabilitated Bela Kun.'

The historians were thrown into disarray. Rather than disobey Pollitt, they decided to disobey the clear instructions of the Executive Committee. Instead of producing a history of the Party, they would produce a series of essays on various periods. And, in spite of Brian's protests, they wrote the minutes of their meeting so as to obscure what had happened.

On December 11 the workers of Hungary began a general strike against the imposition of martial law. Kadar summoned two of the workers' leaders, Sandor Racz and Sandor Bali, both of the Belojanis Electrical Plant, to negotiate with him. Both were arrested. The Belojanis workers refused to start work until they were released. The plant was seized by armed police. The workers sat down for three days. After that they worked, but so slowly that their output was 8% of normal.

On December 12 Peter Fryer's own branch, Hampstead, protested against his suspension. The London District Committee ignored the protest.

On December 13 the *Daily Worker* printed part of a speech by the Indian Premier, Jawaharlal Nehru, who by this time had studied the reports of his Ambassador in Hungary, Krishna Menon. 'Our Ambassador told us that the atmosphere he found in Budapest at this time was reminiscent of the civil disobedience days in India.'

The *Daily Worker* left out the next sentence: 'Mr Menon correctly represented India's policy when he stated that there was no justification for the presence of Soviet forces in Hungary. It was a national uprising; it was not a coup d'état which might have been urged in justification of the Soviet intervention.'

On December 16 the Executive Committee of the Party met and issued another statement on Hungary, even more mendacious than the first. Campbell told us about this at a staff meeting the next day.

He had two difficulties. One was that our own paper, that morning, carried a report from Sam Russell, headed: GRIM STRUGGLE TO LIVE FACES HUNGARIANS. It continued on to the back page. And the bit on the back page contained the words: 'The first death sentence under the martial-law regulation was carried out at Miskolc yesterday, where two men were condemned to death for illegal possession of arms.'

Campbell's other difficulty was that, in the temporary absence of himself and Mick Bennett, the EC had decided not to have its resolution on Hungary published, or even summarised, in the *Daily Worker*. (It was circulated to the Party branches.) Clearly the leaders had so little confidence in their own views that they were not prepared to defend them in public.

Campbell admitted that the EC was so sharply divided on the first Soviet intervention, the one on October 24, that it had not proved possible to mention it in the resolution at all. What I did not know until 1991 was that Campbell, Mick Bennett and five other members of the Political Bureau had wanted to condemn the first Soviet intervention.

As for the report of the delegation to the Soviet Union, Campbell said: 'It contains a number of expressions which I would not personally have used, such as the one comparing the feeling in the Soviet Union to McCarthyism... But I agreed to them to avoid having a majority and a minority report.'

Pat Devine asked in horror: 'Do I understand that you are going to sign a report which suggests that there is McCarthyism in the Soviet Union?'

'You do, my dear comrade, you do,' Campbell replied. 'I had to do that or face a minority report.'

George Sinfield said cautiously: 'I don't say there wasn't McCarthyism in the Soviet Union.'

'It was worse!' exclaimed someone – I think Frank Patterson.

'All right, it was probably worse,' admitted Sinfield.

Campbell interrupted him. 'We have got to diminish our problems, and get the Jewish problem out of our way.'

Pat Devine pleaded: 'We must be very careful in not

lending to such accusations the names of such leaders as the working class has confidence in.'

Campbell said: 'There is not twopennyworth of difference between myself and any other member of the delegation as to the fact that there was persecution. That is, a limited persecution of certain Jews took place. A Yiddish theatre was closed down, the Anti-Fascist Committee was framed and shot, and some Jews had the way to promotion blocked... Wives of Jews who were shot said that there was no great anti-Semitism among the people... Willie Gallacher has independent data.'

John Gritten, a reporter who normally kept his mouth shut at meetings, asked: 'What is the origin of the story about the last plenum, where Joe had his stroke?'

He was referring to a story told to the Poles by the Soviet Ambassador in Warsaw, that Stalin had announced a plan to deport all Jews to Siberia. Molotov, so the story went, muttered a few words of protest. Voroshilov stood up to Stalin, dramatically flinging his Party card on the table. It was a good story, and it got into *The Daily Telegraph* the following Whitsun. But it was not consistent with the other inside story – the one confirmed by the Khrushchov speech – that Voroshilov was not invited to any meetings during the last months of Stalin's life. Campbell said he knew nothing about it.

At this meeting I defended Peter Fryer's action in talking to the *Express*, pointing out that (as we all now knew) the Polish Communists had deliberately given the Khrushchov report to the US State Department, in order to get rid of Stalin's man, Rokossovsky. Campbell nervously interjected: 'Go easy on the Poles!' I thought he was expecting the tanks to roll into Warsaw. But he denied that, when I tackled him about it afterwards. He had meant, he said, that the Poles had many economic problems to face.

I could not believe more than half he said, because the

Campbell who had insisted on signing the report on Soviet anti-Semitism was co-existing with the hard-line Campbell. At this same meeting he exclaimed: 'The Soviet comrades will never do a Twentieth Congress again, because even the most timid Parties have protested violently.'

By 'doing a Twentieth Congress' he meant what George Sinfield had meant by 'the mess'. If only Edith Bone had stayed quietly in her dungeon, if only the millions of people shot had stayed quietly in their graves, leaders like Pollitt and Maurice Thorez could have gone on making their great speeches to gatherings of the faithful. Campbell was not above longing for those days to return.

XIII

Watching a play about Henry VIII on TV, we saw Sir Thomas More resigning the Great Seal. 'No, no!' Jack cried. 'Stay in till Easter.'

That was our advice to all the comrades who were ripping up their Party cards. It would be time to do that if the Congress at Easter 1957 did not bring about a change. 'Be an Easter ripper,' Jack said.

Until 1956, people who left the Party were beyond the pale. Party members did not speak to them – much less ask their opinion.

Now, just as Jack and I had sought out J.T. Murphy, other Party members were seeking out ex-comrades. Pat Dooley was surprised to find himself consulted by people in his old Party branch.

Pat Dooley was a journalist, married to another journalist, Anne Kelly. She had covered the Traicho Kostov trial in 1949 for the *Daily Worker*. (That was the trial that went wrong. Kostov repudiated the confession extorted from him in prison.)

Pat Dooley replied to his former comrades: 'On my return from Romania and from Prague in 1953, I told Pollitt, Campbell and Gollan all that is now publicly being said... Pollitt didn't want to know – treated me as a naive boy who has just heard the facts of life, and smiled at me – told me to keep quiet, don't talk "while at home" and go back and don't get mixed up in anything!

'Gollan said almost the same, word for word. Campbell, too, although Campbell is, in my opinion, still the best of the bunch of them, he knows what's going on: knew before I did, but he thinks the larger issues should predominate…'

The Party members had asked Pat Dooley whether to believe Peter Fryer, whose paperback, *Hungarian Tragedy*, was rushed out by Dennis Dobson early in December.

Dooley wrote: 'I support his views – even to going outside the Party (after the idiotic suppression of *The Reasoner*) to make himself heard. I too should have done it… If you read Fryer's book, as you should, forgive his occasional intemperate language, written white hot to denounce an evil he *saw* for the first time – and remember *his conclusions are not invalidated by the methods he chose to get a hearing.*'

Pat Dooley was expecting to be called 'an enemy of the people' for this. Instead, his old comrades asked him what he had seen when he worked in Czechoslovakia. He replied:

> Almost everyone worked and walked in fear… There was a spy in every office and none knew who it was until experience eliminated the more courageous and left the finger of suspicion pointing in the right direction.

> One thing engendering fear was the refusal of the political management to believe any 'mistakes' could be made. 'Mistakes' were always said to be counter-revolutionary acts with the result that, altho' the country starved for cadres, every capable Communist who could (read dare) leave a responsible position, fled from it (some of my friends into coal mines or on to the factory floor where no large responsibility was expected of them).

> My colleague on the journal I edited, *Czechoslovak Life*, was threatened with arrest because of a mistaken caption under a picture. Incidentally this journal, circulating throughout the world, was allowed to send only 160 copies to Russia, for

Czech embassies etc., because the pictures indicated a higher standard of life than in Russia: this at a time when millions of copies of Russian translations of everything were being produced in Prague in a special institution, at Czech expense.

Every worker has a work dossier, kept by the firm's political cadre. The worker never sees it. Every spy or enemy can report him: down it goes into the report – and if the worker is allowed to leave a job the next firm's political cadre will not take him on without an OK and the dossier from his last job...

Anti-Semitism was rife in Czecho – unloosed by the Minister of Information, Kopecky, who is still in charge. No attempt was made to differentiate between anti-Semitism and Zionism in political propaganda. It was even shared by ex-TU leader Zapotocky, then Premier, now President since the death of the weak, vacillating Gottwald, who 'died' in Moscow after Stalin's funeral. On New Year's Eve, 1953, 27 Jews in my building (the equivalent of Reuter's building in Fleet Street) were sacked because of their birth. They weren't even allowed to come back to the office and clear their desks. One was my secretary...' [The date is ambiguous. Dooley meant 31 December 1952 – shortly after the Slansky trial.]

They walked the streets for months trying for work, fighting against the telling dossier – and these were brave, honest Communists who had the indelible numbers printed on their arms by the Fascists in concentration camps. 'What's the difference, now?' they asked me bitterly. Such as these led the workers who rose in Budapest – and had I been there I would have been with them!

Pat Dooley regretted that he had not, like Fryer, written a book. 'I ought to have done, because only when the British workers *know* these things can they understand Poland and Hungary (and the long-suffering Russian people) and also prevent our bureaucratic little Stalins here from exercising similar excesses. What chance would Fryer have of liberty, had Mahon, Pollitt and E. Burns been vested with *State* power?'

(John Mahon was London District Secretary; Emile Burns was in charge of cultural matters at Party headquarters.)

The comrades who got these two letters from Pat Dooley typed them in single spacing, so as to get both on to one piece of paper, had them duplicated, and gave them out at meetings. I have the blurred, yellowing sheet of what feels like blotting paper, to remind me how badly we needed a printing press.

Campbell's review of Fryer's book, which appeared on December 20, was a farrago of misquotations and lies. (Though he never denied that Peter had seen what he said he saw.) But it was beautifully printed, on that great rotary which we had seen installed with so much pride.

Peter Fryer had now met a man who offered him the use of a printing press. To reject it would have been like turning down a glass of water in Iran.

Peter was to realise within three years that Gerry Healy, the Trotskyist, had all the worst habits of the Communist Party leaders, such as rigging congresses, blackening the names of those who disagreed with him and manipulating young people. (Manipulating literally, if they were girls.) But Healy was in many ways very competent, and he ran the Plough Press at a profit. When Peter issued his appeal against expulsion, it was as a pamphlet, well printed and easy to handle.

Not even a printing press could have won Peter to the side of Gerry Healy, if Healy had not offered him something he wanted even more – a rational explanation. What we hungered and thirsted for then was not so much righteousness, as some way to make sense of the events which had hit us. Peter and Brian Pearce (who was enlivening the columns of the *New Statesman* with learned letters) were drawn to Healy, not only because he had been right about Stalin, but because he boasted of a historical theory which accounted for Stalinism.

In the New Year, 1957, Jack and I went to meetings of

the newly formed Socialist Forum, and heard this view of history several times from Healy's disciples. We were less impressed than Peter and Brian were.

According to these Trotskyists, there was nothing wrong with the Bolshevik Revolution, and nothing wrong with the dissolution of Russia's first attempt at democracy, the Constituent Assembly. As for the suppression of the rising at Kronstadt in 1921 – that couldn't be wrong, since Trotsky had carried it out. The point where everything went wrong was the decision by Stalin to build Socialism in one country. Any friend of Healy's could produce quotations from Lenin, to the effect that there could never be Socialism in Russia, unless at least one of the advanced countries also went socialist.

I never found it possible (though I went right on trying) to convince a Trotskyist that these quotations proved Lenin a mad gambler. What right had he to overthrow Kerensky, if seizing power in Russia was not going to be enough? What right had he to stake millions of lives on a revolution in Germany, which he had no power to bring about?

One of Brian Pearce's letters to the *New Statesman* described Lenin, in conversation with Klara Zetkin, admitting that he had done wrong to order the disastrous march on Warsaw in 1920. Lenin listed all the political reasons against it. 'But, above all, ought we, unless absolutely and literally compelled, to have exposed the Russian people to the horror and suffering of another winter of war?'

Why hadn't he thought of that before? Surely because he had imagined he would win. If he had won, if the Bolshevik armies had swept on through Warsaw and into Germany, he would not have cared what suffering he brought about. Jack and I were accustomed to looking at these events through a romantic haze, because they had, after all, led to Socialism. Now that we knew what they had in fact led to, the effect on us of Brian's researches was not what Brian intended. Every quotation from Lenin made us feel that Stalin was indeed, as he had claimed, Lenin's heir.

As for Trotsky, his book, *Terrorism and Communism* (first published in England under the title *In Defence of Red Terror*) is a do-it-yourself manual. It shows how to construct a morality which will destroy you. Trotsky's biographer, Isaac Deutscher, called him a prophet. If he had been one, he would have entitled this book: *Build Your Own Icepick.*

The attraction of the Trotskyists, that winter, was not that their arguments were good. It was that they were prepared to argue at all. The orthodox were not. The *Daily Worker* was no longer printing critical letters. On January 2 and 3, 1957, it carried two articles from the Chinese Communist Party, the second of which informed us: '...although Stalin committed some grave mistakes in his later years, his was nevertheless the life of a great Marxist-Leninist revolutionary.'

On a Saturday in January 1957 there was a meeting of all the Party members in the *Daily Worker* building – compositors, foundry men and office staff, as well as journalists. The Party leaders may have believed that we, the neurotic intellectuals, would be shamed by the constancy of the manual workers.

One of the manual workers, Ernie Pountney, said it was 'no accident' that those who had left the paper were journalists. They were the comrades most affected by outside influences. He added that he could not understand the attitude of some comrades. They seemed to be suggesting that capitalism had changed its nature.

I said maybe Communism had. The Communism revealed by the Khrushchov speech was not what we thought we had been fighting for all these years. I said thank goodness yes; some of us were susceptible to outside influences. We did notice what was going on the world and what people were saying in the streets. Some comrades seemed to notice nothing outside their own offices.

One of the foundry workers, who belonged to the Southwark branch, said: 'We in Southwark don't believe that Khrushchov ever made that speech.'

I said: 'Christ Almighty!' But my voice was drowned in moans and laughter. Then I noticed that George Matthews and Mick Bennett were not responding. They sat unmoving, unsmiling, as if determined to ignore the whole incident. (Campbell was not present.)

In the rush of events, it was hard to remember who had said what when. Looking at those two stone faces, I thought that the Party leaders had never admitted the authenticity of the Khrushchov speech. Not until 1990, when I went through the back numbers of the *Daily Worker*, did I realise that their admission had been on the front page on 22 June 1956, only 12 days after the *Observer* printed the full text. All of us at the meeting had forgotten that. Or, if Mick Bennett and George Matthews remembered it, they were not going to remind the comrade from Southwark.

Mick Bennett said, about the people who had left the paper: 'Those comrades just weren't strong enough to hold their sector of the front in the class war, that's all.'

Afterwards the reporter John Gritten remarked to me that this military phraseology was an obsession with the Party, and was completely alien to the British working class.

According to Gritten, Ernie Pountney's remarks about 'outside influences' meant that he thought we were influenced by journalists from Fleet Street. 'Sometimes it's only meeting those bastards,' Gritten reflected, 'that keeps us in the Party.'

I asked the young man from Southwark: 'Do you really believe that Khrushchov didn't make that speech?'

'Well,' he said, 'it was doctored.'

'No, it wasn't,' John Gritten said.

In the course of the ensuing argument, the foundry man

said: 'Well, you must admit that Imre Nagy was a traitor.'

'No, he wasn't,' John Gritten and I said in unison.

The foundry man, preparing to get on his bike, said: 'Whatever happens, we mustn't let the Soviet Union down.'

Dora Scarlett (whom I still did not know at this time) had come back to England and discovered that many comrades, like the man from Southwark, did not believe that Khrushchov ever made that speech. Or they argued that Khrushchov must have been lying.

'But in Hungary,' Dora wrote, 'every one of these charges was immediately credible because people had seen the same things happening in front of their eyes for the last eight years – police terror, deportations, staged trials, extorted confessions, the murder of good Communists and honest workers.'

On Monday, 7 January 1957, the comrades in the Muswell Hill branch were presented with a fait accompli. There was a vacancy in the Stroud Green ward of the Middlesex County Council, and for this by-election the Party was putting up a candidate, Mrs Lena Prior. She was a platonic devotee of G. J. Jones (Jonah), and Jonah himself was at the meeting to give us the news. (And to remind us that he got 10,000 votes in 1945.) He was not asking our consent for Lena Prior to stand. The decision, he told us, had been taken, and it was too late now to withdraw the candidate.

I asked what, in that case, we were supposed to be discussing. Dorothea Zemla, a member of the Borough Committee which had taken the decision, said that the purpose of the discussion was to convince us, the rank-and-file members, that the decision was correct.

Several of us had no intention of being convinced. The seat was a marginal one, previously held by a Tory, but possible for Labour to win. Nowhere else in the country had the Party put up a candidate in a marginal seat.

We looked expectantly at David Ainley, Jonah's old opponent. He said: 'While I would normally have opposed the putting up of a Communist candidate, I support it in this instance.' Why? 'It will take comrades away from all this inner-Party discussion, and turn them outwards to the people.'

I said I would be taken away from inner-Party discussion if I took my children for a walk in Highgate Wood, and then at least I would not be doing the Party any harm. But to fight an election where we might split the vote and let the Tory in, thereby antagonising Labour people – that was an activity directly harmful to the Party.

After protesting to the London District Committee, and to John Gollan, I realised that most of the Party leaders (though they would not say so in writing) agreed with David Ainley. They were past caring what harm they did, even to their own organisation, if only they could distract us from asking questions.

And yet here I must except Campbell. It was largely his doing that the report on anti-Semitism in the Soviet Union was published. Not, it is true, in the *Daily Worker*, but in the Party's weekly, *World News*, where it appeared on January 12.

The report admitted that 'the years 1948-52 were known as the "black years", the period during which many Jews were dismissed from their posts, Jewish poets and writers were arrested and charged with treason and executed...'

There was a discrepancy here between the written and the spoken word. From what Campbell had told us, the black years were not 1948-52 but 1948-53. The persecution certainly did not end before Stalin's death, and could it be said to have ended afterwards?

The report in *World News* was otherwise accurate:

> Shortly after his arrest, the immediate relatives of the arrested man would be deported to some distant place and there set to work and often at low wages. Finally the husband would be

shot, perhaps after torture, to try to force him to confess or to intimidate others. In this way, practically the whole of the Jewish Anti-Fascist Committee was liquidated, and this procedure was carried through by the secret police under the direct authority of Beria, with the agreement of Stalin himself... It is unnecessary to give chapter and verse as proof of these crimes. They are known, admitted and accepted as a fact in the Soviet Union today, and no attempt is made to deny them... leading Jewish cultural workers who were done to death have been 'rehabilitated' publicly and officially and... their families compensated.

That Campbell was a ruthless liar I have shown; that he joined in the whispering campaign against Peter Fryer is also true. But it should be remembered that he set his name to the report on anti-Semitism, and that it included the following paragraph:

Crimes and distortions of this type cannot be the work of one man... sectors of the administrative personnel must have been aware of what was taking place and must have taken the steps necessary to implement it. This argues a certain level of deterioration in this sector; a certain measure of indifference to human values which does violence to those of us, brought up in bourgeois capitalist society, who have given our support to the Socialist cause. Rightly or wrongly we have expected something vastly different from this.

The reason this was printed in *World News*, not in the *Daily Worker*, was that *World News* was read only by Party members, whereas the *Daily Worker* could be read by anybody. But print is print; once the report was in *World News*, it was inevitably in the *Observer* the following Sunday.

Though this report was unanimous, though the delegation which produced it was sent to Russia by the Party, the Party's bureaucracy managed to treat it as if it were unofficial. Ray Waterman remembers how difficult it was to publicise a report-back meeting addressed by Professor Hyman Levy. She could not get the chairman of an official Party meeting to mention it. As people were leaving she stood up at the back of the hall and shouted when and where Levy would speak. Then she phoned everybody she knew who might possibly come.

The night I heard Levy, he was addressing a joint meeting of the Cricklewood and Golders Green branches. Several hundred people were present, all Party members. By the morality to which we still adhered, this meant that Levy could speak freely.

He said he had begun by trying to find out whether Beria had had a fair trial. 'But I soon realised how naif I had been.' He talked to people who had been tortured by Beria and his men. 'I said – stop! Stop telling me these things! I'll think you're going mad.' (Yes, Levy said: 'You', not: 'I'.)

He was still leaning over backwards to be fair to the Soviet Union. He thought Beria might have shown Stalin anti-Soviet speeches and writings of the kind that sometimes appeared in the *Jewish Chronicle*. This, he admitted, was only his theory. The meeting thought poorly of it.

Levy said that Zionist feeling among Jews in the Soviet Union was largely the result of the 'black years'. He had refused to talk to the Chief Rabbi of Moscow – 'Chief Rabbis make the same noises in all countries' – and instead had gone out looking for ordinary Jews. The custodian of a museum in Leningrad looked Jewish. Levy spoke to him in Yiddish. The man started, and went to fetch a colleague who spoke Yiddish better than he did. Through this encounter, Levy met Jews of several generations. The old people who had grown up before the revolution spoke Yiddish. The middle-aged people who had grown up in the first years after the revolution did not speak it much, and some of them had married non-Jews.

'We know from our own experience,' Levy said, 'that in an atmosphere of tolerance we do tend to intermarry. When I was a boy I didn't know one Jew who was married to a non-Jew. Now I don't know one who isn't!'

He said that in the Soviet Union the young people, who had grown up during the 'black years' had turned back, inwards, to the Jewish community. They learned Yiddish from their grandparents, and shrank from intermarriage.

Levy said he had tried to discuss these things with the Soviet theoretician, Mikhail Suslov. 'I didn't like him, and he didn't like me. But I kept my temper. One of our Canadian comrades began to throw things.'

(The Canadian comrade was J. B. Salsberg, who had been struggling since 1949 to get at the facts about anti-Semitism in the Soviet Union. During his talks with a Soviet spokesman he asked about the 'quota' interview with Furtseva. The spokesman refused either to confirm or deny it – and then made it clear that the quota did in fact exist.)

Levy was besieged with questions from the meeting. Someone asked: 'All right – suppose that Stalin did think the Jewish Anti-Fascist Committee was plotting against him. So why did he have to shoot them? Why not simply send them to prison?'

Levy said: 'That seems not to have occurred to anybody. I've been to the Soviet Union many times, but this time I felt that I was in a strange land – a land where human life doesn't have the value that we're accustomed to attach to it.'

He added that one man, released from Siberia, had told him: 'Towards the end of Stalin's life it got so bad that, if the Americans had known what they were doing, they wouldn't have invaded – they'd simply have dropped arms into Siberia by parachute. Within a few days they'd have had an army of a million men fighting on their side.'

There were groans and gasps of horror from the hall. When someone asked what we, as members of the British Communist Party, could do about all this, I shouted from the back: 'Sling out the present leaders!'

This was cheered. And yet Levy did not want to go so far. When I talked to him afterwards I found that he did not want to turn any meeting he addressed into a faction for changing the leadership of the Party. He met the Swinnertons later, but he had not at this time linked up with their movement. If he had done so, if the groups then emerging had been able to focus on him, there might have been a transformation at the Easter Congress. But too many rank-and-file comrades were still trying to keep within the rules.

On the bus back to Muswell Hill I talked to a woman comrade about the faked evidence in the Slansky trial. During the war she had worked at a hostel for Czech refugees. Czechs could not be interned, as they were not enemy aliens; they were detained under Regulation 18B, like the fascists. Then they were released one by one, after signing a document promising not to impede the British war effort. All the Communist refugees were happy to sign that. By the time they got out the war had ceased to be an imperialist war, since Hitler had attacked the Soviet Union.At the hostel, each new guest who had signed and been released was greeted with a little party. There were songs and drinks and jokes about the British document.

Some of these refugees were put on trial with Slansky. The evidence against them was that they had been released on signing a document 'promising to work for British intelligence'.

When the woman who had worked in the hostel told me this, neither of us knew that Mick Bennett had protested on just those grounds on behalf of his friend Otto Sling. At the King Street headquarters of the Party, Betty Reid had obtained a transcript of the trial in English (still in the Party archives) and had taken it to Pollitt to protest about this obvious frame-up. We would not, then, have believed this of Betty

Reid. She was Party bureaucracy personified – 'the lady policeman from King Street', as one of the dissidents called her. Like Mick Bennett, she was far too disciplined to talk about this unavailing protest.

On January 19 *World News* published more of the report by the British Communist delegation to the Soviet Union. This part was about the arrests and shootings made possible by the 'Special Conference', set up in 1934. There was also the throwaway line: 'For ten years it was impossible to carry out genuinely scientific work in the field of genetics.'

Such were the events which we were now expected to ignore, in order to 'turn outwards to the people'. Those who tried it – for example by attempting to sell the *Daily Worker* – soon found how little use the people had for the friends of Russian tanks. The drop in our sales was discussed at an editorial staff meeting on 28 January 1957. Cecil Kline, who was in charge of mass sales, reported: 'One comrade says that for years she has shouted: "The only paper that tells the truth." She doesn't feel she can shout that now.'

I said this was hardly surprising. 'Two strikers are shot dead in Hungary and we put it on an inside page at the bottom of a story about something else. Where would we have put it if two strikers were shot dead in England? We have to go to the *Observer* even to get the news about what happens inside our own Party.' The *Observer* had printed, as the *Daily Worker* had not, the Minority Report of the Commission on Inner-Party Democracy. This was the protest by Malcolm MacEwen, the Oxford historian Christopher Hill and a teacher, Peter Cadogan, against the methods by which a small clique of permanent officials had kept the Party on the line laid down by Moscow. Malcolm MacEwen disclosed in this report that he had been forbidden to address meetings outside his own branch. Only people who agreed with the leadership could do that. Peter Cadogan had missed some of the commission's meetings, because he had been suspended from Party membership for writing a letter to the *News Chronicle*. Only people who agreed with the leadership could do that, either. And the *Daily Worker* was of course closed to him.

I reminded the staff meeting that Campbell had recently sneered at the American *Daily Worker* for printing three different points of view in the same issue. 'That's precisely what we should be doing,' I said. 'Why not? Because we're so obsessed with this idea that we're a bloody army.' I pointed out an appeal to the rank-and-file members which Pollitt and Gollan had just issued. 'It's got half a dozen military expressions in the first few pars. "Rally the forces... under enemy fire..." That's not the language of the British working class.'

At this one of the reporters exclaimed: 'Alison can always be relied on to ruin a good case!'

Mick Bennett saw nothing good about my case. It seemed that other people, at other meetings, had been telling him to give more prominence to the shooting of Hungarian strikers. 'I can't imagine anything that would make it harder to sell the paper.'

There had been undermining of confidence among the comrades in the building, Mick went on. 'We have got to put a stop to that.'

Campbell faced us a week later, on February 5. All he could say, in defence of the Russians in Hungary, was: 'These things have been done and we have got to live with them.' For the Easter Congress, he said, the EC had prepared a political resolution. 'That resolution is likely in my opinion to provoke some very lively discussion.'

He meant that the resolution was a blast of unrepentant Stalinism. Probably he had voted against it, but, as a disciplined member of the EC, he had to defend it to us. He also had to defend the EC decision not to allow the Congress to amend the Party rules. Even George Sinfield protested at that.

Just after that meeting, David Gammans, Conservative MP for Hornsey, died. That gave Jonah what he most wanted in the world – a chance to fight a Parliamentary by-election. And it put us rebels in a spot. Jack and I had ignored Lena Prior and her council election, because we did not consider ourselves bound by the decision to put up a candidate. By telling us that there had been no need to consult our branch beforehand, our leaders invited, and got, the response that they could go out and campaign without us.

But our leaders were not going to make that mistake again. They were going to hold all the proper meetings beforehand, and pack them with Jonah's supporters. Then, if we refused to come out and campaign for Jonah, we would be exposing ourselves as wreckers, not real Party members; and everything we said in the branch would be disregarded.

Was this, perhaps, the moment to leave the Party? I felt that, even if I were no longer a Party member, it would still hurt me to see the name of Communism publicly associated with an idiot like Jonah.

Jack and I gritted our teeth, and stayed in till Easter.

XIV

At the first opportunity, the London District Committee voted in favour of Jonah standing for Parliament. At the first opportunity, Jack went to a local Party meeting to protest. Jonah's speech there began: 'What a piece of luck that we have a by-election in Hornsey!' It ended: 'We must make a break from the long period when we were turning in on inner-Party discussion.'

Diana Pym of Highgate branch, where Jonah was not loved, pointed out that Lena Prior had got only 182 votes in Stroud Green a few weeks earlier, at the end of January 1957, as against 250 in 1955. 'This,' Diana pointed out, 'was where we were supposed to have the greatest mass support.'

(I had, in a way, been proved wrong by that Stroud Green vote. Far from splitting the vote and letting in the Tory, Lena Prior made such a miserable showing that she scarcely annoyed the Labour Party. Ted Castle, husband of the Labour leader Barbara Castle, won handsomely in what was previously a Tory ward, with 3,602 votes to the Tory's 3,138.)

Diana argued that, if this was the strongest part of the Hornsey constituency, Jonah could not expect much more than 700 votes in the constituency as a whole.

Bob Ferguson, a Jonah supporter whom I was to encounter again, made a speech beginning: 'If we don't understand the role of the Labour Party to be that of the capitalist class itself...' (Labour's Parliamentary candidate was a particularly lively left-winger, Lyn Mostyn.)

The London District Secretary, John Mahon, had to explain why his committee had not consulted the local comrades before urging Jonah to stand. 'It would have been a failure of leadership if we hadn't expressed our view.'

The opposition to this 'leadership' was so fierce that Mahon made a concession. There would be an aggregate meeting of all Hornsey members, to decide the issue. Jack and I decided that we must both go to this one. Our mothers were in poor health, and the only possible babysitter was my long-suffering Tory father. We no longer felt that we could not tell him why we wanted to go to the meeting.

The school hall at Crouch End was packed. Most of the words uttered were in a sort of code. The people who said they wanted Jonah to stand meant that they wanted the Russian tanks to stay in Hungary. They felt that this proved them to be firm, steady and loyal. 'We, who have weathered Hungary...' one woman began. Jonah himself had just been challenged in the local paper, by a fellow-member of the United Nations Association, to declare his attitude on Hungary.

In his reply, Jonah accused his challenger, a Mr Palmer, of not mentioning Formosa, Kenya, Malaya, British Guiana and Cyprus. Mr. Palmer rejoined: 'I did not, indeed, mention Formosa, Kenya or British Guiana; nor, for that matter, did I mention Omsk, Tomsk and all stations to Vladivostok.'

These exchanges did not give the readers of the local paper any clear view of Jonah's policy about Hungary. As for Lena Prior, she, like the other candidates at the council election in Stroud Green, had been invited to make a speech after the votes were counted. She said: 'The Labour victory was not only a vote against the Conservative action in Suez and the Government's Rent Bill; it was also a vote against the council's differential rent scheme.'

Someone shouted: 'Hungary!' Lena Prior said she was not there to make any further statements.

From this it will appear that, however firm, steady and loyal they felt, those who supported the Party line on Hungary showed some diffidence about saying so in public. Why, then, did they seek to expose themselves to public scrutiny at elections? Because if they were rushing to and fro, shouting through megaphones about the Rent Bill (an easy target, since it raised most working-class rents) they would not have to confront their own real feelings about Hungary. A great deal was said at this meeting about the working class, and about the need to 'show the face of the Party'. It all meant: 'Keep the tanks in Budapest, but, please, don't let's talk about it.'

It did not follow that all those who wanted Jonah not to stand also wanted the Russian tanks out of Hungary. Some were in two minds about it, and did not want to expose either mind to public view.

In his closing speech, Jonah reminded us that he had got 10,000 votes in 1945.

The vote at the end of the meeting was almost exactly divided. By two or three, Jonah won. He was going to stand for Parliament, unless Gollan and the other national leaders decided that he should not. We had little hope of that. It would be a strange campaign, if half the Party members in Hornsey refused to turn out for Jonah. But those were just the Party members whom Gollan would most like to expel.

While Jonah's affairs were in the balance, Jack and I heard from an old friend, Chris Bartlett. She, like so many people we knew in the Party, was both worker and intellectual. If she had been born south of the Border, she would never have got to a university. Her mother was a widow who scraped a living by dressmaking. But Glasgow had university places for the poorest, and Chris worked her way through college, part of the time as a bus conductress. The toughness which enabled her to throw the drunks of Glasgow off her bus was useful to her when she, her husband and their three little girls went to live in Bulgaria. He worked on an English language paper there; she taught English. Now she was back on holiday, and would be able to tell us what Communist Bulgaria was like.

She maintained that it was perfectly all right, if you stood up to the officials. When a pair of children's shoes wore out after a week, she took them back to the shop and protested, just as she would in Britain. As the shop would not replace them she went to the appropriate Ministry. 'But I didn't see the Minister himself,' she said. 'Not that time. I saw him later, when we didn't get the flat they promised us.'

The passionate speeches Chris made, at first in broken Bulgarian, then with ever-increasing fluency, staggered the Bulgarians meekly waiting in government offices. 'The militiaman in the corner looked at me as if he didn't know whether to shoot me or join the revolution.'

Chris told the Bulgarians not to be so timid in making complaints. 'Look!' she pointed out to them. 'I do it all the time, and nothing happens to me.'

Chris did not deny that she and her family, like other foreign Communists, were leading a privileged life. But she maintained that conditions were improving for everyone. The mistakes and abuses of Stalin's day were being put right.

'What about the frame-up of Traicho Kostov in 1949?' we asked her. 'What about his rehabilitation last April? Are people allowed to talk about it?'

We grilled her, like secret policemen, till 2 a.m. Then, suddenly, she exclaimed: 'Those bastards! Those bastards!'

She was talking about the Executive Committee of the Comintern. We now knew that they had unanimously voted to expel the Hungarian leader Bela Kun in 1936. They had thus, in effect, handed him over to Stalin's police.

Among those who turned against Bela Kun was Georgi Dimitrov, then the hero of the Reichstag fire trial and, later, the dictator of Bulgaria. There was a legend that Dimitrov had been murdered by Stalin, since he died in Moscow shortly before the Kostov trial. Was Dimitrov refusing to agree to the framing of Kostov? It was a touching thought, but, as Chris admitted in the small hours, Dimitrov had shown himself ruthless to any comrade whom Stalin wanted out of the way.

I got another view of Eastern Europe when I went to a meeting organised by the British-Polish Friendship Society, to explain what happened when Gomulka came to power.

The chairman was Hyman Levy; the speaker was Dr Len Crome, an old International Brigader.

For us, any man who had joined the International Brigade between 1936 and 1938, and fought for the Popular Front Government of Spain against Franco, was a hero. We were only beginning to grasp that Stalin had hated old International Brigaders, for the same reason that he had hated Jews. They had contacts with the west.

Len Crome had gone to a reunion of International Brigaders in Warsaw, in the autumn of 1956, and found his old comrades just released from camps in Russia. Many of them were crippled by torture.

Also at the reunion in Warsaw was a British Communist leader, Peter Kerrigan. It was now generally known (though not said at the meeting) that whenever one of the Poles tried to describe Stalin's camps, Kerrigan exclaimed: 'I refuse to discuss the Soviet Union with you!'

Len Crome told the meeting what he had heard from one of the old International Brigaders, who had now become a member of Gomulka's Government. On 20 October 1956, when Khrushchov and Marshal Konev flew into Warsaw, they had not bothered to tell the Poles they were coming. The Polish air controllers kept the plane circling round Warsaw

Airport for an hour, before they gave it permission to land. This put Khrushchov in a temper. He marched into the meeting of the Central Committee of the Polish Workers' Party, and shouted: 'Russian blood was shed to liberate Poland! We're not going to hand it over to the Zionists!'

Gomulka said: 'In that case we shall have to adjourn this meeting, so that we can complete our military dispositions.'

Khrushchov simmered down and started to talk. We had all heard a rumour that he said to the Poles: 'There are too many Abramoviches here!' But this was not in Len Crome's version.

When Khrushchov at last consented that Rokossovsky should be sacked, and that Gomulka should be premier, Poland's problems were only beginning. Freedom of speech (though not of the press) came back, and the first thing that came to the surface was anti-Semitism.

Jakob Berman, the secret police chief who had carried out Stalin's atrocities in Poland, *including his anti-Semitic atrocities*, was a Jew. The Natolin Group (supporters of Rokossovsky) had attempted to blame all the unpopular actions of Rokossovsky's government on the Jews.

A Jewish lady in the audience said that her two nephews in Poland had frequently told her that they both had good jobs and were glad they had gone back to Poland after the war. But since Gomulka had come to power they had lost their jobs, and now felt themselves menaced by anti-Semitism.

There was an uncomfortable silence. Brian Pearce, who was next to me, whispered what I had already thought, that her nephews may have been 'little Bermans'.

(Only when I went to Poland, 21 years later, did I discover how widespread had been the practice of giving unpopular jobs to Jews. Stalin had nothing to learn from those mediaeval kings who sent Jews out to collect the taxes.)

Some people angrily contested the truth of Len Crome's

story about Khrushchov. And one man cried: 'I can't believe Stalin was ever anti-Semitic. Because it says in the Soviet Constitution...'

Another man interrupted him, shouting: 'Will nothing shake your patent Stalinist shock-absorber? Professor Hyman Levy there can tell you something about anti-Semitism in Russia.'

Levy, looking embarrassed, called the meeting to order. It was turning into a fight between the two factions of the Party. He would have loved to join in. But there were non-Party people present, and so the matters most on all our minds could not be discussed.

I asked when we could have a full English translation of the document, published in a Polish paper, which gave the whole proceedings of a Central Committee meeting a few days before Khrushchov arrived. Rokossovsky had begged Gomulka's supporters to refute the story that he, Rokossovsky, had been planning to kidnap them all. They had made no comment on this, but had reminded Rokossovsky and Berman of the innocent people arrested and tortured by the secret police.

I was told that the British-Polish Friendship Society had not the money to finance a full translation.

Brian Pearce whispered that there were only four copies of the Polish text in the country. He had been in the Polish Embassy when an emissary came from the British Communist headquarters, to take one of these precious copies to John Gollan. (Later an English translation was published, under the title: *The Polish Road*, by the International Society for Socialist Studies. It could be obtained only by sending a postal order to an address in Bradford. As it was not sanctioned or distributed by the Party, most Party members did not know it existed.)

In a tube train, after this meeting, Brian Pearce told me: 'There's a woman called Dora Scarlett who's come back from

Hungary. She confirms everything Peter Fryer said.'

Swaying in the tube, I took down Dora Scarlett's address. I wrote to her the next day. Even before she replied, I challenged Palme Dutt at a meeting of the Muswell Hill branch. 'You say Peter Fryer's a traitor because he talked to the *Express*. There's a Party member called Dora Scarlett who came back from Hungary and talked to John Gollan. What she has to say won't be published in the *Daily Worker*. She can't talk to any Party branch except her own, because that would be forming a faction. If she talks to the *Daily Express*, she's a traitor. So tell me – what should Dora Scarlett have done?'

Palme Dutt said: 'In 1917 Zinoviev and Kamenev...'

(Thirteen years later Dutt was happily giving the secrets of the Party to the *Sunday Times*. That was different; he'd been outvoted in the Political Bureau.)

At that branch meeting, we were given the welcome news that Jonah would not, after all, be standing. The EC meeting on March 10 had heard a report on his health. His blood pressure was dangerously high, and he had been ordered to rest for several weeks.

On 14 March 1957 Dora Scarlett wrote to me: 'My experiences since returning from Hungary could have been more help to the struggle for inner-Party democracy if only I had realised earlier that such a struggle was going on, and that the forces on this side within the Party were quite strong. But I had been quite isolated from British Party life, and I had a struggle in my own mind, which had been going on long before the rising in Hungary, to decide whether the evils I saw around me were the result of the very nature of the Party or whether they were "mistakes" which would ultimately be rectified. The rising was for me not a decisive point; I had reached that point earlier. My attitude when I came back was therefore too individualistic. My chief concern was to tell the Party what I had experienced, and to resign.'

When she came to see us, Dora described her conversation with John Gollan. She told him all about the Communist bosses, their privileged beach behind barbed wire on Lake Balaton, the long record of arrests, frame-ups, tortures and executions, and the final explosion of popular hatred against the security policemen... Gollan heard her out and said, in his gentle Edinburgh voice: 'Och, I wish we'd known a' this.' He then continued to speak and write as if he did not know it.

What Dora brought from Hungary was the one small suitcase she had been allowed to carry when the British Embassy got her out. She was homeless and unemployed. At first two old comrades put her up. When she tried to tell them what she had seen in Hungary, they screamed that it couldn't be true; it mustn't be true... A family of Communist rebels came to her rescue. They housed her and fed her while she wrote her book, *Window onto Hungary*.

By this time the first draft of the book was almost complete. She could not find a publisher for it. All the journalists' books on Hungary had already been rushed out. There was no room for Dora's careful, scholarly work, based on her three years in the country, her travels to every part of it and her personal experiences of the rising. In the end she had to bring it out at her own expense. It remains the best of all the books written then about Hungary, and probably the least read. There must be a few hundred copies about in the world, but all I can be sure of is the copy in the British Library, the copy in the London Library, the copy Brian Pearce has and the copy on my own shelves.

Whatever Jack and I lost, in 1956 and 1957, is outweighed by one great gain. We came to know Dora Scarlett. Her calmness, her sanity, her fortitude through every setback, gave us the example we needed.

On that same Sunday when it was decided that Jonah could

not stand for Parliament, March 10, the *Observer* carried the news that Professor Wolfgang Harich, of East Berlin University, had been sentenced to 10 years penal servitude for treason. He had led a group which called for the abolition of the secret police, and for freedom of speech. It was alleged, as a black mark against him, that he had been in touch with the Petöfi Circle. He claimed in his defence that the playwright Berthold Brecht had been one of his collaborators. (Brecht had died in August 1956.) It seems to have infuriated the East German authorities that, when they would not read a memorandum Harich submitted, he took it to the Soviet Ambassador and asked him to pass it on to his fellow-Germans, as they would listen to nobody but a Russian.

In that memorandum, Harich mentioned an unmentionable name. 'This first industrialisation of the USSR was necessary; to this extent Stalin was right and Trotsky was wrong. But the methods and forms by which it was achieved implied a political degeneration of the Bolshevik Party and the Soviet State and in seeing this Trotsky was right, while Stalin, in denying it, was wrong.'

The *Daily Worker* contained more information than usual, on March 19. The splash was headed: BUDAPEST ENJOYS SPRING WEEKEND. This was Sam Russell's report that a coup, designed to overthrow Kadar, had been foiled. The story contained no evidence that anyone had been planning a coup. But Sam always did give some information, even if you had to go to the end of the story for it. He admitted that, between December 16 and February 25, 304 people had appeared before military tribunals. Of these, 245 had been sentenced, 40 of them to death. Fifteen of the death sentences had been carried out immediately.

In the same issue of the *Daily Worker* was the news that the New York *Daily Worker* had a new executive editor, Simon Gerson, but that John Gates remained editor-in-chief.

This was the only indication given to our readers of the battle raging in the American Communist Party – a battle which was to result in the destruction of the New York *Daily Worker*.

Two days later, on 21 March 1957, our own *Daily Worker* reported the abolition of the 'Special Conference'. Sam Russell, now back in Moscow, wrote:

> One of the first measures taken after the exposure and execution of former Interior Minister L. Beria and his gang was the abolition of the so-called special conference, the *Osoboye Soveshcheniye*, which was Beria's private and secret Star Chamber and which had existed for almost 19 years.

This was inaccurate. The Special Conference was abolished in September 1953. Beria was probably not shot until December 1953. It was not 'Beria's private and secret Star Chamber'. In 1934, when Stalin set it up, Beria was not a person of any importance. Such inaccuracies do creep into the news, if you report it three and a half years late. But Sam's consistency in blaming Beria looked like something worse than a lapse of memory.

> This conference or commission, composed of officials appointed by Beria himself and responsible only to him, had powers to use extra-legal methods to impose penalties like exile, banishment and confinement to a camp on persons whom Beria decided were 'dangerous to society'. Persons dealt with by this body were often sentenced in their absence, on the basis of documents alone, which no independent body had an opportunity of checking and after very special methods of investigation and with the accused only given the indictment 24 hours before 'trial'.

> When Beria's Star Chamber was abolished in September, 1953, the special military tribunals of the MVD were also abolished.

Sam concluded that the Soviet people and its leaders were 'determined that the terrible nightmare of those years will never be allowed to return'.

Oh, good. But where had Stalin got to all of a sudden? Didn't he have any say in who got shot?

Since the beginning of 1957, the Soviet leaders had been rediscovering Stalin's good points. On January 20 the *Observer* reported Khrushchov as saying: 'In the essential – and the essential is class interests – God grant that every Communist should be able to fight like Stalin to defend them.'

There was another sinister sign. Since the Yugoslavs had protested against the kidnapping of Nagy, they had once again fallen into disfavour. In December 1956 *Pravda* began to attack the Yugoslav leader Edvard Kardelj, without telling its readers what he had said. (He had told the Yugoslav National Assembly: 'The cause of the crisis in Hungarian Socialism was the absence of every democracy. An anti-democratic system of bureaucratic despotism, against the will of the working masses, for years pursued the policy of a clique.') Since then several attacks on the Yugoslavs had been printed in the *Daily Worker*, which omitted every Yugoslav reply.

It was consistent with re-Stalinisation that we had not had a staff meeting at the *Daily Worker* for seven weeks. When Campbell confronted us again, he wanted to talk about the engineering strike. Some of the rebels who had stayed on the paper did indeed think this important. John Gritten specialised in industrial disputes, and became very much bound up with the strikes he reported. Then why didn't he protest about the shooting of Hungarian strikers? He did, but only in a quiet, 'disciplined' way. In private he remarked: 'When you come to think of it, you and I owe our lives to the fact that our efforts have been unsuccessful.'

Of all the rebels who stayed on the *Daily Worker* through that winter, the most impressive was George MacDougall. He had arrived from Scotland in 1949, an unsophisticated lad. On his first visit to Paris, he was taken aback to find that the attendant at the men's lavatory was a woman. She held out two pieces of toilet paper to him, and demanded money. Trying to explain that he didn't need the toilet paper, George cried: 'Non, non! Wee-wee!'

He had matured since then, as a journalist and as a man. He was now deputising for Allen Hutt, and considered likely to be his successor. With a wife and two little girls, he could not live on the Party rate, £8.50 a week. So Campbell had found him spare-time jobs. George earned about another £15 a week by acting as London correspondent for the East German paper, *Neues Deutschland*, and for two Polish dailies. He cannot have had any spare time at all. But he never failed to turn up at staff meetings, where his denunciations of the Party line were clear, measured and forceful.

However, at the March 25 meeting, George had nothing to say. He listened in silence while I asked Campbell what he thought of the 10-year sentence on Wolfgang Harich, and got the reply: 'We are not going to defend everything that happens in Socialist countries.'

Walter Holmes showed a disposition to defend it. The heavy sentence, he said, was 'due to the circumstances'.

Afterwards I asked George MacDougall why he was so silent. 'Perhaps I'm becoming a cynical journalist,' he said.

At a Muswell Hill branch meeting, Jack remarked to Palme Dutt: 'I've been seeing an old friend of yours – J. T. Murphy.' Dutt's face brightened. Then he remembered that Murphy had left the Party. With a grave shake of the head he whispered to Jack: 'It was his wife, you know.'

Like the rest of the orthodox, Dutt would never discuss what reason a person had for leaving the Party. It could not be done for a reason; it must show a weakness of character.

As Jack and I were already suspected of some such weakness, we had no hope of being elected to represent the branch at the Party Congress. However, we did what we could.

Jack moved, in Palme Dutt's presence, that Palme Dutt should no longer be a member of the EC. Jack was outvoted there, but not by much. I may have given the impression that the members of my local branch were not very bright. Some of them were not, but Palme Dutt's part in their debates had shocked even the dullest. He would soar into stratospheric follies which they had never dreamed of. Only Dutt could have argued (as he did during the rows about elections) that the feelings of Labour Party people did not matter.

As we drew near to the Easter Congress, I moved to delete, from the draft political resolution, the words: 'In Hungary, imperialism took advantage of grave internal difficulties to attempt long-prepared counter-revolution. But... imperialism was decisively rebuffed.' The branch voted to leave the words in. But the branch voted with me (and against Palme Dutt) to change 'Stalin's errors' to 'Stalin's crimes'. I also got the branch to deplore the recent worsening of relations between the Soviet Union and Yugoslavia, and to condemn the failure of the Party press to carry the statements of Yugoslav leaders.

The political resolution declared: 'In Poland, where a difficult situation developed, the Party remained united.' When I tried to explain to the branch what had happened in Poland, I was met with stares of blank disbelief. They knew about Yugoslavia; they'd been had that way before. But what I said about Poland couldn't be true. Never mind that I was quoting the proceedings of the Polish Central Committee. My comrades were not going to believe that Berman's prisoners had been released 'unfit to continue their lives' after being made to stand three weeks in their own excrement, or having water poured over them in winter and being kept in the prison yard until they froze solid.

Somebody moved: 'Next business!' and this was carried. Then I moved that the EC should be asked to reconsider all its past statements on Hungary, in the light of the eye-witness reports now available, including those of Dora Scarlett. There, too, I was defeated.

But it was Palme Dutt who got defeated when I moved that we should renounce the putting up of Communist candidates in marginal seats.

Some of the local comrades reproached me for being obsessed with the past. Why didn't I join in the present, the really urgent campaign, to prevent the testing of the British hydrogen bomb? Didn't I care about the poisoning of the atmosphere, the genetic damage to future generations?

I did care. And I cared still more when the Russians, without warning, began to let off their own hydrogen bombs.

XV

On Friday, 5 April 1957, George MacDougall finished his night's work. That included subbing the news that the Russians had let off their second hydrogen bomb. On Saturday morning he rang up Campbell, to say that he wasn't coming back.

He also wrote Campbell a letter, which Mick Bennett read to us at the staff meeting on Monday April 8.

'I write this with great personal regret... At least the Tory Government has given us the opportunity of carrying out a protest against this... The Russians do it without warning... The Russian attitude smells of hypocrisy...'

'Well, to me that letter smells of hypocrisy!' Mick exclaimed. He was bitter because George had gone without notice, thus breaking the NUJ code. 'Allen Hutt, I know, feels personally stabbed in the back,' Mick went on.

Not until 1990 did I know that Mick's account was incomplete. George had in fact given notice, shortly before I questioned him about his silence at a meeting. He told Hutt that he would have to leave, on political grounds, but not for another six months. Campbell then called George into his office and said that, if only he would stay, he stood a good chance of becoming foreign editor. Besides, there would be other little extra jobs, to provide him with more money. George turned the offer down. He had then every intention of working out his notice, but the Soviet hydrogen bomb tests were the last straw.

George, in his letter to Campbell, said he knew the *Daily Worker* would not protest against the Soviet tests. 'What made him say that?' Mick asked indignantly. 'We have protested.' And he pointed to that morning's editorial, written by himself. 'We are against all further tests, whoever makes them. For that reason we do not condone tests by the Soviet Union either.'

I did wonder whether this was OK by the Party leaders.

From that staff meeting I had to dash back, pick up Stella from her morning nursery, take her for a run in the woods, be at home when Cathy came back from school, cook a great deal of food and leave everything ready for that night's babysitter. There was, once again, a meeting Jack and I wanted to attend together.

This was the annual shareholders' meeting of the People's Press Printing Society, which owned the *Daily Worker*.

David Ainley, who was an expert of the co-operative movement, had worked out the statutes of the society, just after the Second World War. That was when the *Daily Worker* ceased to carry on its masthead: ORGAN OF THE COMMUNIST PARTY, and began to carry instead: THE ONLY DAILY PAPER OWNED BY ITS READERS.

Technically, therefore, the paper was no longer the property of the Party, but of a co-op, formed in the proper manner and approved by the Registrar of Friendly Societies. This meant that the shareholders could, if they wished, make the paper independent of the Party.

This did eventually happen, but almost 30 years later. By that time the Party had gone 'liberal', standing up to the Russians over Czechoslovakia and Afghanistan. The people who succeeded in wresting the paper away from the Party were the old Stalinists.

Our attempt in 1957 was not well organised. For a start,

nearly 7,000 people had left the Party, which now numbered only 26,742. Many of the non-Party trade unionists who had read the paper for its industrial news were now so sickened by its attitude to Hungarian strikers that they no longer cared what it said about Britain. Any ex-supporter who still held a share had probably not made the effort to write and ask for his pound back. He was even less likely to make the effort to go to a meeting. The Party machine, still strong and efficient, had rallied all comrades considered reliable. So the vast majority of those who turned up were the orthodox.

And those who came hoping for a change had not met beforehand. Nor had anyone worked out who should say what. I rang up Derek Kartun and suggested that he should tell the meeting what happened when he left the *Daily Worker*. He was thinking that over when one of his children caught measles and kept him at home. I could not myself get up and say that the Russians had deprived us of our foreign editor. I knew from my experience in the Muswell Hill branch that nobody would believe it.

So Jack and I went intending simply to back the resolution proposed by Malcolm MacEwen, 'that the management and policy of the paper must be firmly under the control of the elected management committee, according to rule'. The resolution also called for 'a conference representative of the entire left movement', to discuss how the paper should be run.

Outside the Conway Hall stood Peter Fryer, selling his appeal against expulsion for a shilling a time. I had written to assure him of my sympathy, but this was the first time since the previous summer that we had met face to face. Jack and I would in any case have been glad to shake him by the hand, but it gave us particular pleasure to do so amid the hate-filled glances of the orthodox.

We sat in the second row, behind Isabel Brown. She

turned to us and said that she knew we were sincere comrades, but what about some of the others? Look at Dennis Swinnerton! Had we seen his letter in the *Observer*?

We said yes, we had. It had appeared the previous day. Dennis was replying to another Party member, Karl Mathews, who had asked what British Communists could do about the ten-year sentence on Wolfgang Harich. Dennis described how he, his wife and their friend Leslie Sewell had been suspended from Party membership for challenging the Party line. Dennis added: 'We were fortunate; in a Communist country we, like Professor Harich, would now be serving sentences for treason.'

Isabel Brown had made her name with her great speeches about the injustice of putting Dimitrov on trial. But Dimitrov was an officially approved hero. She must surely have felt some indignation about Harich, but she had managed to channel all her feelings into hatred of Dennis Swinnerton. 'A man with a past like that!' she cried, adding some details about his past which we suspected (rightly) to be untrue. 'And his wife! What a reputation they've got – both of them!'

By this time Jack and I were both talking at once. Jack said it was a pity that some of us with better reputations hadn't done something about Wolfgang Harich. I said: 'There's none of us who couldn't have something dragged up from the past.'

Isabel drew herself up and said: 'Nothing can ever be dragged up against me.'

I was so angry that I was about to tell her something that could be. Just in time, I realised that the man sitting beside Isabel was her husband, Ernie Brown. So, by a hair's breadth, I avoided following her example.

The meeting began. Campbell made an astute speech, omitting to mention the resignation of George MacDougall. He claimed that the circulation of the *Daily Worker* had recently gone up. A voice from the hall asked whether this was because of extra orders from East European embassies. Campbell said: 'The increase is irrespective of any orders from outside this country.' This was a masterpiece of evasion. Embassies are not outside the country.

(At the beginning of 1990 the Soviet Union crippled the *Morning Star* – the successor to the *Daily Worker* – by cutting the daily order from 12,000 copies to 6,000. By that time only 6,000 copies a day were being sold in Britain.)

Peter got up and challenged Campbell to say why George MacDougall had resigned. Campbell replied by telling the meeting who Peter was. He began gently, calling Peter 'Comrade', although Peter had been expelled from the Party. Then the speech worked up to a climax. (Years before, I had heard Campbell say of another comrade: 'He's no such a rabble-rouser as – er – as I am.')

'Comrade Fryer was one of those who resigned from our paper because they thought the Hungarian rising was a real people's movement, though how any movement led by Cardinal Mindszenty…'

Mindszenty's name was the talisman which brought roars of happy, comforted applause from the majority. The minority, however, shouted: 'Answer the question!' They were so persistent that Campbell had to say something about George MacDougall. He succeeded in conveying that he was surprised, shocked and pained by George's sudden action. George hadn't, he suggested, ever given a hint of his disagreement with Party policy. In his best bluff, honest manner, Campbell concluded: 'If a man has differences of policy with me, I expect him to come to me and say so.'

After so many staff meetings where I had heard George clearly and forcefully putting his point of view, in Campbell's presence, I could not let this pass. I got up and shouted: 'On a point of order!'

That stopped everything, long enough for me to say: 'I

object to attacks on the character of George MacDougall.'

'That's not a point of order,' said the chairman.

I knew it wasn't, but I had made my protest.

Jack made a speech about the first issue of the *Daily Worker*, in 1930. He had been one of those who waited up for it all night, and then dispersed to sell it around London. 'We didn't think that night,' Jack said, 'that we should see the time when our *Daily Worker* would be telling lies. We didn't do all that work so that we should have to wait for Sunday, to get the truth from the *Observer*.'

Campbell replied that, since the *Observer* didn't report strikes truthfully, Comrade Selford ought to realise that it wasn't truthfully reporting the affairs of those countries ruled by the working class.

This argument (greeted with wild applause) made me all the angrier because I had been taken in by it for so many years.

Campbell added that in 1930, as today, people had said that the *Daily Worker* took Russian orders. 'Yes,' Jack muttered, 'and they were probably right both times.'

We went home on the bus with David Ainley. He was clutching the sealed box of ballot papers, which were to be counted the next day. He was doubtless capable of sitting up all night to falsify them, but there was no need. The majority had been convinced by Campbell. (Malcolm MacEwen's attempt to get on the committee did, however, attract about a fifth of the votes.)

Ainley had a theory that Peter Fryer, George MacDougall and the others who had left were 'all in it together'. How did Peter know of George's resignation, if they hadn't been in touch?

Party discipline still had a hold on me. I had no doubt that Peter Fryer was in the right, and that what had been done to him was infamous. All through that winter, I had never felt the cold. I was kept warm by burning indignation.

And yet, when Ainley spoke, I felt a faint, residual pang of guilt that I had been in touch with Peter Fryer. I did not tell Ainley that I had. I said only that people who had never even met George MacDougall knew about his resignation. Rumours were flying around the Party so fast that everybody heard everything. (Peter Fryer and his wife were staying with George, but I did not know that then.)

We argued with Ainley about the *Observer* and the Soviet Union. He said that of course people had been sent to Siberia. But Edward Crankshaw of the *Observer* gave the numbers as hundreds of thousands when it was really only thousands. One of those cases where a quantitative change leads to a qualitative change... I quoted Levy, and the man who told him that the Americans need only have dropped arms into Siberia. 'Then they'd have had a million men fighting on their side.'

'*Who* said this?' Ainley asked.

'Some Russian, to Levy,' I told him.

I could see Ainley making a mental note. Report Levy to the leadership...

That was the day when, in Budapest, three leaders of the rising were sentenced to death.

During all this time nobody mentioned the departure of Phil Piratin, the former MP, who had ceased to be circulation manager in February. He did not admit to any political disagreement; the point at issue between himself and Campbell was supposed to be whether the circulation should be organised from the *Daily Worker* office or from King Street.

In 1991 I persuaded Phil to talk. He said that, even when he was a member of the Politburo, he had felt excluded from the Party's inner circle. He was shocked by the extra ten shillings a week the Politburo members paid themselves, and protested, successfully, when they took it away from Willie Gallacher.

In 1956, Phil said, he drove to Oxford, to defend the Party line on Hungary at a meeting of undergraduates. He got as far as the outside of the hall, stopped – and drove home again.

Phil remained in the Party, but he never again worked for it full time. He became a businessman, and, with his brains and energy, a successful one.

On April 13 the *Daily Worker* published a profile of John McLoughlin, shop steward and strike leader. The headline was MAN OF PRINCIPLE. McLoughlin had been sacked from Briggs Bodies, causing a strike. At the ensuing enquiry he told Lord Cameron, who had asked about his political views: 'That is between me, my conscience and the ballot box.' So he was probably the inspiration for Fred Kite, the character played by Peter Sellers in *I'm All Right, Jack*.

Jack and I had one more night out together, before the Easter Congress. We were invited to a left-wing literary party. There I met my predecessor as TV critic, Honor Arundel. She could not understand what the rest of us were talking about. What had we all got against the Party leadership? Honor, formerly a Hampstead intellectual, had been living for the past three years in Scotland. Her local Party branch was happily campaigning against the Rent Bill. 'The Political Resolution? Oh yes, we passed that. Why? Was there something wrong with it?'

I realised with a jolt that most of the Party branches outside London were like that. There wasn't a hope of the Congress unseating our present leaders.

But what should I do if the dissidents had some limited success? It seemed possible, for example, that Levy might be elected to the EC. If that happened, I would have to stay in the Party, in order to back him up.

I realised that I was dreading the prospect. I had, for a whole year, attended meetings, argued far into the night,

ALISON MACLEOD

hunted out obscure pamphlets, caught up with books that I
should have read years before (the works of Arthur Koestler,
for example) and sought out anyone who had a first-hand story
to tell. That I never failed to get my column written on time,
that I covered every news story connected with TV, that we
ate well-cooked meals and wore clean clothes, that the hedge
was, now and again, clipped, the lawn occasionally mown,
does not prove that I was a superwoman. I had a daily help to
clean the house. Jack was not just a willing but an enthusiastic
baby-entertainer.

For all that, I was very tired. I did not see how I could
keep up the same pace for another year.

I had to go to one more staff meeting, on Monday, April
15. Throughout that meeting, Mick Bennett sat silent, hunched
into his pullover. I could see by looking at him that he had
been in trouble over his editorial on the Soviet H-bomb.
Campbell, too, was obviously choosing his words with great
care. The Government had issued a Defence White Paper,
announcing that the call-up of 1960 would be the last. That left
only the Communist Party still supporting conscription.
Campbell tried to prove to us that a conscript army was more
progressive than a small regular army, yet in the same breath
told us: 'That does not mean that we oppose the running down
of the present National Service system.'

As for the hydrogen bomb: 'We are receiving letters
every day supporting our saying that we do not condone the
Russian H-bomb tests.' However: 'We are not for a long-term
policy where the Russians don't have tests and the other two
nuclear powers do have tests. We cannot be for the unilateral
disarmament of the Soviet Union.' Some 'misguided readers'
were calling for the Soviet Union to abandon the tests
unilaterally. (He hadn't published any of those letters.)

Then he admitted: 'There is one snag in our argument.
Either the letting off of these weapons poisons the atmosphere

247

or it does not. If it does, then a Soviet hydrogen bomb poisons the atmosphere just as much as a British one.'

When Campbell called for questions, there was a gloomy silence. I said: 'Well, if nobody else will have a bash, I will. This little snag in your argument, Johnnie, isn't a snag – it's a bloody great hole right through it. You admit that a Soviet hydrogen bomb poisons the atmosphere just as much as a British one. They've let off four in ten days. You're putting the short-term military advantage of the Soviet Union before the future of humanity.'

At this there was a cry of protest from Peter Zinkin. He said he couldn't understand what I meant. I tried to explain.

'We've said in the paper that children are going to be born deformed and idiotic because of one British H-bomb. Then what's the use of talking as if this was an ordinary weapon of defence that the USSR has got to have its fair share of?'

Peter Zinkin declared that my point of view was that of the right-wing leaders. He accused me of saying: 'Everything the Russians do is wrong.'

I am not sure when I knew – or when I admitted to myself that I knew – the reason for Peter Zinkin's unsackability. He was the Russians' man in the office. I now know that he made regular reports to the Soviet Embassy on all of us. (What can they have been like? He could barely construct a sentence.)

Several other speakers expressed their concern at the Russian tests. At the end of the debate Campbell allowed me to speak again. I said: 'I think what George MacDougall did was wrong, because it's wrong to leave the British Communist Party on account of what the Russians do. If I'm driven out of the Communist Party, it won't be because of the Russians. I'm past being surprised at anything the Russians do.' (Someone said: 'Hear, hear!') 'It will be because I think the British Party is betraying the interests of the British people. And we shall be, if we don't protest against these tests.'

After I had said that I might be driven out of the Party, Campbell was particularly sweet to me. He came up to me and talked about my protest at the shareholders' meeting. 'I did not make a cowardly attack on the character of George MacDougall,' he said.

'I didn't use the word 'cowardly',' I told him. 'But you told the meeting that he never discussed his differences with you, and you know as well as I do that he talked and talked and talked, until he was tired of talking.'

Campbell did not answer me, but smiled. I found him later, in the canteen, having his lunch alone. I sat down opposite him and said: 'You're a shocking old demagogue, aren't you?'

All Campbell's wrinkles creased up in delight. 'Och!' he said. 'Naebody's called me a demagogue for years and years.'

I had loved him like a father. I loved him all the more because we were about to be parted, as finally as by death. But I was not going to let him off the hook.

'How could you use that old gag?' I said. 'The *Observer* doesn't tell the truth about a strike, so how can it tell the truth about the Soviet Union? We know that in fact it has told the truth about the Soviet Union. It printed the Khrushchov speech. We didn't. We laughed at Crankshaw – those incredible numbers of people sent to Siberia. Now we know all that was true.'

Campbell, better informed than Ainley, admitted everything with a tired: 'Ay.' Defending the last ditch, he went on: 'But Crankshaw doesna see the positive side.'

Mick Bennett sat down at the table and tried to interest Campbell in a comic poem he had written. Campbell grunted, and left.

Up to this moment, we dissidents had all been such clean fighters that we were no match for our leaders. Now I began to play dirty. I pretended I liked Mick's poem. Then I said: 'I understand you've been in trouble, over this leader of yours.' I understood nothing of the sort; it was a guess. The gossip I heard a few days later was that Mick had taken his editorial to John Gollan before it went into the paper. But Gollan, after reading the first two sentences, began to criticise Mick's literary style. Mick, who was vain about his style, flared up. Gollan then threw the article on the floor, and never did read the part about the Soviet tests, until it appeared in the paper. But I knew nothing of this when I was talking to Mick in the canteen.

Mick drew himself up and said: 'I cannot discuss what goes on in the Political Committee.'

That was all I wanted. I rang up every Congress delegate I knew and said that the Politburo had had Mick on the carpet for his leader – which meant that our leaders did condone the Soviet H-bomb tests.

The Communist Party Congress opened on Good Friday, April 19. As the delegates arrived at Hammersmith Town Hall, they saw, painted on the ground outside the entrance, a slogan devised by Peter Fryer: FREE HARICH – SACK HARRY. 'Who's Harich?' some delegates asked. They knew Harry meant Pollitt. Sheila Lynd had another slogan for him. When the old Stalinist leaders of Hungary fled to Russia, it was said that they had been sent to a retirement home in Sochi, by the Black Sea. Sheila launched the slogan: 'Pollitt for Sochi!' But it never caught on.

Watching the delegates arrive, just as a year before, was the Trotskyist leader Gerry Healy. And, as a year before, he spoke to Campbell. This time it was to warn him of his precarious situation. Gerry Healy needed no spies to tell him this; it was notorious that Campbell's insistence on facing the facts about Soviet anti-Semitism had antagonised the other leaders. They blamed him, too, for the turmoil in the *Daily Worker* office. Somehow, he must have recruited the wrong people. Or he had told them too much at meetings. Gallacher had said he did not know how to handle the staff.

Peter Fryer could have made things even worse for Campbell, if he had said that he was working out his notice, when Campbell sent him to Hungary. But he never mentioned that. Was he too clean a fighter? Or (as he now thinks) just naive?

Campbell quietly listened to Healy's warning, and did not dispute it. He asked only: 'But where can I go?'

Levy, and some of the other Congress delegates, tried to put an emergency motion about the Soviet H-bomb tests. The chairman of the Standing Orders Committee, Syd Abbott, at first told Levy that no motion could be put before the Congress unless he, Syd Abbott, agreed with it. Later another motion was put before the Congress. Levy's motion called on all powers, including the Soviet Union, to suspend the tests. The motion selected in its place was one calling on the Soviet Union to suspend them unilaterally. The leaders calculated that this would be rejected as too extreme, and they were right. Throughout the Congress, the same tactics were followed, in most cases with the same result.

Where the leaders failed was in their attempt to keep Peter Fryer off the press table. The left-wing weekly *Tribune* had chosen him as its reporter. At the last moment it was announced that there would be no room on the press table for the weeklies, but only for national daily and Sunday papers. Peter therefore missed the Good Friday proceedings, including a speech denouncing the leaders' policy on Hungary by 'the man of principle', the shop steward John McLoughlin.

McLoughlin said: 'We have collections for people who are victimised, but not for Edith Bone.'

One of the orthodox cried: 'The *Daily Express* did.'

McLoughlin replied: 'Yes, but they didn't put her in the nick.'

Peter also missed an exchange which directly concerned him. One of the delegates asked whether the Appeals Committee would hear Peter's appeal against his expulsion. George Matthews said that the Appeals Committee would decide that for itself. There was uproar in the hall, as delegates pointed out that to be heard by the Appeals Committee was Peter's right under the rules. George Matthews, who had been saying only what Gollan told him to say, was embarrassed. He was even more embarrassed when Pollitt said: 'Of course the committee will hear Peter Fryer.' It did, the following morning, at the Party headquarters. In the afternoon Peter took his place at the press table, having got a press card from the *Observer* man, who no longer needed it.

Before the Appeals Committee, Peter said that he had no apologies for attacking the leadership. The Appeals Committee therefore confirmed his expulsion.

At the end of the confidential document which this committee circulated to the Party leaders was a carefully worded paragraph:

> On the question of Fryer addressing this Party Congress, the Appeals Committee discussed this question and decided unanimously that it was unnecessary for him to do so. Although prior to Congress he had raised the question of addressing Congress, he did not mention the matter in our discussions with him or request to do so.

That is, the members of the committee knew that Peter had already expressed his wish to address the Congress. (He had in fact expressed it in writing.) But, since he did not repeat his request when he was before them, they decided that it was 'unnecessary' to grant him the right which the rules of the Party gave to every expelled member. Hence the statement made by a full-time Party official to the delegates on Sunday, that Peter had not asked to address them.

Why didn't Peter rise from the press table and contradict? Because the statement was made in a closed session, from which the press was excluded.

Far from not wishing to address the Congress, Peter had prepared a speech which contained a remarkable prophecy.

XVI

Peter Fryer's undelivered speech was duplicated and handed out to the Congress delegates. In it he pointed to 'signs of an approaching show trial of the Hungarian Communists who resisted Stalinism.' He quoted a speech made by Marshal Bulganin on 27 March 1957, reported in *Soviet News* but not in the *Daily Worker*. Bulganin said:

> One must make particular mention of the sinister role which was played by the Imre Nagy-Losonczy group in the staging of the counter-revolution in Hungary. The undeniable facts make it abundantly clear that, long before the October events in 1956, Imre Nagy, masquerading as a Communist, was in fact in the service of the enemies of the Hungarian people...

Bulganin's accusations of treason and counter-revolution against Imre Nagy and Geza Losonczy were, as Peter pointed out, quite new. He could have added, but did not, that on February 26 the Kadar Government had declared it was not going to put Nagy on trial.

Peter continued: 'If Nagy and Losonczy were placed on trial while the infamous Rakosi, Farkas and Gerö went scot-free this would be a crime no less monstrous than the murder by Stalin of the leaders of the Bolshevik Party and of Rajk, Kostov and Slansky. And should we then be told, after five, ten, twenty years, that Nagy and Losonczy, too, were victims of a "violation of Socialist legality", of a "mistake"?'

Peter was wrong on two counts. Losonczy was not tried, but murdered in his cell. Sandor Kopacsi, who was in the next cell, heard it happening. (Kopacsi survived by a series of extraordinary chances, to write his great book: *In the Name of the Working Class*.)

And it wasn't ten years, or twenty, but thirty-two years and two months after Peter's undelivered speech that Imre Nagy and those executed with him were rehabilitated and given a state funeral. This event in June 1989 set off what Peter also forecast in his undelivered speech, 'further political revolutions, which will not be confined to the outer rim of the Stalinist regime'. By the beginning of 1990, out of all Eastern Europe, only Albania remained in the hands of self-styled Communists. In February 1991 even the Albanians brought the statue of Enver Hoxha crashing down.

It turned out that the creaking old show had been kept on the road by the ringmaster's whip. Nothing else. Not one shred of moral authority, not one vestige of the ideals which had consumed our youth, was recognisable in the ruins. Of all the causes Jack and I campaigned for in our Party days, we could feel completely happy only about the National Health Service, which kept us alive and well and able to enjoy the TV pictures of young people dancing on the Berlin Wall. On 10 July 1990 we had the further pleasure of seeing Mikhail Gorbachov round on his critics, at the 28th Congress of the Soviet Communist Party, with the words: 'What did you want us to do? Send the tanks in again? Do we try to teach them again how to live?'

Some of those who voted for Peter's expulsion in 1957 thought that it was indeed the job of the Russians to teach us how to live. Their own job was to help the Russians do it. There are people still alive who went on thinking so, up to that moment in August 1991, when the tanks of the old Stalinists turned back, defeated by the Russian people.

There were some good moments in the 1957 Congress, as when John McLoughlin, the 'man of principle', shouted at Andréw Rothstein: 'You are the enemy, you lying old swine!' McLoughlin never got another admiring headline in the *Daily Worker*.

Peter's expulsion was carried by 486 votes to 31, with 11 abstentions. As he had expected this it made no difference to his activity, which included producing a 'Congress Special' every night, on the duplicator in Healy's house. It was given out to the Congress delegates as they arrived each morning. Thus, on Easter Monday, the delegates received the full text of the speech which Hyman Levy made on Easter Sunday, April 21.

Levy was supporting the minority report on inner-Party democracy, the one written by Malcolm MacEwen, Christopher Hill and Peter Cadogan.

He told the Congress: 'We have lost 7,000 members this year. But have we had an analysis of how we have lost them? Where is that analysis?'

Levy also wanted an analysis of the terror under Stalin. 'All this did not spring into existence suddenly, out of the blue, out of one half of Stalin's character, as we are told. I have been a Marxist too long to believe that kind of thing. It had been growing and developing for years. It was part of the history of Socialism that we Marxists had to know about and to understand. Without this understanding our Marxist education was incomplete.'

Levy argued that the failure of the Party leadership to cope with the Stalin revelations was responsible for the low level of Marxist understanding among Party members, which he had found on his visits to branches. At this there were noisy interruptions. It was tactless of Levy to tell the rank-and-file what nits they were. Several specialist comrades, who for years had met only the intellectually presentable Party members, were shocked when, in the months before the Congress, they began to attend their local branch meetings. But only Levy had the nerve to say so. 'He's talking rubbish!' cried one delegate, as Levy ran out of time.

Campbell, in the chair, ruled that Levy could have another two minutes. Levy then began to speak so fast that no shorthand writer, except Peter Fryer, could follow him. 'I went to the Soviet Union, and I saw and heard things that shook me to my foundations. In the fortnight I was there I literally got my belly full of what will last me for the rest of my life. I have been to branches. I have not told all but I have told them sufficient. During the period that this has been happening, how much of that did our Party leadership know? If they knew and kept quiet then they were misleading you as regards your Marxist education. The subject was taboo.

'I asked Johnnie Campbell did he know about it before. I could see the relief on his face. At last someone was going to talk about it. That was the impression I got... I must have the truth about this matter. I am not the only member of the Party who has been deluded by the leadership, by Pollitt. How often has he told people to keep their mouths shut?... Isn't it the truth that the leadership knew what was going on, didn't trust you, didn't trust the working class, thought you couldn't take it? Is this what you call Marxism?'

Campbell commented: 'I've always thought I had a poker face.'

He had not, as I can testify. After the Congress had elected a solidly Stalinist leadership, and adopted solidly Stalinist resolutions, with few amendments of any consequence, I went to see Campbell and told him I was leaving.

I also told him that the other leaders were gunning for him. (I did not know that Healy had said the same thing.) They thought him a bloody old liberal. Campbell turned pale and asked me how I knew. Who had I heard calling him a bloody old liberal?

I said I didn't need to hear it; I'd been seeing enough of Palme Dutt and the full-time officials (two of whom were in our branch) to know how their minds worked.

It would have been cruel to labour the point. Campbell was 62. If he ceased to be editor of the *Daily Worker*, he had no prospect of being anything else. (In fact, he was to last another two years in the job.)

I was 37. My political life had begun at 13. I do mean 13. That was when Hitler came to power, and I began to tell my schoolmates that nobody was doing anything against Hitler, except the Communists.

So I reckoned that half my political life was over. If I were to spend the other half in fighting a useless leadership, I would rather do it inside the Labour Party. There, at least, I'd have company.

I said so, to Campbell. He replied: 'I wish all these comrades who are going into the Labour Party would come back after three months and tell me what it's like. I've always heard ye can't have any real political discussion there. The chairman rules ye out of order.'

I said that if I worked for any other paper nobody would think I believed in the proprietor's political line. (Gabriel, who was now working for the *Evening Standard*, was allowed complete latitude.)

Campbell said: 'Now, now – don't make excuses for Gabriel that ye wouldna make for me.'

This remark did not strike me so forcibly at the time as it did when I thought it over. Campbell meant that he needed excuses for staying on a paper whose line he did not believe in.

Had he ever believed in it? When he came back from

Moscow, with the facts about Soviet anti-Semitism, the other leaders had already decided to support the Soviet invasion of Hungary. One of Peter Fryer's despatches had already been suppressed, another mangled. When Campbell suppressed the third, was he acting in accordance with his own convictions? Did he know what his own convictions were? The nearest he got to telling me was to say: 'Ye know what I think. I think Stalin was a bad old boy.' He used freely to admit that, while he was in Moscow in the late 1930s, he had known about the arrest of innocent people. But he had not said so then because what mattered most was to defend what he still called Socialism.

My convictions on that day – 29 April 1957 – still included Socialism as a necessary aim. I said to Campbell: 'It's such a good system that it's bound to triumph, even when it's led by scoundrels, just as capitalism is bound to fail, even if it were led by saints. But I insist on being free to say when Socialism is led by scoundrels – or even by a drunken old fool who can't keep his mouth shut.'

This allusion to Khrushchov made Campbell chuckle. We shook hands. I said: 'I love you very much. I think you know that.' He smiled.

Then I said farewell to Florence Keyworth, whom I also loved. She did not attempt to argue; she only looked at me sadly. What hurt me most was that I could not say farewell to Allen Hutt. He was not speaking to me. I remembered him as he was once, late at night, when we were friends. He was heartbroken because his wife had left him (I do not say without cause). In the daytime he used to flirt with both me and Sheila Lynd, who was as conspicuously thin as I was fat, and say that he could not choose between us. That night he said suddenly: 'In spite of all these elaborate jokes, we both know that there's no physical attraction between us. And because of that we can talk to each other, can't we?' To me that memory was more moving than any past love affair.

I did see Hutt again, a few months later, and we were reconciled in a personal way, though never politically. Shortly before his death I went to see him, to thank him for giving me such a marvellous training that the *Times Business News* had welcomed me with open arms. We had sometimes worried in our office – were we really up to Fleet Street standards? Thanks to Allen Hutt, we were.

I was still a Party member while I was talking to Campbell. That evening I went to a meeting of the Muswell Hill branch, and listened while our Congress delegate gave her report. She said that the section on Poland, in the Political Resolution, had been altered 'to be more in accordance with the facts'. I seethed silently, because, a few weeks before, when I had pointed out how extremely unaccordant with the facts that section was, I had been made to sit down. Everyone seemed to have forgotten that.

After this report, a full-time organiser who worked at Party headquarters, Kay Loosen, said: 'Don't we now feel, comrades, that the decks have been cleared for action?'

I said: 'Yes, comrade, we do; and one of the things that have been cleared off the decks is me.' Then I said, more or less, what I had said to Campbell that morning. This time, when I described Khrushchov as a drunken old fool, there were no chuckles, but gasps of horror.

I said the Congress had put an end to the hope some of us had cherished, that a British Communist Party might emerge that would be British, and free from Russian domination. The meaning of the Congress had been re-Stalinisation. Peter Fryer had been wrong when he wrote in *Tribune* that the portraits of Stalin were going back on the walls at Party headquarters. They had never been down. The leaders of the Party were unrepentant Stalinists. Since I was not prepared to defend them before the British workers, I was leaving the Party and the *Daily Worker*.

After that speech Palme Dutt never spoke to me again. Roy Zemla, the man who had said I was 'vaguely connected' with the *Daily Worker*, spoke of 'immature statements, like the one we have just listened to'. Immature I certainly was, by comparison with the people who had seen through Stalin in his lifetime, but not, I thought, by comparison with Roy Zemla, who could not bear to read an evening paper. (He never read a morning one either, except the *Daily Worker*; nor did he allow TV in his house.)

Beatrix Tudor-Hart, a much respected expert on child care, rose and said that she agreed with me, and that she was leaving too.

The branch wrote me a friendly letter afterwards, thanking me for my past work, and in particular for speaking on our local street corner. The letter concluded: 'We sincerely hope that you will eventually rejoin our Party.'

Another person who hoped that was a Jonah supporter, Bob Ferguson. He phoned me to suggest that I should come round for a chat. There were some fine working-class comrades where he lived, at Finsbury Park. Wouldn't I like to meet them?

Jack could not understand why I went. Enough, he felt, was enough. We had followed Ben Smith's advice and gone to every possible meeting. Because of that, we were cured. Comrades like Roy Zemla had cured us.

But I was (and still am) always happy to chat about politics when invited. Bob Ferguson, it turned out, had exactly one working-class comrade to meet me. This worker did not get a word in edgeways. Bob and his wife Dorothy were busy telling me that if only I'd met more working-class people...

I said that all the friends I'd made in Bristol during the war, when I was a shipyard welder, were workers. My closest friend was a bus conductress, a great organiser of *Daily*

Worker bazaars. She met a bus driver who told her that he had been in Russia during the war, and that he had seen trainloads of starving, freezing people, on their way to Siberia. 'I nearly knocked his face off his head,' she said. 'I told him not to talk such rubbish; I wasn't going to believe it.' Now she knew that there had been trainloads of starving, freezing people on their way to Siberia.

'Well?' said Dorothy Ferguson, in a tone suggesting that she would have sent them there herself. 'Well?'

'She thought it mattered,' I said. 'She left the Party and married the bus driver.'

Bob Ferguson asked if I supported British colonialism in Cyprus, Kenya and Malaya. I said no. I said I might really have been able to do something about it, all these years, if I'd belonged to the Labour Party and, for example, supported Fenner Brockway.

'Fenner Brockway!' exclaimed Bob derisively, and turned for support to the token worker, who was sitting silent in the corner. 'Why, you know about Fenner Brockway, don't you?' The worker did not respond. He was listening only to me.

Bob Ferguson mentioned Gomulka. I said he was the one man who had been keeping me in the Party. But I had begun to notice that in all his speeches he begged his supporters for moderation because of 'Poland's geographical position'. He was stuck between Khrushchov and Ulbricht. We weren't. I thought that, if Gomulka had a nice cosy English Channel to protect him, he'd be in the Labour Party.

'Gomulka in the Labour Party!' exclaimed Bob Ferguson in horror.

When I began to talk about the Rajk trial, Dorothy Ferguson said that, of course, what fascist agents would do was worm their way into the security police and make it unpopular. I said that the Rajk frame-up was arranged by

Soviet security police, sent directly from Stalin. Dorothy refused to believe it. By this time she was in full scream. I am not normally good at keeping my own temper. But, the louder Dorothy Ferguson screamed, the calmer I got. She was what I was leaving. Not until 1992 did I discover that the Fergusons were among the few people who knew the story of Rosa Rust and her journey in the cattle truck.

I worked out my notice at the *Daily Worker*, until Whitsun. The last time I went into the office and saw Campbell was on 2 May 1957. He shook his finger at me and said: 'Ye're a bad girl!' I knew what he meant. Palme Dutt had reported my shocking remarks at the branch meeting, and Campbell was in trouble for having employed me so long. 'But the people at the branch meeting were my comrades,' I said. 'I had to give them an explanation.'

This was the last time I said to Campbell: 'How could you?'

In the *Daily Worker*, that morning, John Mahon had reviewed a book, *The Stalin Era*, by the American Communist Anna Louise Strong. Mahon wrote: 'She does not accept at its face value the State Department version of the Khrushchov "secret" speech.'

'How could you let that go in?' I said to Campbell. 'You know as well as I do that the State Department version is the speech.'

He said: 'If you're so exacting in your standards, you aren't likely to be happy anywhere.'

Mahon's phrase was a lie in another way, besides the lying implication I noticed then. Anna Louise Strong did accept the State Department version as authentic, but she thought Khrushchov was lying about Stalin's military knowledge. Mahon could not bear to mention that any American Communist had called Khrushchov a liar.

Campbell's prophecy was not fulfilled. I did, some years

later, discover a field of work which demands the strictest truthfulness – financial journalism. Bankers want to know whether a country will pay its debts; they are not interested in propaganda. Telling the readers of *Euromoney* that the Shah would fall, that Poland would default, that Roberto Calvi was a crook, I had every inducement to tell the truth. Journalists do incessantly make mistakes, because they work in a hurry, but the good ones apologise. In my experience the serious newspapers and magazines are staffed by people much more truthful than Campbell.

I was the thirteenth person to leave the *Daily Worker* over Hungary. And I was the only one whose farewell statement was carried in the paper. It appeared on 4 June 1957.

'This is my last article for the *Daily Worker*. I deeply regret leaving the paper which I first joined in 1944, and the many fine comrades with whom I have worked so happily. I have no personal quarrel with them whatever. But I believe the policy of the Communist Party, as confirmed at its Easter Congress, to be mistaken.'

I was well out of it. The following day, the leading article contained the sentence: 'What kind of a workers' revolution was it in which Cardinal Mindszenty re-emerged and was allowed to broadcast a demand for the restoration of capitalism?'

This was six months after the monitored text of the speech had shown that Mindszenty made no such demand.

Mick Bennett's departure from the paper, which took place a few days earlier, was not (he maintained until his death in 1997) due to his protest about the Soviet H-bomb. His farewell statement said only that his way of writing leaders had been criticised. 'I do not accept these views, nor can I help but adhere to my own natural style of writing.'

The historian Christopher Hill left the Party when I did. The Swinnertons left before they could be expelled. Brian

Pearce courted expulsion, and got it. Sheila Lynd left when Imre Nagy was executed, in June 1958. Malcolm MacEwen was expelled. Hyman Levy was expelled. He told Ray Waterman that this made him feel like an orphan. (Surely a man in his seventies ought to be an orphan?) The occasion of Levy's expulsion was that in 1958 he wrote a book, 'Jews and the National Question', in which he asked: 'Can the Soviet Union not afford to publish Yiddish poetry in the original language?' So that nobody could accuse Levy of going to a capitalist publisher, his friend Chimen Abramsky published the book, under the imprint 'Hillway Publishing Company'. When Levy was expelled, Abramsky left the Party in sympathy.

Dora Scarlett, who had left the Party on her return from Hungary, went to India. In the foothills of the Western Ghats, 50 miles west of Madurai, she founded a clinic, Seva Nilayam. It flourishes in every sense; the people who come for free treatment are sheltered from the sun by tall trees, all of Dora's planting. She has made sure that there is never a day in the year without blossom. Young people, inspired by her example, have taken health care into remote villages. In 1994 she was awarded the M.B.E.

Ray Waterman left the Party when I did, but Alec Waterman stayed, struggling to make the Party leaders protest against the treatment of Soviet Jews. On the National Jewish Committee of the Party he had one like-minded comrade, Wolf Arnold. Then Wolf Arnold died and Alec Waterman battled on alone. He died in 1966, the day after completing a detailed memorandum on the suppression of Jewish culture. His ghost may now rest easy. In 1989 a Russian Jew was allowed to open a school of traditional Jewish dancing, and groups of Jews now travel to Israel to learn about their own folk music. There are Yiddish theatres in Russia, somewhat hampered by a lack of actors who can still speak Yiddish. In 1990 the article in *Folks-sztyme*, which sent Alec Waterman reeling back from his front door, was published in the Soviet Union.

At Whitsun 1957, for a week, Jack and I recuperated in a holiday camp near Oxford. There we met a Labour man who had known the Dutch Communist George Fles and his English wife Pearl Rimmel in the 1930s.

'They were at a summer school,' the Labour man said. 'They were very young, and very keen on each other, and thrilled that they were going to the Soviet Union. Then, a couple of years later, I met Pearl at the same summer school, with her baby. 'Where's George?' I said. She said: 'Oh, he had to stay on for a bit. He'll be back.' There was a debate between a Communist and a Trotskyist, about the trials in Moscow. I thought the Trotskyist wiped the floor with the Communist. But Pearl was very fierce on the Communist side. I was listening to her, and suddenly I thought – this is phony. She thinks that she's being watched. She's trying to prove that she's loyal. Where's George?'

A little later he heard that Pearl had given up pretending. (That must have been when her letters to George began coming back, marked: 'Address unknown'.) The Labour man met a Party member who said: 'Pearl? Oh, she's gone completely Trot. Well! You can't tell me her old man was arrested for nothing.'

In our local Labour Party, far from finding that we were under suspicion as ex-Communists, Jack and I were warmly welcomed. A councillor pointed out, with great pride, another ex-Communist. 'Used to be on the Moscow Soviet, that chap.'

This was George Aitken, once a member of the Central Committee of the Party, and a political commissar with the International Brigade. He had known Campbell well. Not long after Aitken came back from Spain, completely disillusioned, he and his wife went to see Campbell to tell him that they were leaving the Party.

'Campbell thought he was out of the Party too,' Aitken said. 'He told us what he'd seen in Russia during the purges. It was the time of the change of line, you remember, at the beginning of the war. Campbell said: 'I shall never accept this criminal bloody line.' And then, the next we heard, he had accepted it.'

'What made him do it?' I asked.

'It was his stepson,' Mrs. Aitken said. 'He'd become a Soviet citizen. So, when the war started, he couldn't get out of Russia. Johnnie had brought the boy up; he loved him like his own. That was what made him accept the change of line.'

I asked the Aitkens about Pollitt, whose volte face at the beginning of the war was no less spectacular than that of Campbell. What made him accept that it was an imperialist war? As he said on television 17 years later, he had always believed it was an anti-fascist war.

The Aitkens did not like Pollitt. They thought he was capable of accepting a line he did not believe in, simply in order to keep his prestige with the Russians.

But there is another possible explanation. Pollitt's first love, Rose Cohen, had been condemned to ten years in prison without the right to a visit. This was a code. It meant she had been shot immediately. But Pollitt did not know that. Rose Cohen's sister in London did not know it. At the outbreak of war she might, for all Pollitt knew, have been alive. As I have not found anything good to say of Pollitt, so far, I would be happy to think that, when he argued for a line he did not believe in, he was doing it, as Pearl Rimmel did, in the hope of saving one beloved life.

That Campbell did the same thing for the sake of his stepson is credible. He was devoted to his family; when I knew him he spent every spare moment with a beloved grandson. If the Aitkens' supposition is true, Campbell's stepson may have affected the course of history. If Campbell had left the Party in 1939, when he was in his forties, he would not have said, as he did in 1957: 'But where can I go?' He would have gone into the Labour Party. There, his rise would have been unstoppable. Campbell was the stuff of which cabinet ministers are made.

Anybody can judge his quality, now that it is possible to read (in the book *About Turn*) the speeches made in the Central Committee of the British Communist Party at the beginning of the war. The difference between Campbell and the other leaders is obvious. Pollitt (who was arguing on the same side) seems boastful and self-obsessed by comparison.

Campbell read aloud articles from *Pravda* and *Izvestiya* which blamed Poland for starting the war. The other leaders were upset, not by these articles, but by the contempt with which Campbell treated them. 'I think the statements are correct,' said Gollan, 'else they would not be in *Pravda*.'

On that occasion Bill Rust was whole-hearted in his support of the Russians. If he was moved by anxiety for his daughter, then fourteen years old and still at her Soviet boarding school, he succeeded in keeping it far more secret than Campbell kept his anxiety for his stepson.

Campbell's stepson is now dead. His story was more complicated than the Aitkens knew. He came back to England with his Russian wife in 1977, and wrote an excellent autobiography, *Villi the Clown* (Faber, 1981). He admitted that his decision to become a Soviet citizen, in 1939, was a terrible mistake. It did not even save him from being considered a foreigner. In Stalin's last years he was banned from appearing on the stage because of his British origin. What is missing from William Campbell's book is the fact that, shortly before Stalin's death, he was in prison. (There are still people alive who remember that.)

Surely Campbell would go to Moscow and try to get him out? I think he did, and I think I know when.

In the first chapter I mentioned the notes I have, dated 12 September 1952, of a *Daily Worker* staff meeting. The notes indicate that Campbell had just been to Russia. He told us: 'Every Party member has the right to criticise every other Party member, however high up.' Campbell knew very well what would happen to a Party member who criticised Stalin, or who looked as if he might be about to criticise Stalin.

Embedded in this rubbish is a nugget of real information. Talking about the proposed new rules for the Communist Party of the Soviet Union, Campbell told us to read an article about them in the next issue of *For a Lasting Peace, For a People's Democracy*. He told us the name of the author, a name which then meant nothing to us – Nikita Khrushchov. (The article did appear, but anonymously.) How did Campbell know Khrushchov was writing such an article? Surely because he had been talking to Khrushchov. Though he was then unknown outside Russia, Khrushchov was already a powerful figure in Stalin's entourage. Did he get William Campbell out of prison? Somebody did, and before Stalin's death. William Campbell has written a vivid eye-witness account of the streets of Moscow on the day Stalin died.

If Khrushchov did this, it might well account for Campbell's inclination to look with favour on anything else Khrushchov did – even the sending of the tanks into Hungary.

This is deduction, and I cannot prove it. There are still people alive who know far more about these events than they have been willing to tell me. Until I know that the last one has died, I cannot be sure that I am justified in writing:

THE END